Stepping into Virtual Reality

Mario A. Gutiérrez A. • Frédéric Vexo •
Daniel Thalmann

Stepping into Virtual Reality

 Springer

Mario A. Gutiérrez A., PhD
Frédéric Vexo, PhD
Daniel Thalmann, PhD

EPFL VR Lab
Lausanne
Switzerland

ISBN: 978-1-84800-116-9   e-ISBN: 978-1-84800-117-6
DOI: 10.1007/978-1-84800-117-6

British Library Cataloguing in Publication Data
A catalogue record for this book is available from the British Library

Library of Congress Control Number: 2008920949

Printed on acid-free paper

9 8 7 6 5 4 3 2 1

Springer Science + Business Media
springer.com

Acknowledgments

Most of the images included in this book are part of the research work of the following people, they are members or former members of the research team of the Virtual Reality Laboratory at EPFL:

Mireille Clavien, Achille Peternier, Pascal Glardon, Marcelo Kallmann, Ramon Mas, Ronan Boulic, Tom Molet, Zhiyong Huang, Hansrudi Noser, Amaury Aubel, Tolga Abaci, Michal Ponder, Sebastien Schertenleib, Pablo De Heras Ciechomski, Branislav Ulicny, Alejandra Garcia-Rojas, Etienne De Sevin, Barbara Yersin, Jonathan Maim, Julien Pettré, Damien Maupu, Tolga Capin, Guillaume Gauby, Luca Vacchetti, Patrick Salamin, Patrick Lemoine, Bruno Herbelin, Helena Grillon, Anderson Maciel, Sofiane Sarni, Jan Ciger, Rachel de Bondeli, Fatih Erol, Stephanie Noverraz, and Olivier Renault.

Preface

This book is the fruit of many years of experience on the creation of synthetic worlds and virtual realities. Our goal is to transmit this experience to students and ease the learning curve required to master the creation of Virtual Reality (VR) applications. We start by providing some brief answers to key questions such as: where did VR come from? what are the main concepts that help us understand this research field? what are the current VR trends? and last but not least, how can we create virtual worlds?

Throughout the book we consider the terms "virtual environment," "virtual world" and "VR application" as equivalent concepts: computer-generated environments mainly composed of interactive computer graphics, designed to physically and/or psychologically immerse one or more users in an alternative reality.

The first part of the book makes a review of the basic theoretical and practical concepts involved in the visual aspect of virtual environments. We start by presenting the basic mathematical foundations for the synthesis of 3D graphics, including basic modeling and rendering techniques. A comprehensive review of the state of the art of computer animation closes this part.

The second part provides more details on the components, structure and types of virtual worlds that can be created. We provide a detailed explanation of the main modeling and animation techniques for virtual characters, which are one of the most important actors in a virtual world. A review and discussion of the main types of VR system architectures serve to define the different alternatives for organizing and designing a VR application. Virtual Reality is only one of the different types of mixed reality environments that belong to the "reality continuum," defined in Chapter 1. This part of the book provides more details on how to create mixed reality applications, such as augmented reality.

The third part covers the main principles of Virtual Reality hardware. Instead of providing an exhaustive review of the state of the art of VR hardware, which would get outdated very soon due to the fast pace of this research area, we present a generic classification of interaction devices using a human-centered approach, based on the five main human senses: vision, audition, touch, smell, and taste. Each chapter explains the importance of a specific human sense and describes the different types of input and output devices that can exploit a given modality to establish a dialog between human users and virtual worlds.

The last part deals with the present and future of Virtual Reality. Successful VR systems and applications are reviewed and discussed. We highlight how the basic principles explained throughout the book were applied and analyze the practical and theoretical problems that were addressed.

This work was conceived as a guided tour that will give a practical explanation of each step in the process of creating a Virtual Reality application. It can be used both as a textbook for a Virtual Reality course and as a reference for courses covering computer graphics, computer animation, or human-computer interaction topics.

Mario A. Gutiérrez A.
Frédéric Vexo
Lausanne
September 2007
Daniel Thalmann

Contents

List of Figures XIII

1 Introduction 1
  1.1 Virtual Reality: The Science of Illusion 1
  1.2 Basic Concepts 2
     1.2.1 Immersion 2
     1.2.2 Presence 3
  1.3 A Brief History of Virtual Reality 4
  1.4 Reality-Virtuality Continuum 7

Part I Fundamentals

2 Computer Graphics 11
  2.1 Mathematics 11
     2.1.1 Coordinate Systems 11
     2.1.2 Vectors, Transformations and Matrices 14
     2.1.3 Angular Representations 18
     2.1.4 Projections 24
  2.2 3D Modeling 25
     2.2.1 Geometric Representations 26
     2.2.2 Curves 26
     2.2.3 Surfaces 33
  2.3 3D Rendering 34
     2.3.1 Local Illumination Model 35
     2.3.2 Global Illumination Model 37
     2.3.3 Textures 41
     2.3.4 Rendering Pipeline 44

3   Computer Animation 49
   3.1   Introduction 49
      3.1.1   Animation Types: Real Time and Image by Image 49
      3.1.2   Articulated Bodies and Virtual Characters 50
   3.2   Motion Control Methods 51
   3.3   Motion Capture and Performance Animation............... 52
      3.3.1   Optical Motion Capture Systems 53
      3.3.2   Magnetic Trackers and Systems 53
      3.3.3   Motion Capture Advantages and Disadvantages 55
   3.4   Key-Frame Animation 57
      3.4.1   Shape Interpolation and Parametric Keyframe
            Animation....................................... 57
      3.4.2   Kochanek-Bartels Spline Interpolation 58
   3.5   Inverse Kinematics 60
   3.6   Motion Retargeting 62
   3.7   Procedural Animation................................... 64
   3.8   Physics-Based Animation 65
   3.9   Behavioral Animation 66

Part II Virtual Worlds

4   Virtual Characters....................................... 71
   4.1   Virtual Humans in Virtual Environments 71
   4.2   Character Skinning 72
      4.2.1   Skeleton-Based Deformations 72
      4.2.2   Data-Driven Methods 75
      4.2.3   Physics-Based Approaches 76
   4.3   Locomotion... 76
      4.3.1   Locomotion Generation 76
      4.3.2   PCA-Based Locomotion 78
   4.4   Virtual Human-Object interaction 81
      4.4.1   Feature Modeling and Smart Objects 81
      4.4.2   Grasping 82
      4.4.3   Motion Planning 88
   4.5   Facial Animation 90
   4.6   Autonomous Characters 92
      4.6.1   Why Autonomous Virtual Characters? 92
      4.6.2   Properties of Autonomous Virtual Characters 94
      4.6.3   Behaviors for Autonomous Virtual Characters 96
   4.7   Crowd Simulation 100

5   Architecture of Virtual Reality Systems 107
      5.1   Scene Graph-Based Systems 108
      5.2   Semantic Virtual Environments 109
      5.3   Generic System Architecture for VR Systems 111
      5.4   Distributed Virtual Environments 112
             5.4.1   Communication Architecture 113
             5.4.2   Interest Management 113
             5.4.3   Concurrency Control......................... 114
             5.4.4   Data Replication 115
             5.4.5   Load Distribution 116

6   Mixed Realities 117
      6.1   Augmented Reality and Augmented Virtuality 117
      6.2   Tracking Techniques 118
             6.2.1   Markers-Based Tracking...................... 118
             6.2.2   Marker-Less Tracking 119
      6.3   Mixed Reality Tool Kits............................. 122

Part III Perceiving Virtual Worlds

7   Vision 125
      7.1   Graphical Display Technologies........................ 125
             7.1.1   Cathode-Ray Tubes 125
             7.1.2   Liquid Crystal Displays 126
             7.1.3   Plasma Displays........................... 129
      7.2   Virtual Reality Displays 130
             7.2.1   Head-Mounted Displays 130
             7.2.2   Fish Tank VR 133
             7.2.3   Handheld Displays......................... 133
             7.2.4   Large Projection Screens 135
             7.2.5   CAVE Systems............................ 135

8   Audition 139
      8.1   The Need for Sound in VR 139
      8.2   Recording and Reproduction of Spatial Sound............. 140
      8.3   Synthesis of Spatial Sound.......................... 140
             8.3.1   Sound Rendering 140
             8.3.2   Head-Related Transfer Function 141
             8.3.3   3D Sound Imaging......................... 142
             8.3.4   Utilization of Loudspeaker Location 142
      8.4   Sound Systems for VR 142
             8.4.1   Sound Hardware 143
             8.4.2   Sound Engines 146

9   Touch 147
  9.1 The Need for Touch in VR 147
  9.2 Data Gloves 148
  9.3 Haptic Rendering 148
    9.3.1 History of Haptic Rendering 149
  9.4 Haptic Interfaces 150
    9.4.1 Vibrotactile Displays 151
    9.4.2 Tactile Displays 151
    9.4.3 Kinesthetic Displays 153

10   Smell and Taste 157
  10.1 The Need for Smells and Tastes in VR 157
  10.2 Smell Interfaces 158
  10.3 Taste interfaces 159

Part IV Applications

11   Health Sciences 165
  11.1 Virtual Surgery 165
  11.2 Virtual Rehabilitation and Therapy 166
    11.2.1 Physiotherapy 166
    11.2.2 Psychological Therapy 168
  11.3 Virtual Anatomy 169

12   Cultural Heritage 173
  12.1 Virtual Campeche and Calakmul 173
  12.2 Virtual Dunhuang 175
  12.3 Terracotta Soldiers 175
  12.4 EU-INCO CAHRISMA and ERATO 177
  12.5 EU-IST Archeoguide 178
  12.6 EU-IST Lifeplus 180

13   Other VR Applications 181
  13.1 Vehicle Simulators 181
  13.2 Manufacturing 183
  13.3 Entertainment 185

References 189

Index 211

List of Figures

1.1   The first Virtual Reality systems 5
1.2   Reality-virtuality continuum 7

2.1   Point and shapes in polar coordinates 12
2.2   Triangle-based 3D shape 13
2.3   Non-commutativity of transformations composition 18
2.4   Gimbal lock 19
2.5   Rotation about an arbitrary axis in space 20
2.6   Projection 26
2.7   Conic sections 27
2.8   A cubic Bézier curve and its defining polygon 30
2.9   Spline surfaces: Bézier patches 34
2.10 Shading algorithms for local illumination 37
2.11 Ray tracing example 39
2.12 Radiosity example 41
2.13 Mix of ray tracing and radiosity rendering 42
2.14 Texture mapping 42
2.15 Texture mapping techniques 43
2.16 Rendering pipeline 44

3.1   H-ANIM skeleton 51
3.2   Principles of optical motion capture 54
3.3   Motion capture using magnetic sensors 56
3.4   Interpolation between two drawings 58
3.5   Tension, continuity, and bias on Kochanek-Bartels spline 59
3.6   Direct and inverse kinematics 61
3.7   Use of an intermediate skeleton for motion retargeting 64
3.8   Dynamics-based motion [48] 66
3.9   Direct and inverse dynamics 66
3.10 L-system-based environment 68

4.1   JLD deformations   73
4.2   Metaball-based deformations   74
4.3   Walking generated using PCA   80
4.4   Defining and using smart objects   83
4.5   Grasping taxonomy   84
4.6   Grasping   85
4.7   Multi-agent carrying   86
4.8   Active and passive agents   87
4.9   Reaching examples   89
4.10   A singing facial expression   91
4.11   FDP feature points   93
4.12   Virtual assistant for basic life support   94
4.13   Reflex reactions to a ball   98
4.14   Motivational model for virtual humans   98
4.15   Virtual life simulation   99
4.16   Intercommunication   101
4.17   Crowd simulation   102
4.18   Crowd simulation   104
4.19   Hybrid motion planning architecture for pedestrians   106

5.1   Semantic representation of virtual environments   110
5.2   Cybertennis in Telecom Interactive 97, by MIRALab,
       University of Geneva and EPFL VRlab [199]   113
5.3   Interest management in collaborative worlds   114

6.1   Markers-based tracking using ARToolkit   119
6.2   Playing checkers with a virtual human   121

7.1   Human field of view   131
7.2   Different types of head-mounted displays   132
7.3   Use of handheld devices in VR applications   134
7.4   A CAVE system with four screens   137

8.1   Pioneer sound field control system   144

9.1   Data gloves for touch and force-feedback   149
9.2   PHANTOM® haptic interfaces   150
9.3   The Haptic Workstation™   154

10.1   Food simulator   160

11.1   VR-based telerehabilitation systems for physiotherapy   167
11.2   VR-based treatment of social phobia   169
11.3   Virtual model of the musculoskeletal system   170

12.1   Latin American Virtual Reality applications   174

12.2 Flashlight interaction in a CAVE 176
12.3 EU-INCO ERATO (2006) and CAHRISMA (2004) 178
12.4 Augmented reality and cultural heritage 179

13.1 A car driving simulator 181
13.2 Virtual vehicle simulators 182
13.3 Augmented reality for operator training 184
13.4 Simulator or advanced video game 186
13.5 "Enigma of the Sphinx" 187

1

Introduction

What You Will Learn:
This chapter provides definitions of basic concepts that are essential to understand the field of Virtual Reality. By the end of the chapter you should have a good understanding of the fundamental concepts of Virtual Reality, be familiar with the history of the field, and be aware of the multiple disciplines involved in the development of Virtual Reality applications.

1.1 Virtual Reality: The Science of Illusion

When the term Virtual Reality (VR) started to be used, it produced great expectations. The idea was that this technology would be able to create imaginary worlds that would be indistinguishable from the real world.

During the 1990s other related terms emerged: *virtual environments* and *synthetic environments*. Now, much of the original hype of VR has disappeared due to unfulfilled promises. Technology was not ready to make computer-generated worlds as believable as reality. Today we consider that Virtual Reality is about creating "acceptable" reproductions of real objects or environments for training, entertainment or design purposes.

Virtual Reality uses computers to create 3D environments in which one can navigate and interact. Navigation implies the ability to move around and explore the features of a 3D scene, such as walking through a forest. Interaction means the ability to select and manipulate objects in the scene, for instance, grabbing and examining a flower found in the forest.

Virtual Reality in its most "classical" form requires real-time graphics, a stereoscopic display, used to produce the illusion of 3D, and a tracking system to acquire head and hands motion. Commonly used technologies include head-mounted displays (HMD) and stereoscopic glasses. Interaction can be achieved using a tracking device, which may be integrated in the HMD itself, for tracking head and body movement. A "data glove" can be used to track hand movements. The glove lets the user point to and manipulate objects in the virtual scene.

VR is about simulating reality. The aspect of reality that has been most frequently addressed is the visual one. Sight is, for most people, the dominant perceptual sense and the principal means for acquiring information. However, reality is not limited to what we can see. Other important components of our perceptual experience are sounds and tactile feedback.

Developing VR systems involves different disciplines that address each of the human senses: computer graphics (sight), 3D sound synthesis (hearing), and haptics (touch). Smell and taste play important roles in our daily life, but have been less exploited in VR due to the complexity of the required technology.

In this book we dedicate separate chapters to explain how to generate 3D graphics, 3D sound, and haptic feedback. Smell and taste are grouped in a single chapter because related research is still in a pioneering stage.

But before explaining how computers can synthesize stimuli for each of the human senses to produce the illusion of an alternative reality, we discuss some important concepts that help us to understand and measure the effects of Virtual Reality on users.

1.2 Basic Concepts

The main goal of VR is to create in the user the illusion of being in an environment that can be perceived as a believable place with enough interactivity to perform specific tasks in an efficient and comfortable way. There are two main factors that describe the VR experience from the physical and psychological points of view: immersion and presence.

1.2.1 Immersion

Immersion is related to the physical configuration of the user interface of the VR application. VR systems can be classified as fully immersive (those using an HMD), semi-immersive (large projection screens), or nonimmersive (desktop-based VR). The classification depends on how much the user can perceive (see, hear, touch) the real world during the simulation.

The first VR systems were fully immersive and used variants of head-mounted displays. The idea was to completely isolate the user from the real world, with the hope that this would contribute to the believability and efficiency of the simulation. Early fully immersive systems had different levels of success in creating the illusion of an alternative reality, and some of them were difficult to use. When using an HMD, some people may suffer from motion sickness-related problems. This is known as cybersickness [1]. Several factors that cause it have been identified, but there is still no definite method to prevent it. Cybersickness seems to appear more often with fully immersive systems.

Semi-immersive systems, such as the CAVE designed by Cruz-Neira et al. in 1992 [2], provide 3D sound and high-resolution graphics. A CAVE is a multi-user workplace surrounded by screens where the virtual world is projected. Images are displayed according to the position and gaze direction of the main user. For additional information about CAVE systems, see Section 7.2.5. In general, semi-immersive systems let several users share the simulation; this opens interesting possibilities for collaborative work.

Nonimmersive systems have gained popularity due to their lower cost, ease of use, and ease of installation. They are sometimes called desktop-based VR systems; the most representative examples are video games. The good combination of interactivity, ease of use, and appealing graphics and sound can produce in the users a great level of interest and involvement in the simulation. Few VR systems can compete with a good video game in terms of -psychologically- isolating the user from the world and producing strong emotional responses.

Psychological aspects of the VR experience are an active research area. It is not completely clear which are the factors in a simulation that can produce specific user reactions in terms of emotional response, involvement, and degree of interest. One of the most important concepts that helps us understand the psychology of the VR experience is the "sense of presence."

1.2.2 Presence

Presence is a subjective concept, associated with the psychology of the user. According to Slater and Wilbur, "Presence is a state of consciousness, the (psychological) sense of being in the virtual environment" [3]. Professor M. Slater is one of the most known researchers on this subject. There are several journals[1] and international conferences where the psychology of the VR experience is explored and discussed.

Presence is when the multimodal simulations (images, sound, haptic feedback, etc.) are processed by the brain and understood as a coherent environment in which we can perform some activities and interact. Presence is achieved when the user is conscious, deliberately or not, of being in a virtual environment (VE). For example, when playing a video game, a person knows the world in the game is not real, but decides to behave as if it were a real situation. A sign of presence is when people behave in a VE in a way that is close to the way they would behave in a similar real-life situation. However, presence can be achieved in a VE that does not resemble any real-life environment, for example, fantasy worlds in video games are taken by users as if they existed in reality and users behave accordingly.

---

[1] One of the main publications on the topic is the MIT Press journal *Presence: Teleoperators and Virtual Environments* (http://www.mitpressjournals.org/loi/pres).

Presence can lead to involvement and emotional reactions from the user. Once the brain integrates the 3D images, sounds, and other kinds of feedback in the form of a coherent environment, different reactions can arise. It can occur that we feel deeply involved in the simulation and experience a variety of emotions. A well-crafted virtual world could change our emotional state and make us feel anxiety, happiness, or sadness. This phenomenon is what has motivated many researchers to use VR as a therapeutic tool for treating phobias, such as arachnophobia or social phobia. In this sense, research tries to discover what sensory input is needed for people to feel as if they were present in an environment. Depending on the situation, some senses can be more important than others. For instance, when simulating surgery to train doctors, having accurate tactile haptic feedback is more important than the image quality of the simulation. In other scenarios, an accurate 3D sound synthesis can be the key factor to induce a sense of presence. For example, when simulating an orchestra in a concert hall, presence will be achieved if the sound is accurately reproduced, taking into account the acoustics of the hall. In this case, the realism of the 3D graphics has a lower priority for the sense of presence. In fact, when listening to a high-quality sound recording, it is easier to feel like you are in the concert hall when you close our eyes, because the visual input is less important in this situation.

It has been observed that user involvement can induce a sense of presence. It is important to distinguish presence and involvement. As in real life, one can be present but not involved, for example, being in a stadium watching a game that is boring, we know we are in the stadium, but we don't behave accordingly; even though we are there, we don't feel present. Involvement depends on the content, for example, watching an important game of my favorite team on TV can make me react and behave as if I were in the stadium. The content of a simulation can induce presence. This explains the high levels of presence that can be achieved by players of some video games. The content of the VE produces so much involvement in the user that despite the fact that the system is nonimmersive and there is no sophisticated user interface, usually keyboard, mouse and/or joystick, the user feels like he or she is in the virtual world and gets isolated from reality.

1.3 A Brief History of Virtual Reality

The history of Virtual Reality as a multisensory simulation of the real world can be traced back to the 1960s. The "Sensorama" (see Figure 1.1a), created by the cinematographer Morton Heilig in 1962, was a multisensory vehicle simulator. The system allowed users to sit in front of a screen where they could choose from different rides prerecorded using motorcycles, bicycles, and even a helicopter. Sensorama used wide field of view optics to view 3D photographic slides and had stereo sound, as well as smell and wind generators. At that time, computers were not ready to be used for such applications. The system had almost no interactivity; the user was a passive observer.

In 1965, Ivan Sutherland published a paper entitled "The Ultimate Display" in which he described how one day the computer would provide a window into virtual worlds. In 1968 he built a head-mounted display (see Figure 1.1c) that presented to the user left and right views of a computer-generated 3D scene. The system tracked the user's head movement to update the images accordingly, giving the illusion of being in a virtual world. Images were far from being realistic; they were simple line drawings. However, the stereoscopic view produced the impression of looking at solid 3D objects. Sutherland also developed the "Sketchpad" (see Figure 1.1b), considered to be the ancestor of modern computer-aided drafting (CAD) programs. Sutherland is commonly recognized as the "father of Virtual Reality systems."

(a) Norton Heiling Sensorama (1962)   (b) Sutherland Sketchpad (1963)   (c) Sutherland's head-mounted display (1968)

Fig. 1.1: The first Virtual Reality systems

In 1978 A. Lippman, Scott Fisher, and other researchers from MIT developed the "Aspen Movie Map." The application allowed users to view a simulated ride through the city of Aspen, Colorado. The system used photographs of all the streets of the city, taken with four cameras pointing in different directions mounted on a truck. The user could move in four directions within the simulation; these were the beginnings of interactive virtual environments.

In the early 1970s Myron Krueger experimented with computer-generated environments and developed several computer art projects. Computers responded to gestures of the audience by interpreting and anticipating actions. Audience members could "touch" their video-generated silhouettes and interact with them. The system was called "Videoplace" and was used to generated what Krueger called "artificial reality" [4].

In the mid-1980s, different technologies converged to create the first true VR systems. Researchers at NASA's Ames Research Center worked on the creation of an affordable pilot training system for manned space missions. The people involved included Scott Fisher, Stephen Ellis, Michael McGreevy, and Warren Robinett. Their efforts led to the development of the Virtual Interface Environment Workstation (VIEW). The VIEW system consisted of a wide-angle stereoscopic display unit, glove-like devices for multiple degree-of-freedom tactile input, speech-recognition technology, gesture-tracking devices, 3D audio, speech synthesis, computer graphics, and video image generation equipment. In the words of Stephen Ellis, "The technology of the 1980s was not mature enough."[2] At that time, VR helmets (HMD) were too heavy, computers didn't have enough processing power, and touch feedback systems weren't reliable enough.

Another important pioneer VR project is the work started in 1967 by Frederick Brooks at the University of North Carolina at Chapel Hill. Brooks selected as a "driving problem" the manipulation of molecules. The objective of project GROPE was to develop a haptic interface for molecular forces. The idea was to allow molecule designers to "feel" force constraints when trying to create new molecule combinations. Force feedback was provided by the Argonne Remote Manipulator (ARM) a large ceiling-mounted mechanical device that was used to "grasp" and manipulate molecules. Project GROPE stayed active until 1990 [5].

The first initiatives to commercialize VR products started in the early 1980s. VPL Research was one of the first companies focused on developing VR hardware and software. VPL developed the "DataGlove," a glove-based input device. Other VPL products included head-mounted displays and software for graphics and sound rendering. VPL Research was founded by Jaron Lanier, who is recognized as having coined the term "Virtual Reality." Sun Microsystems acquired the patent portfolio of VPL Research in 1998.

Other companies that have played a role in the history of commercial VR products are Polhemus, Ascension, Virtual Technologies, and Immersion. Polhemus, a private company since 2002, was previously owned by major aerospace companies (Northrop, McDonnell Douglas, Kaiser Aerospace). Founded in the late 1960s, Polhemus pioneered electromagnetic position tracking. Ascension Technology was founded in 1986 by Ernie Blood and Jack Scully, former Polhemus employees. Ascension specializes in 3D tracking devices; the "Flock of Birds" set of magnetic trackers, one of their most popular products, is used in animation and medical applications. Virtual Technologies Inc., developers of the CyberGlove™, a glove-based interface, was acquired by Immersion Corporation in 2000. Immersion Corp. sells force-feedback devices and software.

---

[2] "Whatever happened to... Virtual Reality"
http://science.nasa.gov/headlines/y2004/21jun_vr.htm (accessed August 2007)

The 1980s saw a boom in VR research and commercialization, however, as mentioned before, the technology was not ready to fulfill all the expectations. Unreliable hardware, slow computers, and cybersickness were common problems. In the early 1990s, a change of paradigm in VR interfaces occurred with the design of the CAVE [2]. A CAVE is a room with graphics projected from behind the walls. It was invented at the Electronic Visualization Laboratory of the University of Illinois at Chicago Circle in 1992. The images projected on the walls were in stereo to provide a depth cue. In a CAVE, the user is surrounded by the projected images, offering a field of vision that is much wider than that of an HMD. Instead of wearing an uncomfortable VR helmet, CAVE users put on lightweight stereo glasses and can freely walk inside the CAVE. CAVEs are multi-user systems where people can see their own hands and bodies as part of the virtual world, enhancing the sense of presence and allowing for collaboration and exchange of ideas.

VR systems continue to use HMDs, which are now less heavy and have wider fields of view and higher resolution. However, the use of multiple projection screens with stereo images has gained popularity.

1.4 Reality-Virtuality Continuum

In [6], Milgram et al. proposed the idea of a reality-virtuality continuum, a way to understand and classify different types of display technologies. This helps to classify VR simulations with different degrees of reproduction fidelity, presence, and interactivity; see Figure 1.2.

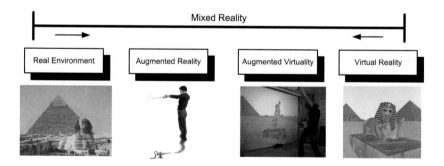

Fig. 1.2: Reality-virtuality continuum

On one end of the continuum, we can situate "pure" Virtual Reality: everything one can perceive is artificial; the user is isolated from the real world. On the opposite end, we have real reality, no computer generated stimuli. In the middle, we find mixed reality, simulations that combine real and virtual images: augmented reality and augmented virtuality. In augmented reality, most of the images are real. For example, using transparent headsets, you could see how new furniture would look in your house or view the 3D schematic of a car engine while working on the engine itself. In augmented virtuality, most of the imagery is computer-generated, such as, virtual sets, commonly used in TV shows, where presenters are projected into an imaginary environment.

In the last part of this book we describe VR applications, which are specific examples of simulations situated in different positions along the reality-virtuality continuum.

Part I

Fundamentals

2

Computer Graphics

What You Will Learn:

The objectives of this chapter are quite ambitious; you should refer to the references cited in each Section to get a deeper explanation of the topics presented. By the end of this chapter you will be familiar with the main building blocks of a 3D graphics interactive application and will be able to use this knowledge to build your own VR projects.

In particular, we will give a brief overview of the following topics:

- **Mathematics**: coordinate systems, vectors, and transformation matrices. These are used to represent, visualize, and animate 3D objects, characters, and the like.
- **3D modeling**: 3D primitives and geometric representations. This is how we actually create objects with a particular 3D shape.
- **Image rendering**: illumination models, lighting, colors and textures. These are used to visualize 3D shapes in a realistic and believable way.

This knowledge will give you the foundation required to understand any 3D graphics system, be it a software API like OpenGL or DirectX, a modeling/animation tool such as Maya, Blender 3D, or 3DS MAX, or a game engine like Torque or Unreal.

2.1 Mathematics

2.1.1 Coordinate Systems

A coordinate system is a way to determine the position of a point by a set of numbers (coordinates) that can be distances from a set of reference planes, angles subtended with an origin, or a combination of both [7].

Different coordinate systems have been defined, each of them allows representation of 3D shapes; however, depending on the shape, it may be easier to represent using one coordinate system than another. The most commonly used coordinate systems are the cartesian and the polar or spherical coordinate systems. Both allow for specifying the position of a point in a 3D Euclidean space, a space in three dimensions just like the world we know. It was named Euclidean after Euclid of Alexandria, a Greek mathematician whose treatise *The Elements* defined the principles of geometry. There are also non-euclidean geometries, but the kind of shapes we will work with will be represented in a 3D Euclidean space.

Cartesian Coordinate Systems

This is the most commonly used coordinate system in computers. The position of a point is determined by three distances, from each of the planes. The axes are at right angles (orthogonal) and are typically used to specify spatial dimensions: width, height, and depth (x, y, z). Cartesian coordinates are the most common data to represent real, theoretical, and artistic worlds.

Spherical Coordinate Systems

A spherical coordinate system is a called polar coordinate system when used in two dimensions. The position of a point is specified using one distance (ρ from the origin) and two angles (θ and ϕ) measured from the reference planes at right angles (see Figure 2.1a). Spherical coordinates are commonly used in applications that need to define positions relative to the surface of the Earth, such as meteorology, geography, and oceanography. In such cases, the angles are better known as latitude and longitude. The origin is at the center of the planet and the reference planes are the Equator and Greenwich meridian. Spherical coordinates are also used in astronomy to specify the position of celestial objects. In this case, the angles are called right ascension and declination.

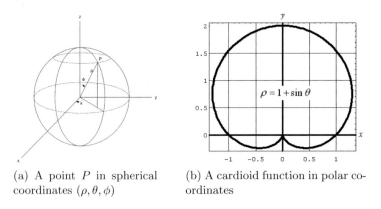

(a) A point P in spherical coordinates (ρ, θ, ϕ)

(b) A cardioid function in polar coordinates

Fig. 2.1: Point and shapes in polar coordinates

As shown in Figure 2.1b, some shapes are easier to specify and plot using polar coordinates than using Cartesian coordinates. However, most computer visualization systems, which are programmed using graphics APIs like OpenGL, use Cartesian coordinates. Thus, it is necessary to convert positions defined in polar/spherical coordinates to Cartesian coordinates through the following formulas:

$$x = \rho \sin \phi \cos \theta \quad y = \rho \sin \phi \sin \theta \quad z = \rho \cos \phi$$

In the rest of the book we will use Cartesian coordinates; as mentioned earlier, they are the most commonly used and are better "understood" by 3D APIs and other computer graphics-related tools.

In general, 3D virtual worlds are created out of 3D polygons, usually triangles or squares arranged in 3D space to form 3D surfaces that comprise more complex objects; this is illustrated in Figure 2.2. The simplest polygon and the most efficient to represent, process, and visualize with current graphics hardware is a triangle. A triangle is defined by specifying the three points or vertices that compose it (see Figure 2.2). Commonly available hardware (graphics cards) is able to take these three vertices and use them to draw a colored triangle on the screen at very fast speeds. Currently, graphics cards can draw hundreds of millions of colored triangles per second; for example, the NVIDIA Quadro FX 4600 card can render 250 million triangles per second (March 2007). The complete "drawing" process is called rendering; it involves computing the effects of color and textures assigned to each triangle in addition to lights and possibly shadows and reflections. We explain this process in Section 2.3.4.

Fig. 2.2: Triangle-based 3D shape

Triangles are the basic primitive for creation of 3D shapes, the building block of virtual worlds. In order to understand how to visualize and animate virtual entities in 3D space we must be able to visualize and animate each triangle comprising the environment in a coherent way. We will provide more details on animation in Chapter 3.

2.1.2 Vectors, Transformations and Matrices

To illustrate the basic mathematical principles behind visualization of 3D shapes, we start with a single triangle. In order to represent a triangle shape in a computer we use a Cartesian coordinate system and three points in the space to delimit the shape; we call them vertices. A vertex $\mathbf{v}$ is composed of three cartesian coordinates (v_x, v_y, v_z). This set of three coordinates is a 3D vector, an array of three values, which are the vector components. A triangle can thus be defined by three 3D vectors that specify the coordinates of each vertex in the space: $\mathbf{v_1}, \mathbf{v_2}, \mathbf{v_3}$.

In a 3D environment, triangles and any other 3D shape can suffer three basic coordinate transformations: they can be translated, rotated, or scaled. When combined, these three basic transformations allow us to produce a great variety of animation, from simple linear motion to complex trajectories and surface deformations. Some important questions to answer are: how can we translate/rotate/scale a 3D shape? what happens to the vertices forming the shape?

Translating a 3D shape means adding a vector $\mathbf{T}$ to each of its composing vectors. The addition of two vectors consists of summing each of its components: $\mathbf{a}+\mathbf{b} = \mathbf{c}$, where the components of vector $\mathbf{c}$ are: $(a_x+b_x, a_y+b_y, a_z+b_z)$.

Scaling affects the components of each vertex by multiplying them by a scale factor s. The components of vector $\mathbf{v}$ when scaled by a given factor are $(v_x \times s_x, v_y \times s_y, v_z \times s_z)$.

The rotation transformation is a combination of addition and multiplication operations that result from basic trigonometry. It is easier and computationally efficient to use a matrix representation and matrix multiplication to perform a rotation transformation over a vector. In fact, the most convenient way of processing coordinate transformations is to set up matrices containing the parameters of the transformations and use matrix multiplication to reduce a series of transformations to a combined single transformation matrix.

Homogeneous Coordinates

In order to process transformations in a uniform way, it is necessary to add a component to the vectors and increase the dimensions of the matrices. For 3D space, 4D vectors are used, the four components are called homogeneous coordinates. The components of a 4D homogeneous vector are reduced to three dimensions by the following normalization operation:

$$\left[x,\, y,\, z,\, h \right] \longrightarrow \left[\tfrac{x}{h},\, \tfrac{y}{h},\, \tfrac{z}{h} \right]$$

Any vertex in 3D space can be represented as $\left[x,\, y,\, z,\, 1 \right]$; 4×4 matrices should be set up in such a way that multiplying a transformation matrix M by a vector $\mathbf{v}$ will give as the result a vector $\mathbf{v'}$ whose components $\left[x',\, y',\, z',\, 1 \right]$ correspond to the coordinates of $\mathbf{v}$ after applying the transformations parameterized in M.

The fourth dimension (fourth component) will normally remain 1. Most of the graphical transformations can be broken down into products of the three basic ones. Transformation matrices are defined as follows.

Translation

Vector $\mathbf{v}'$, which is the position of $\mathbf{v}$, after a translation of t_x units over the X axis, t_y units on Y, and t_z units on the Z axis is calculated as follows:

$$\mathbf{v}' = T \cdot \mathbf{v} = \begin{bmatrix} 1 & 0 & 0 & t_x \\ 0 & 1 & 0 & t_y \\ 0 & 0 & 1 & t_z \\ 0 & 0 & 0 & 1 \end{bmatrix} \cdot \begin{bmatrix} x \\ y \\ z \\ 1 \end{bmatrix} = \begin{bmatrix} x + t_x \\ y + t_y \\ z + t_z \\ 1 \end{bmatrix}$$

When applied to all the vectors (vertices) that comprise a 3D shape, this transformation will move the shape by the magnitude and direction of vector $[t_x, t_y, t_z]$. Note that translation cannot be achieved using 3×3 matrix multiplication with a 3D vector. This is one of the most important reasons for using homogeneous coordinates: they allow composite transformations to be handled by a single matrix.

Scale

The scaled version of $\mathbf{v}$ is calculated as follows:

$$\mathbf{v}' = S \cdot \mathbf{v} = \begin{bmatrix} s_x & 0 & 0 & 0 \\ 0 & s_y & 0 & 0 \\ 0 & 0 & s_z & 0 \\ 0 & 0 & 0 & 1 \end{bmatrix} \cdot \begin{bmatrix} x \\ y \\ z \\ 1 \end{bmatrix} = \begin{bmatrix} s_x \cdot x \\ s_y \cdot y \\ s_z \cdot z \\ 1 \end{bmatrix}$$

A scaled 3D shape normally changes both its size and its location. Only shapes centered on the origin will remain in the same position. Scaling may also be done with reference to a point $P_o = [x_o, y_o, z_o]$, which may be the center of the 3D shape.

Translating a 3D shape centered at P_o can be done through a combined transformation: translating all the vertices of the shape to the origin, scaling, and then translating the vertices again to restore the shape to its original position. The vertices comprising the 3D shape can be arranged in a matrix M with n columns (one per vertex) and four rows (homogeneous coordinates). The transformations will be applied by multiplying the following matrices by M: T^{-1} (the inverse of T), for the initial translation to the origin, S for scaling, and T for restoring the original position:

$$M' = T^{-1} \cdot S \cdot T \cdot M$$

$$M' = \begin{bmatrix} 1 & 0 & 0 & x_o \\ 0 & 1 & 0 & y_o \\ 0 & 0 & 1 & z_o \\ 0 & 0 & 0 & 1 \end{bmatrix} \cdot \begin{bmatrix} s_x & 0 & 0 & 0 \\ 0 & s_y & 0 & 0 \\ 0 & 0 & s_z & 0 \\ 0 & 0 & 0 & 1 \end{bmatrix} \cdot \begin{bmatrix} 1 & 0 & 0 & -x_o \\ 0 & 1 & 0 & -y_o \\ 0 & 0 & 1 & -z_o \\ 0 & 0 & 0 & 1 \end{bmatrix} \cdot \begin{bmatrix} x_1 & x_2 & \dots & x_n \\ y_1 & y_2 & \dots & y_n \\ z_1 & z_2 & \dots & z_n \\ 1 & 1 & \dots & 1 \end{bmatrix}$$

$$M' = \begin{bmatrix} s_x & 0 & 0 & x_o(1-s_x) \\ 0 & s_y & 0 & y_o(1-s_y) \\ 0 & 0 & s_z & z_o(1-s_z) \\ 0 & 0 & 0 & 1 \end{bmatrix} \cdot \begin{bmatrix} x_1 & x_2 & \dots & x_n \\ y_1 & y_2 & \dots & y_n \\ z_1 & z_2 & \dots & z_n \\ 1 & 1 & \dots & 1 \end{bmatrix}$$

$$M' = \begin{bmatrix} s_x x_1 + x_o(1-s_x) & s_x x_2 + x_o(1-s_x) & \dots & s_x x_n + x_o(1-s_x) \\ s_y y_1 + y_o(1-s_y) & s_y y_2 + y_o(1-s_y) & \dots & s_y y_n + y_o(1-s_y) \\ s_z z_1 + z_o(1-s_z) & s_z z_2 + z_o(1-s_z) & \dots & s_z z_n + z_o(1-s_z) \\ 1 & 1 & \dots & 1 \end{bmatrix}$$

where M' contains the vertices of the 3D shape scaled with reference to P_o.

At this point it is important to note that matrix multiplication is associative but not commutative: the order in which the transformations are applied must be carefully observed. If the order of the transformations were irrelevant, it would be possible to rearrange the equation $M' = T^{-1} \cdot S \cdot T \cdot M$ as follows:

$$M' = S \cdot T \cdot T^{-1} \cdot M = S \cdot I \cdot M = S \cdot M$$

which is clearly false[1]. This *reductio ad absurdum* argument shows that, in general, exchanging the multiplication order of transformation matrices produces different results.

Rotation

Let us consider rotating a vertex $\mathbf{v}$ over the plane formed by the $X-$ and $Y-$ axes: $\mathbf{v} = [x, y, 0]$. Rotation transformation will be applied about the origin by an arbitrary angle θ. To calculate the transformed coordinates $\mathbf{v'}$, we should consider the position vector from the origin to point $\mathbf{v}$. The length of $\mathbf{v}$ is r at an angle ϕ to the X axis. The position vector $\mathbf{v}$ is rotated about the origin by the angle θ to $\mathbf{v'}$.

Since the $z-$ coordinate of $\mathbf{v}$ is 0, we can write the position vectors as follows:

$$\mathbf{v} = [x, y] = [r \cos \phi, r \sin \phi]$$
$$\mathbf{v'} = [x', y'] = [r \cos(\phi + \theta), r \sin(\phi + \theta)]$$

---

[1] Multiplying a square matrix by its inverse (e.g., $T \cdot T^{-1}$) yields the identity matrix I (a matrix that has a 1 for each element on the main diagonal and 0 elsewhere), the identity for matrix multiplication.

Using trigonometric identities[2] allows writing $\mathbf{v'}$ as:

$$\mathbf{v'} = [x', y'] = [r(\cos\phi\cos\theta - \sin\phi\sin\theta), r(\cos\phi\sin\theta + \sin\phi\cos\theta)]$$

Using the definitions of x and y allows rewriting $\mathbf{v'}$ as:

$$\mathbf{v'} = [x', y'] = [x\cos\theta - y\sin\theta, x\sin\theta + y\cos\theta]$$

Thus, for a vertex on the plane $X - Y$, the transformation matrix for a general rotation about the origin by an arbitrary angle θ is:

$$R = \begin{bmatrix} \cos\theta & -\sin\theta \\ \sin\theta & \cos\theta \end{bmatrix}$$

This corresponds to a rotation around the $Z-$ axis. Any 3D vertex rotated around the $Z-$ axis will keep unaltered its $z-$ coordinate. Thus, we can convert the previous 2×2 matrix into a 4×4 matrix with homogeneous coordinates:

$$R_z = \begin{bmatrix} \cos\theta & -\sin\theta & 0 & 0 \\ \sin\theta & \cos\theta & 0 & 0 \\ 0 & 0 & 1 & 0 \\ 0 & 0 & 0 & 1 \end{bmatrix}$$

Notice how this transformation matrix only modifies the $x-$ and $y-$ coordinates of a 3D vector. Following an analogous procedure, we can obtain the transformation matrices for rotations around the $X-$ and $Y-$ axes:

$$R_x = \begin{bmatrix} 1 & 0 & 0 & 0 \\ 0 & \cos\theta & -\sin\theta & 0 \\ 0 & \sin\theta & \cos\theta & 0 \\ 0 & 0 & 0 & 1 \end{bmatrix} \quad R_y = \begin{bmatrix} \cos\theta & 0 & \sin\theta & 0 \\ 0 & 1 & 0 & 0 \\ -\sin\theta & 0 & \cos\theta & 0 \\ 0 & 0 & 0 & 1 \end{bmatrix}$$

As in the case of the scaling transformation, the rotation matrices we have defined allow us to rotate a 3D shape centered at the origin of the coordinate system. If the shape we want to rotate is not centered, it must first be translated to the origin, rotated and then translated back to its original position: $M' = T^{-}1 \cdot R_z \cdot R_y \cdot R_x \cdot T \cdot M$, where M and M' contain the n vectors corresponding to the original and transformed vertices that comprise the 3D shape; see the example for the scaling transformation.

As we have shown before, the order in which transformation matrices are multiplied is critical; Figure 2.3 shows the different results obtained by exchanging the order of translation and rotation transformations.

---

[2] $\cos(\phi \pm \theta) = \cos\phi\cos\theta \mp \sin\phi\sin\theta$
$\sin(\phi \pm \theta) = \cos\phi\sin\theta \pm \sin\phi\cos\theta$

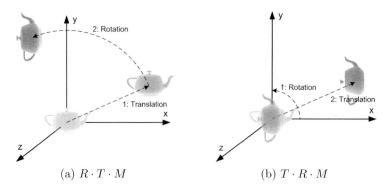

(a) $R \cdot T \cdot M$ (b) $T \cdot R \cdot M$

Fig. 2.3: Noncommutativity of transformations composition

2.1.3 Angular Representations

The rotation matrices defined earlier correspond to a particular angular representation called Euler angles. Angular representations are mathematical approaches to specify the orientation of a 3D shape. Each angular representation has pros and cons; some are more "intuitive" than others, as is the case of Euler angles, but present some problems when specifying certain types of orientation. Other representations are more robust, in the sense that they allow for representing complex orientations without ambiguity, such as quaternions, but can be more difficult to understand when you are not familiar with them.

Euler Angles

The Euler angles are one of the most intuitive angular representations. It was developed by Leonhard Euler to describe the orientation of a rigid body in a 3D Euclidean space. The orientation of an object (3D shape) can be expressed as a sequence of three rotations described by the Euler angles. The order and the axes around which the rotations are applied can be specified in different ways. Other descriptions of rotations in 3D space equivalent to Euler angles are the Tait-Bryan angles, also called Cardano angles or nautical angles. Such representations are used to describe the orientation of an aircraft and name the angles as roll, pitch, and yaw. A common definition of Euler angles is as follows:

- θ, the angle between the $X-$ and $Y-$ axes, roll angle
- ϕ, the angle between the $Z-$ and $X-$ axes, the yaw angle
- ψ, the angle between the $Z-$ and $Y-$ axes, the pitch angle

Precaution must be observed when applying rotation transformations using Euler angles. A well-known problem called "gimbal lock"[3] occurs when applying rotations of 90°. As illustrated in Figure 2.4, when a 90° rotation around the $X-$ axis is applied, subsequent rotations on the $Y-$ or $Z-$ axes give unexpected results. The local coordinate system of the shape is in such a position that, after rotation around $X-$, the $Z-$ axis has the same orientation as the original Y, but rotations using Euler angles are applied according to the global coordinate system, hence the unexpected result. Other angular representations try to avoid the gimbal lock and provide more flexibility to describe 3D shape orientations.

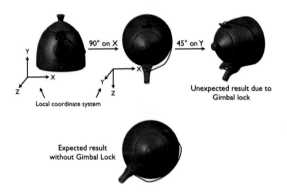

Fig. 2.4: Gimbal lock

Axis Angle

This angular representation is an alternative way to describe the orientation of an object in 3D space. Rotations are represented by a unit vector and an angle of revolution around the vector; see Figure 2.5. This angular representation is commonly used in robotics, animation, and simulation. Rotation about an arbitrary axis in space can be calculated using translations and rotations about the coordinate axes if we have an arbitrary axis in space passing through the points $O(x_0, y_0, z_0)$ and $P(x_1, y_1, z_1)$. The rotation about this axis by an angle δ is calculated as follows:

- Translate point (x_0, y_0, z_0) to the origin of the coordinate system.
- Perform necessary rotations to make the axis of rotation coincident with the $Z-$ axis (the choice of axis is arbitrary). This implies a rotation about the $X-$ axis and a rotation about the $Y-$ axis.

---

[3] A gimbal is a mechanical device that allows the rotation of an object in multiple dimensions. A gimbal lock occurs when two of the three gimbal rings align together so that one of the rotation references is canceled.

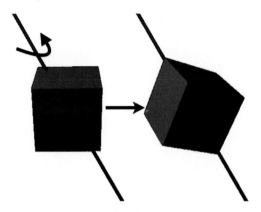

Fig. 2.5: Rotation about an arbitrary axis in space

- Rotate about the $Z-$ axis by the angle δ.
- Apply the inverse of the rotation transformations to put the axis of rotation back to its original orientation.
- Perform the inverse of the translation to leave the shape and its rotation axis at the original position.

The complete axis-angle transformation can be calculated as follows:

$$M' = T^{-1} \cdot R_x^{-1} \cdot R_y^{-1} \cdot R_\delta \cdot R_y \cdot R_x \cdot T \cdot M$$

where M and M' contain the n vectors corresponding to the original and transformed vertices that compose the 3D shape we want to transform.

The required matrices are:

$$T = \begin{bmatrix} 1 & 0 & 0 & -x_0 \\ 0 & 1 & 0 & -y_0 \\ 0 & 0 & 1 & -z_0 \\ 0 & 0 & 0 & 1 \end{bmatrix}$$

$$R_x = \begin{bmatrix} 1 & 0 & 0 & 0 \\ 0 & \cos\alpha & -\sin\alpha & 0 \\ 0 & \sin\alpha & \cos\alpha & 0 \\ 0 & 0 & 0 & 1 \end{bmatrix} = \begin{bmatrix} 1 & 0 & 0 & 0 \\ 0 & c_z/d & -c_y/d & 0 \\ 0 & c_y/d & c_z/d & 0 \\ 0 & 0 & 0 & 1 \end{bmatrix}$$

$$R_y = \begin{bmatrix} \cos(-\beta) & 0 & \sin(-\beta) & 0 \\ 0 & 1 & 0 & 0 \\ -\sin(-\beta) & 0 & \cos(-\beta) & 0 \\ 0 & 0 & 0 & 1 \end{bmatrix} = \begin{bmatrix} d & 0 & -c_x & 0 \\ 0 & 1 & 0 & 0 \\ c_x & 0 & d & 0 \\ 0 & 0 & 0 & 1 \end{bmatrix}$$

$$R_\delta = \begin{bmatrix} \cos\delta & -\sin\delta & 0 & 0 \\ \sin\delta & \cos\delta & 0 & 0 \\ 0 & 0 & 1 & 0 \\ 0 & 0 & 0 & 1 \end{bmatrix}$$

We will now review other more compact angular representations that have interesting properties for robotics, computer graphics, and Virtual Reality applications.

Quaternions

Quaternions were discovered and described by Sir William R. Hamilton in 1844 [8]. In 1985, Ken Shoemake proposed using them as an efficient way to represent 3D rotations of objects in computer animation applications [9].

Quaternions were conceived by Hamilton as extended complex numbers: $w+ix+jy+kz$, composed of imaginary numbers: $i^2 = j^2 = k^2 = -1$, $ij = k = -ji$ and real numbers: w, x, y, z. Quaternions can be treated as quadruples of real numbers: $[w, x, y, z]$, with operations of addition and multiplication suitably defined. The components can be grouped into a real part, w, called scalar and an imaginary part, (x, y, z) which Hamilton named vector. We usually write a quaternion as $[w, \mathbf{v}]$, with $\mathbf{v} = (x, y, z)$. A real number s can be represented as a quaternion: $[s, 0]$, a vector $\mathbf{v} \in R^3$ can also be represented as a quaternion: $[0, \mathbf{v}]$.

Unit quaternions have unit norms: $| q | = 1$, $x^2 + y^2 + z^2 + w^2 = 1$.

Quaternion multiplication is defined as follows:

$$q_1 q_2 = \begin{bmatrix} w_1 \\ \mathbf{v}_1 \end{bmatrix} \begin{bmatrix} w_2 \\ \mathbf{v}_2 \end{bmatrix} = \begin{bmatrix} w_1 w_2 - \mathbf{v}_1 \cdot \mathbf{v}_2 \\ w_1 \mathbf{v}_2 + w_2 \mathbf{v}_1 + \mathbf{v}_1 \times \mathbf{v}_2 \end{bmatrix}$$

Quaternion multiplication is associative but not commutative:

$$q_1 q_2 \neq q_2 q_1$$
$$q_1(q_2 q_3) = (q_1 q_2)q_3$$

The multiplication identity quaternion is:

$$q_i = \begin{bmatrix} 1 \\ (0,0,0) \end{bmatrix}, \quad qq_i = q$$

The conjugate of a quaternion is written q^*, and is defined as:

$$q^* = \begin{bmatrix} w \\ \mathbf{v} \end{bmatrix}^* = \begin{bmatrix} w \\ -\mathbf{v} \end{bmatrix}$$

$$(q^*)^* = q$$

$$(q_1 q_2)^* = q_2^* q_1^*$$

Based on these definitions, the inverse of a quaternion is:

$$q^{-1} = \frac{q^*}{|q|} \quad qq^{-1} = \begin{bmatrix} 1 \\ 0 \\ 0 \\ 0 \end{bmatrix}, \text{ the unit length quaternion}$$

Given a point $\mathbf{p}$ in 3D space (a 3D vector), represented by a quaternion $q_p = \begin{bmatrix} 0 \\ \mathbf{p} \end{bmatrix}$, and a unit quaternion $q = \begin{bmatrix} \cos(\theta/2) \\ \sin(\theta/2)r \end{bmatrix}$, the product $qq_p q^{-1}$ results in $\mathbf{p}$ rotating about an arbitrary axis r by an angle θ:

$$qq_p q^{-1} = \begin{bmatrix} w \\ \mathbf{v} \end{bmatrix} \begin{bmatrix} 0 \\ \mathbf{p} \end{bmatrix} \begin{bmatrix} w \\ -\mathbf{v} \end{bmatrix} = \begin{bmatrix} w \\ \mathbf{v} \end{bmatrix} \begin{bmatrix} \mathbf{p} \cdot \mathbf{v} \\ w\mathbf{p} - \mathbf{p} \times \mathbf{v} \end{bmatrix}$$

$$= \begin{bmatrix} w\mathbf{p} \cdot \mathbf{v} - \mathbf{v} \cdot w\mathbf{p} + \mathbf{v} \cdot \mathbf{p} \times \mathbf{v} = 0 \\ w(w\mathbf{p} - \mathbf{p} \times \mathbf{v}) + (\mathbf{p} \cdot \mathbf{v})\mathbf{v} + \mathbf{v} \times (w\mathbf{p} - \mathbf{p} \times \mathbf{v}) \end{bmatrix}$$

Thus, we can calculate $\mathbf{p}'$ which is the new position of point $\mathbf{p}$ after a rotation about an arbitrary axis with normalized coordinates (x_r, y_r, z_r) by an angle θ as follows:

$$\mathbf{p}' = R_{(q)} \cdot \mathbf{p}$$

where $R_{(q)}$ is the matrix form of quaternion $q = \begin{bmatrix} w = \cos(\theta/2) \\ x = x_r \sin(\theta/2) \\ y = y_r \sin(\theta/2) \\ z = z_r \sin(\theta/2) \end{bmatrix}$:

$$R_{(q)} = \begin{bmatrix} 1 - 2y^2 - 2z^2 & 2xy - 2wz & 2xz + 2wy & 0 \\ 2xy + 2wz & 1 - 2x^2 - 2z^2 & 2yz - 2wx & 0 \\ 2xz - 2wy & 2yz + 2wx & 1 - 2x^2 - 2y^2 & 0 \\ 0 & 0 & 0 & 1 \end{bmatrix}$$

If q_1 and q_2 are unit quaternions, the combined rotation of rotating first by q_1 and then by q_2 is expressed as $q_3 = q_2 \cdot q_1$. Any unit quaternion multiplied by the identity quaternion will not be changed.

Representing a rotation as a quaternion requires four numbers. It is easy to construct the quaternion corresponding to any given axis and angle, and vice versa. This is more difficult using Euler angles. Another important advantage of quaternions is that they allow us to produce "smooth rotations," slow rotations commonly used to control the point of view (camera motion) in a video game or virtual environment. Techniques such as spherical linear interpolation (SLERP) are commonly used with quaternions to interpolate camera rotations between an initial and a final orientation.

When multiplying several rotation matrices, rounding errors accumulate due to the finite precision of the microprocessor. When rounding errors have surpassed a threshold, quaternions or matrices do not represent the required rotations any more and lead to unpredictable results. In order to solve problems due to rounding errors, quaternions can be normalized; an analogous but harder procedure is required to fix a rotation matrix (make it orthogonal again).

Exponential Maps

Exponential maps require only three parameters to describe a rotation. This representation does not suffer from the gimbal lock problem, and its singularities occur in a region of the parameter space that can easily be avoided [10]. The exponential map represents rotations as vectors in R^3 (vector with three components), where the axis of rotation is defined by the vector direction (components) and the rotation angle is the magnitude of the vector.

A detailed discussion of the benefits of exponential maps, compared to quaternions and rotation matrices is presented by F. Sebastian Grassia in [11].

Choosing the Best Angular Representation

We have presented different approaches to represent the orientation of a shape in 3D space. A very important question to answer is which angular representation to use in a Virtual Reality application. In fact, the answer depends on the part of the application we are referring to: user interface, animation constraints, interpolation, composition, or rendering.

User interface implies input data; this is where we "manually" set up the orientation of shapes in a virtual environment or control the camera to watch the virtual scene from different points of view. Common ways to input this information is through keyboard, joystick, mouse or more sophisticated devices such as magnetic trackers. For the user interface we need to have an intuitive representation that allow us to easily visualize the orientation, this is commonly achieved with Euler angles.

Animation constraints are different restrictions that we impose on the virtual world to achieve useful results. Constraints can be, for example, the joint limits of a virtual character, that prevent the legs or arms from adopting unnatural postures. We can also constrain the camera orientation to ease navigation within a virtual world. This is easily done using Euler angles, sometimes quaternions are used, but they are more difficult to handle.

Interpolation refers to the calculation of intermediate orientations to create a smooth transition between two postures/orientations. Interpolation is used when changing the camera point of view or when animating 3D shapes. We have already mentioned that quaternions give very good visual results when interpolated using spherical linear interpolation, commonly known as SLERP. Exponential maps are also suitable for interpolation.

Composition is the process of accumulating different transformations to achieve a desired goal; it can be the series of transformations required to move from point A to point B within a virtual environment: translation, interpolation of camera orientation, and the like. Quaternions and matrices are particularly useful for compositing transformations because they can be multiplied to accumulate (compose) complex series of consecutive translations, rotations, and/or scaling operations.

Rendering is the process used to display on the screen the virtual environment when viewed from a specific point of view. It is the final phase of the visualization pipeline of any computer graphics application. Orientation matrices are the most suitable representation since they can be processed in a very efficient way (hardware acceleration of the graphics card).

2.1.4 Projections

At this point we have presented the fundamentals of representing points in 3D space that can be used to create 3D shapes. We have also described how to transform those points to translate them, scale them, and rotate them. The next step in this overview is to describe some details about how to actually "draw" 3D shapes on the screen. So far we have considered a 3D space; however, the screen is only 2D, we need a way to transform 3D coordinates to 2D. This is known as the projection transformation. Since most computer displays are planar viewing surfaces, the most commonly used projection surface is a plane. Other projection surfaces, such as spheres or cylinders, could also be useful for Virtual Reality applications displayed on hemispherical or cylindrical screens. We will concentrate on planar projections. The viewing surface is also called the plane of projection, transformation projections are also performed on a vertex basis. Straight lines, called projectors, are traced through the points in 3D space, and the projected point is the intersection between the projector and the plane of projection. There are two main types of planar projections: orthographic and perspective, with their associated transformation matrices.

Orthographic Projection

For this projection, we specify a square or rectangular viewing volume formed by the far, near, left, right, top, and bottom clipping planes. Anything outside this volume is not drawn. All objects that have the same dimensions appear the same size, regardless of whether they are far away or near; see Figure 2.6a. Orthographic projection is frequently used in architectural design and computer-aided design (CAD). Orthographic projections are also used to add text or 2D overlays on top of 3D graphic scenes. The most commonly used plane of projection is one that is parallel to the $X - Y$ plane; in such a case, the transformation matrix R_z with projectors in the z direction is defined as:

$$P_z = \begin{bmatrix} 1 & 0 & 0 & 0 \\ 0 & 1 & 0 & 0 \\ 0 & 0 & 0 & 0 \\ 0 & 0 & 0 & 1 \end{bmatrix}$$

In this projection, all the projectors go through a fixed point, the center of projection, which is sometimes referred to as the eye or viewpoint. The center of projection is usually placed on the opposite side of the plane of projection from the object being projected. Perspective projection works like a pin-hole camera, forcing the light rays to go through one single point. This projection adds the effect that distant objects appear smaller than nearby objects. The viewing volume is like a pyramid with the top shaved off. The remaining shape is called the frustum. Objects nearer to the front of the viewing volume appear close to their original size, but objects near the back of the volume shrink as they are projected to the front of the volume; see Figure 2.6b. This type of projection gives the most realism for simulation and 3D animation.

The matrix representation of a perspective transformation is:

$$P_p = \begin{bmatrix} 1 & 0 & 0 & 0 \\ 0 & 1 & 0 & 0 \\ 0 & 0 & 1 & 0 \\ 0 & 0 & 1/f & 0 \end{bmatrix}$$

where f is the distance between the viewpoint and the plane of projection. Transforming a point $\mathbf{p} = [x, y, z, 1]$ using transformation matrix P_p will yield $\mathbf{p'} = [x, y, z, z/f]$. Applying the rules of homogeneous coordinates, 3D coordinates are obtained by normalizing the 4D vector, dividing its components by z/f. Thus, the coordinates of $\mathbf{p'}$ projected on a 2D plane at a distance f from the viewpoint are: $[fx/z, fy/z]$.

2.2 3D Modeling

This Section will focus on how to actually "draw" 3D graphics on the computer screen, considering different ways to describe and visualize 3D curves, surfaces, and volumes. This is known as 3D modeling.

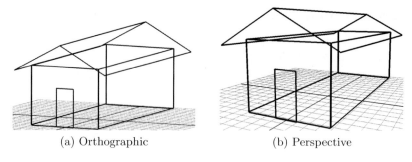

(a) Orthographic   (b) Perspective

Fig. 2.6: Projection

2.2.1 Geometric Representations

Geometric representations are ways to describe the arrangement of 3D vertices to create 3D shapes. There are three basic primitives or fundamental ways to create a 3D shape: points, curves, and polygons. Points are the simplest primitive; a 3D shape can be composed of a large amount of points to cover the whole 3D surface, where each point can be represented by a 3D vertex. A more practical and compact way of representing 3D shapes is using curves, which can be approximated by lines or points. We will dedicate most of this Section to explaining different ways to describe curves, since these are some of the most powerful geometric representations. Curves can be used to describe complex 3D surfaces. In the end, computer graphics cards use polygons to approximate any 3D surface. The simplest polygon and the most efficient one to render is a triangle. Thus at the lowest level, any 3D shape should be represented by a set of triangles. The more triangles used, the more accurate is the surface.

2.2.2 Curves

A curve can be represented as a collection of points lying on a 2D or 3D plane. If the points are properly spaced, they can be interconnected using short straight line segments, yielding an adequate visual representation of the curve. Curves could be represented as a list of points; the higher the number of points used to represent a curve, the more accurate and smooth will be its visualization. However, using an analytical representation has several advantages in terms of precision, compact storage, and ease of calculation of intermediate points. Any point on an analytically represented curve can be precisely determined. When represented by a collection of points, intermediate points must be obtained using interpolation, which leads to losses in drawing precision. In most of the cases, interpolated points do not lie on the curve. Analytically represented curves are easily reproduced, and such representation is useful when continuous alteration of the curve shape is required during the design phase. Thus we will concentrate on analytical definition of curves in 3D space, and we will see that this allows us to describe 3D surfaces. From the mathematical point of view, a curve can be represented in a parametric or nonparametric form.

Nonparametric Curves

Nonparametric representations are either explicit or implicit. For a 2D curve, an explicit, nonparametric form is given by $y = f(x)$. A typical example is the equation for a straight line, $y = mx + b$. In this form, for each value of x, only one value of y is obtained. Closed or multiple-value curves, for example, circles, cannot be represented explicitly. Implicit representations of the form $f(x, y) = 0$ overcome this limitation. For instance, the general second-degree implicit equation, $ax^2 + 2bxy + cy^2 + 2dx + 2ey + f = 0$, describes a variety of 2D curves known as conic sections; see Figure 2.7. A straight line is obtained by setting $a = b = c = 0$. In this case the equation is:

$$dx + ey + f = 0$$
$$y = -\frac{d}{e}x - \frac{f}{e} = mx + b'$$

Nonparametric curve representations present some limitations. First, they are axis-dependent; the choice of coordinate system affects the ease of use. Moreover, when points on an axis-dependent nonparametric curve are calculated at equal increments in x or y, they are not evenly distributed along the curve length. An unequal point distribution affects the quality and accuracy of the visualization. Despite these issues, nonparametric representations are useful for several applications. Parametric representations overcome these limitations.

Fig. 2.7: Conic sections

Parametric Curves

In parametric form, the coordinates of each point in a curve are represented as functions of a single parameter that varies across a predefined range of values. For a 3D curve with t as the parameter, the Cartesian coordinates of a point on the curve are:

$$x = x(t) \quad y = y(t) \quad z = z(t)$$

The vector representing the position of a point on the curve is:

$$P(t) = [x(t), y(t), z(t)]$$

Since a point on a parametric curve is specified by a single value of the parameter, the parametric form is axis-independent. The curve endpoints and length are fixed by the parameter range. In many cases it is convenient to normalize the parameter range for the curve segment of interest to $0 \leq t \leq 1$.

Being axis-independent, a parametric curve can be manipulated using the transformations we have previously discussed.

A typical example of a curve in parametric form is the equation of the circle:

$$P(t) = [r \cos t, r \sin t], \quad 0 \leq t \leq 2\pi$$

where r is the radius of the circle and the parameter t is associated with the geometric angle(in radians) measured counterclockwise from the positive $X-$ axis. Equal increments in t produce equal arc lengths along the circumference of the circle, and the visual appearance is good.

For a detailed discussion on the parametric forms of the circle and other conic sections, you can refer to chapter 4 of *Mathematical Elements for Computer Graphics* by Rogers and Adams [12]; many other printed and electronic sources are also available on this subject.

Splines

Our interest in curve representation will focus on a particularly useful type of parametric curve known as splines. The name spline comes from the shipbuilding industry, where flexible strips of wood, plastic, or metal were used to create full -or almost- full-size drawings of the boat shape and its parts. The splines were held in place with lead weights, called ducks. Before the development of computers, physical splines were the most common way to reliably draw smooth curves. Computers made possible the development of mathematical models and tools to reproduce and accelerate the process of drawing and manufacturing complex shapes.

Pierre Bézier and Paul de Faget de Casteljau developed a way to represent curves and surfaces by specifying a small set of control points. This greatly simplifies the design process of 3D shapes visualized in a computer system, allowing interactive adjustments to the shape of the curve or surface. Such curves have kept the name of Bézier because he was the first to publish his results.[4]

Bézier Curves

The simplest Bézier curve requires only two control points B_0 and B_1 and produces a straight line between such points. It is a curve of order 2 and degree 1. Control points can be 2D or 3D vectors for curves on a plane or in 3D space, respectively. The parametric form of a linear Bézier curve is:

Linear Bézier: $P(t) = B_0 + (B_1 - B_0)t = (1 - t)B_0 + tB_1$ $0 \leq t \leq 1$

It is interesting to point out that this formula is equivalent to a linear interpolation.

A quadratic Bézier is a curve of order 3 and degree 2, requiring three control points; it corresponds to the square of the basis equation $(1-t)+t = 1$:

$$((1 - t) + t)^2 = 1$$

$$(1 - t)^2 + 2(1 - t)t + t^2 = 1$$

where each term is weighted by a control point:

Quadratic Bézier: $P(t) = (1 - t)^2 B_0 + 2(1 - t)t B_1 + t^2 B_2$

Figure 2.8 shows an example of a cubic Bézier curve. These are one of the most frequently used splines. They are used in imaging, animation, and typesetting and are defined as

Cubic Bézier: $P(t) = (1 - t)^3 B_0 + 3(1 - t)^2 t B_1 + 3(1 - t)t^2 B_2 + t^3 B_3$

Thus, a Bézier curve of order $n + 1$ and degree n can be defined as:

$$P(t) = \sum_{i=0}^{n} B_i J_{n,i}(t) \qquad 0 \leq t \leq 1$$

where the Bézier basis or blending function is defined by the Bernstein polynomials:

$$J_{n,i}(t) = \binom{n}{i} t^i (1 - t)^{n-i}$$

with $\binom{n}{i} = \frac{n!}{i!(n-i)!}$

Some important properties of Bézier curves are the following:

---

[4] An interesting review of the history of mathematical splines can be found in "A History of Curves and Surfaces in CAGD," by G. Farin in *Handbook of Computer Aided Geometric Design* [13].

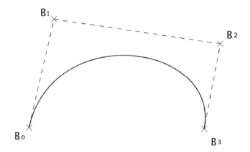

Fig. 2.8: A cubic Bézier curve and its defining polygon

- The curve generally follows the shape of the polygon formed by the control points.
- The first and last points on the curve are coincident with the first and last control points.
- The curve is contained within the convex hull of the polygon defined by the control points (see Figure 2.8).
- The tangent vectors at the ends of the curve have the same direction as the first and last points of the defining polygon. This is important for achieving continuity.
- The curve can be transformed (translation, scale, rotation) by transforming only its control points.

Applications of Bézier Curves

Bézier curves introduced the concept of vector graphics as opposed to raster images. A raster image is described in term of pixels. Each pixel is coded with a color, depending on various algorithms (jpg, gif, png, bmp). The two major problems of raster images is that they are generally big in terms of file size and they are not scalable, meaning that if you zoom into the image, you will see the square pixels getting bigger and bigger.

Bézier curves provided a solution to describe an image in terms of its mathematical representation. A vector graphics file will contain the coordinates of control points to describe a series of curves. The viewer application (renderer) will then draw the graphic. If the user wants to zoom in, the renderer will increase the space between the control points and redraw a smooth curve. Vector graphics are therefore scalable. Up to a certain degree of image complexity, it is generally more size-effective to store control point coordinates rather than pixel information.

Nowadays, Bézier curves are the standard for the typesetting industry. The lines and curves required to define the shape (glyphs) of TrueType fonts, used to display and print high-quality text, are described by quadratic Bézier curves. Cubic Bézier curves are frequently used to define curved shapes in imaging, modeling, and animation applications.

The advantages described earlier make mathematical splines one of the most useful and versatile tools for 3D shape modeling and animation, which are key elements of a Virtual Reality application. They allow for interactive design; remember they were created to solve precisely this problem: helping automobile designers create new shapes and describe them in a precise and formal (mathematical) way so that computers can process them.

B-Spline Curves

Curves generated by using control points are dependent on the interpolation or approximation scheme being used to establish the relationship between the curve and the control points. This scheme is provided by a basis function. As we have explained, the basis function of Bézier curves is defined by the Bernstein basis. The use of Bernstein polynomials as basis functions limits the flexibility of the resulting curves. One of the most important limitations is that any point of a Bézier curve is a result of blending the values of all control points, a change in one control point is felt throughout the entire curve. This makes it impossible to produce a local change within a curve. This kind of local change is very useful for 3D modeling and animation, because they give the designer much more flexibility.

There is another basis: the B-spline basis (Basis spline), which contains the Bernstein basis as a special case. In a B-spline curve, each control point B_i is associated with a unique basis function. Thus, each vertex B_i affects the shape of a curve only over a range of parameter values where its associated basis function is nonzero. The B-spline basis also allows us to change the order and degree of the resulting curve without changing the number of control points; this is impossible using the Bernstein basis.

The parametric form of a B-spline curve is defined as:

$$P(t) = \sum_{i=1}^{n+1} B_i N_{i,k}(t) \qquad t_{min} \leq t < t_{max}, \ \ 2 \leq k \leq n+1 \qquad (2.1)$$

where the B_i are the position vectors of the $n+1$ control points of the defining polygon and the $N_{i,k}$ are the normalized B-spline basis functions.

For the ith normalized B-spline basis function of order k and degree $k-1$, the basis functions $N_{i,k}(t)$ are defined by the Cox–de Boor recursion formulas [14],[15]:

$$N_{i,1} = \begin{cases} 1, & \text{if } x_i \leq t < x_{i+1} \\ 0, & \text{otherwise} \end{cases}$$

$$N_{i,k}(t) = \frac{(t - x_i)N_{i,k-1}(t)}{x_{i+k-1} - x_i} + \frac{(x_{i+k} - t)N_{i+1,k-1}(t)}{x_{i+k} - x_{i+1}}$$

The values of x_i are elements of a knot vector satisfying the relation $x_i \leq x_{i+1}$. The parameter t varies from t_{min} to t_{max} along the curve $P(t)$. The convention $0/0 = 0$ is adopted.

The knot vector has a significant influence on the B-spline basis functions $N_{i,k}(t)$ and hence on the resulting B-spline curve. The only requirement for a knot vector is that it should be an increasing series of real numbers. There are three types of knot vectors: uniform, open uniform (or open) and nonuniform.

Uniform Knot Vectors

In a uniform vector, knot values are evenly spaced, for example, [0 1 2 3 4], [−0.2 − 0.1 0 0.1 0.2]. In practice, knot vectors usually begin at zero and are incremented by one to some maximum value or are normalized in the range [0..1].

Open Uniform Knot Vectors

Open uniform knot vectors have multiple repeated knot values at the ends. The number of repeated values is equal to the order k (in Equation 2.1) of the B-spline basis function. Examples: $k = 2 : [0\ 0\ 0.25\ 0.5\ 0.75\ 1\ 1]$, $k = 3 : [0\ 0\ 0\ 0.33\ 0.66\ 1\ 1\ 1]$.

B-splines using open uniform basis functions are very similar to Bézier curves. When the number of control points is equal to the order of the B-spline basis and an open uniform vector is used, the B-spline basis can be reduced to the Bernstein basis. In such a case, the resulting B-spline is in fact a Bézier curve. For example, using four control points and the fourth-order ($k = 4$) open uniform knot vector [0 0 0 0 1 1 1 1] yields a cubic Bézier/B-spline curve.

Nonuniform Knot Vectors

Nonuniform knot vectors have no specific arrangement; they can be unequally spaced and/or have multiple repeated values. They may be periodic or open, for example, [0 0 1 3 3 4], [0 0.10 0.6 0.7 1]. Nonuniform knot vectors allow us to vary the influence region of each control point so that some control points can affect the shape of the curve more strongly than others.

Nonuniform Rational B-Spline Surves

Nonuniform rational B-splines, commonly called NURB curves are the most general form of mathematical splines. To give the definition of NURB, we must first define what a rational B-spline is.

A rational B-spline curve is the projection on 3D space of a 4D nonrational B-spline. Nonrational B-splines are polynomial B-splines, just like the ones we have already described. They are represented using homogeneous coordinates; each control point has three Cartesian coordinates plus the homogeneous coordinate h: $[x, y, z, h]$. Rational B-spline curves are defined as:

$$P(t) = \frac{\sum_{i=1}^{n+1} B_i h_i N_{i,k}(t)}{\sum_{i=1}^{n+1} h_i N_{i,k}(t)} \qquad h_i \geq 0 \qquad (2.2)$$

If $h_i = 1, \forall i$ the NURB equation reduces to the definition of nonrational B-splines (equation 2.1). Increasing h_i pulls the curve closer to point P_i, while decreasing it pushes the curve farther from P_i. Setting $h_i = 0$ eliminates the effect of P_i on the curve.

Nonuniform rational B-splines are a generalization of nonrational B-splines and share with them most of their analytic and geometric characteristics. NURBs provide a precise way to represent common analytical shapes such as lines, conic curves, planes, free-form curves, quadratics, and sculptured surfaces, which are frequently used in Virtual Reality applications and computer-aided design.

2.2.3 Surfaces

Virtual Reality applications usually require complex and visually appealing 3D shapes in order to create the illusion of being in an alternative but believable environment. We usually require modeling everyday objects like furniture, vehicles, tools, structures like houses and all kinds of buildings, and of course living beings, like animals and humans. These shapes can be modeled as 3D surfaces created with splines. Other modeling strategies exist (e.g., surfaces of revolution), but we will focus on surface creation using splines since this is a powerful and versatile method. Modeling with splines provides high interactivity at design time and a compact storage of the models. As we have explained, to reconstruct a spline all we need are the control points, and in the case of NURBs, the knot vector. Very complex surfaces can be created with piecewise surfaces composed of Bézier, or more generally, NURB patches.

How do we create a surface out of spline curves? We usually define a mesh of polygons out of a grid of splines. Splines are calculated from a net of control points; see Figure 2.9. For each row of the grid we calculate a spline at fixed intervals of parameter t; remember this is in fact a linear interpolation between control points. Each point of this spline will serve as a control point for the vertical splines. This way we create a grid of splines whose points can be used to create a mesh of triangles. Triangles are the basic 3D primitive for current graphic cards. This means that the most common way to visualize a 3D shape is by representing it as a polygonal mesh; this process is called tessellation. The more polygons we use, the more accurate and smooth the surface will be.

Formally a Bézier surface can be defined as the tensor product of Bézier curves, also known as Bézier patches:

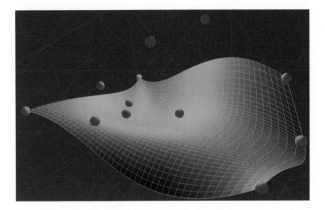

Fig. 2.9: Spline surfaces: Bézier patches

$$P(s,t) = \sum_{i=0}^{n} \sum_{j=0}^{m} B_{i,j} \binom{n}{i} s^i (1-s)^{n-i} \binom{m}{j} t^j (1-t)^{m-j}$$

Similar definitions based on the tensor product of the corresponding curve equations are used to define NURB patches.

Other techniques, such as recursive subdivision, can provide even more accurate and smooth surfaces. Instead of generating a mesh of polygons from a grid of splines, it is also possible to render directly from the patch definitions. In this algorithm, described by Catmull and Clark [16], a set of control points is divided into two smaller patches, and this procedure is recursively applied until each subpatch projects to less than one pixel on the screen. Then each patch is rendered by filling in the single pixel it projects to. While this method produces higher quality surfaces, it is also computationally intensive and hence slower. However, subdivision techniques can be hardware-accelerated using modern graphics cards with programmable GPU (graphics processing unit), see the work of Shiue et al. [17] and Loop and Blinn [18].

2.3 3D Rendering

3D rendering is the process of generating 2D projections of 3D shapes, taking into account the effects of color, light, surface, and other characteristics of the shapes. If we want them to be believable and visually appealing, 3D shapes should be colored, reflect light when illuminated, cast shadows, and so on. Light reflected from objects is what makes them visible for us. Different illumination models have been developed to simulate light reflections. An illumination model is the set of equations used to compute the color and brightness of a point on the surface of an object. It should determine how much light is reflected to the viewer from a visible point on a surface. Reflected light is a function of light source direction, color and intensity, viewer position, surface orientation, and surface properties [19]. Surface properties usually include colors, an opacity factor, a reflectance, a specular power parameter, and the like.

Light reflections can be performed at three different scales: microscopic, local, and global. The exact nature of reflection from surfaces is best explained in terms of microscopic interactions between light rays and the surface. However, simplifications at the local level usually provide acceptable results in real time, an essential requirement for Virtual Reality applications.

In addition to the illumination model, a shading model can be used to avoid the faceted aspect of polygonal surfaces. The most popular shading models are Gouraud and Phong shading, although Phong shading is less frequently used because of its computational cost.

2.3.1 Local Illumination Model

As mentioned earlier, local illumination is an incomplete method, from the physics point of view, but the simplification produces acceptable results for real-time interaction. The model considers that the light intensity (I) at one point on a surface has three components: ambient, diffuse, and specular reflections: $I = I_{ambient} + I_{diffuse} + I_{specular}$. Rasterization-based algorithms apply this model and are implemented in current graphics boards.

Ambient Reflection

The ambient term considers background illumination of unlit surfaces. It allows for some global control of brightness in a scene: $I_{ambient} = I_a k_a$, where I_a is an ambient illumination constant defined for the entire scene and k_a is an ambient reflection coefficient, usually restricted to values in [0..1].

Diffuse Reflection

Diffuse reflection is characteristic of light reflected from a dull, matte surface. Objects illuminated only by diffusely reflected light exhibit an equal light intensity from all viewing directions. The reflected light intensity is independent of the position of the viewer and is proportional to the incident light energy I_i. The incident light energy per unit area depends on the cosine of the angle θ between the incident light direction and the outside normal[5] to the surface **n**. This is known as Lambert's cosine law: $I_{diffuse} = I_i k_d \cos \theta$, where k_d is the diffuse reflection coefficient. If we calculate the normalized direction vector from the object surface to the light source **s**, the same equation can be expressed by the dot product of **s** and **n**: $I_{diffuse} = I_i k_d (\mathbf{s} \cdot \mathbf{n})$

---

[5] The normal vector of a surface, e.g., a triangle, is a normalized vector perpendicular to the surface plane.

Specular Reflection

Specular reflection is characteristic of light reflected from a shiny surface, where a bright highlight appears from certain viewing directions. Mirrors reflect incident light in one direction only and are considered perfect specular reflectors. Specular reflection depends on the perfect reflection direction $\mathbf{r}$, the viewer direction $\mathbf{v}$, and the surface normal $\mathbf{n}$: $I_{specular} = I_i k_s (\mathbf{r} \cdot \mathbf{v})^n$, where I_i is the incident light energy, k_s is the specular reflection coefficient, and n can be considered a surface roughness parameter. The parameter n determines how close the surface is to a perfect specular reflector. Values of n larger than 100 specify mirror-like surfaces, values around 1 are used for matte surfaces. The reflection vector $\mathbf{r}$ can be expressed in terms of the surface normal and the light source vector $\mathbf{s}$: $\mathbf{r} = 2\mathbf{n}(\mathbf{n} \cdot \mathbf{s}) - \mathbf{s}$.

Color

The local illumination model we have reviewed calculates the light intensity per surface unit (e.g., per triangle); it is a scalar value that does not represent a specific color. Current display devices generate colors by mixing the three primary colors: red, green, and blue. This is known as the RGB model, in which the maximum intensities for the three primary colors are normalized to the range [0..1]. Different colors are obtained by specifying different intensity levels for each color component.

Other color models have been proposed, such as the HSV or the CIE models. The HSV model uses the concepts of hue, saturation, and brightness to define colors. The CIE model was proposed by the Commission Internationale de L'Eclairage (CIE) in 1931. The CIE model specifies colors as the mixture of the three primary colors with different intensities whose sum is 1. There are formulas to specify a given color using any of the three color models. However, in computer graphics and Virtual Reality applications, colors are usually described using the RGB model.

Producing a colored image requires calculating the light intensity (ambient + diffuse + specular reflections) three times, once for each color component. Surfaces reflect the three color components with different reflection coefficients. White light contains equal intensities for each primary color. However, diffuse reflection of white light will not necessarily have equal intensities on the three components. The color of diffuse reflection depends on the diffuse reflection coefficients of the surface; this gives the illuminated object its color. Different object colors are obtained when scenes are illuminated using colored light.

Gouraud Shading

Light intensity is usually calculated on a per-polygon basis; this is known as flat-shading, see Figure 2.10. To reduce the visual effect of discontinuous

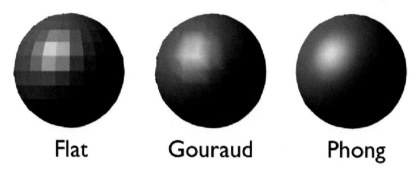

Flat   Gouraud   Phong

Fig. 2.10: Shading algorithms for local illumination

changes in light intensity, known as the mach band effect, intensity interpolation techniques are applied. Gouraud shading[6] is an intensity interpolation algorithm that partially eliminates intensity discontinuities. Light intensities are calculated for each vertex of the polygon; the normal of each vertex is the average of the surface normals of the adjacent polygons. Linear interpolation is used to determine the color at each point inside the polygon.

Phong Shading

Not to be confused with the Phong illumination model, which considers the addition of ambient, diffuse, and specular reflections. Phong shading[7] interpolates the surface normals, rather than the intensities of polygon vertices, as is the case with Gouraud shading. At each point on the polygon, the normal is calculated as an interpolation of the normal vectors at the vertices of the polygon. Each vector is then normalized and for each point, an illumination model is used to determine the light intensity; see Figure 2.10. Phong shading usually produces better results than Gouraud shading, but it is also more expensive in terms of computation.

2.3.2 Global Illumination Model

The global illumination model produces the most realistic images and has two main components:

- **Direct illumination**: light arriving directly from sources such as lamps or the sun.

---

[6] This algorithm was proposed by the French computer scientist Henri Gouraud in 1971 [20]. Gouraud shading is hardware-accelerated in current graphics cards.

[7] Both the illumination model and the shading algorithm were proposed by the Vietnamese computer scientist Bui Tuong Phong in the 1970s [21].

- **Indirect illumination**: effects of light reflecting off surfaces in the environment.

A general global illumination equation, also called the rendering equation describes all energy (light) exchanges between surfaces. This equation describes the flow of light throughout a scene. In contrast to local illumination models, which are approximations, the rendering equation is based on the physics of light and provides theoretically perfect results. The equation states that the transport intensity of light from one surface point to another is the sum of the emitted light and the total light intensity that is scattered toward x from all other surface points [22]:

$$\underbrace{L_o(x, \mathbf{w})}_{\text{total light}} = \underbrace{L_e(x, \mathbf{w})}_{\text{emitted light}} + \underbrace{\int_\Omega f_r(x, \mathbf{w}', \mathbf{w})L_i(x, \mathbf{w}')(\mathbf{w}' \cdot \mathbf{n})d\mathbf{w}'}_{\text{reflected light}}$$

where $L_o(x, \mathbf{w})$ is light leaving point x in direction $\mathbf{w}$; $L_e(x, \mathbf{w})$ is the light emitted, a property of the surface at point x; $\int_\Omega \cdots d\mathbf{w}'$ is an infinitesimal sum over a hemisphere of inward directions. $f_r(x, \mathbf{w}', \mathbf{w})$ is the bidirectional reflectance distribution function (BRDF), the proportion of light reflected at point x; $L_i(x, \mathbf{w}')$ is the incident light on point x from direction $\mathbf{w}'$; and $(\mathbf{w}' \cdot \mathbf{n})$ is the attenuation of light due to the incident angle (see diffuse reflection).

Some of the most frequently used algorithms for solving the rendering equation are ray tracing, radiosity, and photon mapping.

Ray Tracing

The basic principle in ray tracing is to simulate the trajectories of light rays emitted by light sources and reflected by objects in the scene until some of them reach the eye or the camera. In order to optimize the algorithm, only rays arriving at the eye are simulated. A set of rays are generated from the viewpoint and the algorithm looks for intersections with objects in the scene. A recursive approach can be applied to simulate reflections: rays intersecting an object generate reflected rays, which are then checked for intersections with other objects. At each intersection the rays contribute a color intensity, the sum of the contributions defines a color for each pixel on the screen. Figure 2.11 shows an example of the kind of images that can be generated. Ray tracing produces very realistic results, including the effects of reflection, refraction, and shadows, which are difficult to generate using local illumination. Although this technique has been traditionally considered too slow for real-time applications, several optimizations have been implemented. The most common optimizations of ray tracing include the use of binary space-partitioning data structures such as k-d trees to speed up the search for ray intersections [23], [24]; the parallelization of the algorithm and its execution on PC clusters [25]; and the use of programmable hardware (GPU) [25], [26].

It is now possible to have interactive ray tracing; a few images per second, enough for examining a complex scene [27]. In the near future, this technique is expected to be used in real-time applications requiring at least 30 images per second, such as video games [28].

Fig. 2.11: Ray tracing example

Radiosity

The radiosity method was originally introduced in the 1950s as a method for computing radiant heat exchanges between surfaces. In 1984, Goral et al. [29] proposed the application of this method to the simulation of light transfer between surfaces. This method considers that the majority of surfaces in a real environment are diffuse reflectors: an incident ray of light is reflected or scattered in all directions within the entire hemisphere above the reflecting surface. The basic principle of radiosity is the energy balance in a closed scene: the radiosity (energy per unit surface) of a surface depends on its self-emitted radiosity and on the energy (light) emitted by all the other surfaces, received and reflected (re-emitted) by the surface. A very representative characteristic of images generated using radiosity is the effect of diffuse color bleeding; see

Figure 2.12. Color bleeding cannot be obtained using classical ray tracing methods. If the scene is subdivided into discrete surface elements or patches with constant radiosity, the energy balance can be expressed by the following equation:

$$B_i = E_i + \rho_i \sum_{j=1}^{N} F_{ij} B_j$$

Where B_i is the radiosity of patch P_i; E_i is the self-emitted radiosity of patch P_i; ρ_i is the reflectivity of P_i, $(0 < \rho_i < 1)$; and F_{ij} is the form factor of patches P_i and P_j; the proportion of the light emitted by P_i that is received by P_j. Writing this equation for each patch leads to a linear system of N equations.

The most computationally expensive part of the radiosity method is the computation of the form factors. Several techniques for the computation of form factors have been proposed: projection methods with z-buffer schemes or exploration methods with ray tracing schemes. Efforts have also focused on parallelization of the algorithm [30]. A comprehensive review of the radiosity method and optimization algorithms is presented by Sillion and Puech in [31]. Radiosity methods calculate light interactions in an environment in a view-independent way. Different views can be rendered in real time; this characteristic makes of radiosity a very interesting method for realistic visualization in Virtual Reality applications [32]. Implementations using programmable graphics hardware are making it feasible to generate images in real-time using radiosity [33].

Photon Mapping

The classical ray tracing algorithm does not handle diffuse interreflections that produce color bleeding nor caustics (e.g., shimmering waves at the bottom of a swimming pool). Photon mapping is able to handle such effects. Diffuse interreflections and caustics are due to indirect illumination of diffuse surfaces. The photon mapping method estimates this kind of illumination using precomputed photon maps. This method was proposed by Jensen [34], [35], [36] and is implemented as an extension to ray tracing. Photon mapping is a two-pass method. In the first pass, photons are shot into the scene and stored in a photon map when they hit nonspecular objects. The second pass, the rendering pass, uses statistical techniques on the photon map to extract information about incoming light and reflected radiance at any point in the scene. The photon map is decoupled from the geometric representation of the scene. This means that the algorithm can simulate global illumination in complex scenes containing millions of triangles. Modified versions of this algorithm have been implemented using programmable graphics hardware [37].

Fig. 2.12: Radiosity example

In order to render the most realistic images, artists use a mix of all the techniques we have explained. Figure 2.13 shows an example of mixing radiosity and ray tracing.

2.3.3 Textures

The creation of believable images for Virtual Reality applications requires more than complex 3D shapes and realistic illumination. Most of the objects in the real world are composed of a variety of materials that affect their appearance; Fo example, objects are made of wood, marble, metal, fur, and so on. Materials can have very complex colored patterns that are difficult to reproduce. One of the most frequently used techniques to improve the visual appearance of 3D shapes is texture mapping [38]. The basic principle is to map a 2D image (texture) to a 3D shape, in such a way that the 3D surface gets colored by the image; see Figure 2.14.

Texture mapping can also be the basis for other sophisticated rendering algorithms for improving visual realism and quality. For example, environment mapping is a view-dependent texture mapping technique that supplies a specular reflection to the surface of objects [39]. This makes it appear that the environment is reflected in the object; see Figure 2.15a.

Fig. 2.13: Mix of ray tracing and radiosity rendering

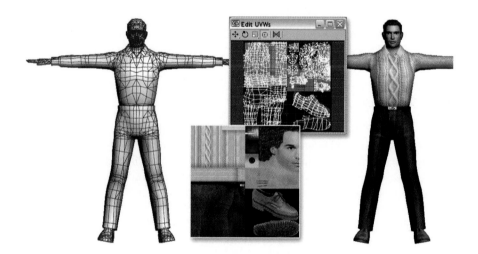

Fig. 2.14: Texture mapping

(a) Environment Mapping

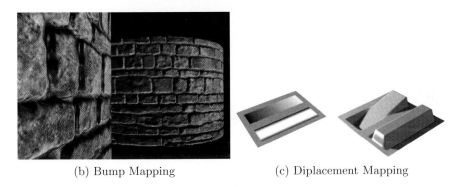

(b) Bump Mapping   (c) Diplacement Mapping

Fig. 2.15: Texture mapping techniques

Texture mapping can be considered as a method for modifying parameters of the shading equation such as the surface normal. This technique is known as bump mapping, it allows us to produce an effect of 3D relief [40], [41] or wrinkles [42] on a surface (see Figure 2.15b).

The coordinates of the point being shaded can be modified based on a parameterization of the surface defined by the texture coordinates. This technique is known as displacement mapping [43], [44], [45]; see Figure 2.15c. In displacement mapping, the surface is actually modified, in contrast to bump mapping where only the surface normal is modified. This means that displacement mapped surfaces produce correct self-occlusions, shadows, and silhouettes. The drawback of this technique is the large number of micropolygons required to deform the surface, which is undesirable for Virtual Reality applications due to the performance penalty that this induces.

Texture mapping, including environment mapping and bump mapping, are implemented in hardware in current graphics cards and supported by the most common 3D graphics APIs: OpenGL 2.0 and DirectX 10.0. Texture mapping is a very cheap way to produce realistic images: scenes with or without texture mapping usually take the same time to be rendered.

2.3.4 Rendering Pipeline

We will explain how standard computer graphics application programming interfaces (APIs) such as OpenGL and DirectX process data in several steps in order to render 3D images; this process is known as the rendering pipeline and is the main purpose of graphics hardware. If no graphics hardware is present (e.g., no OpenGL; DirectX-compatible graphics card), then data processing is emulated in software, which usually results in slow performance.

We will focus the discussion on the OpenGL API because it is now the standard supported by most operating systems and computer architectures, including Windows, Mac OSX, Linux and all UNIX systems, in contrast to Microsoft's DirectX, which is only supported by Windows PCs.

OpenGL is an industry-standard, cross-platform API whose specification was finalized in 1992. The first implementations appeared in 1993. It was largely compatible with a proprietary API called Iris GL (Graphics Library), designed and supported by Silicon Graphics, Inc. To establish an industry standard, Silicon Graphics collaborated with various other graphics hardware companies to create an open standard: OpenGL.

All versions of OpenGL through 1.5 were based on a fixed-function pipeline: the user could control various parameters, but the underlying functionality and order of processing were fixed. OpenGL 2.0 (September 2004), provided users with the ability to program data processing at the level of vertices and pixels (fragments). With this version of OpenGL, application developers are able to implement their own rendering algorithms, using a high-level shading language: GLSL.

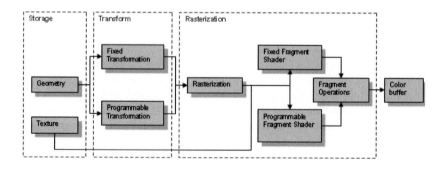

Fig. 2.16: Rendering pipeline

Fixed Rendering Pipeline

Figure 2.16 shows a simplified version of the rendering pipeline according to the OpenGL specification. The process starts with primitives (points, lines, polygons) formed by vertices and their associated attributes such as color and surface normals. Different transformation matrices, as defined in Section 2.1.2, are applied to convert vertices into "eye coordinates."

There are two kinds of transformations: modeling transformations, used to place/move 3D shapes in the scene; and viewing transformations, which specify the location of the viewer or the camera (transforming the whole scene to view it from a specific position and angle). Both modeling and viewing transformations are combined (multiplied in the required order: viewing x modeling) into a single transformation called the modelview matrix.

If lighting is enabled, the lighting calculations are performed using the vertices in eye coordinates, surface normals, light source positions, material properties, and other lighting information to produce a primary and a secondary color for each vertex. OpenGL uses a local illumination model; see Section 2.3.1. The final step of vertex operations involves texture coordinates.

Lit and textured vertices in eye space are transformed by a projection matrix (see Section 2.1.4) into "clip coordinates." Vertices out of the clipping volume are discarded. Depending on the type of primitive, new vertices may be generated at the intersection of the primitive and the view volume. Colors, texture coordinates, and other vertex attributes are assigned to the newly generated vertices by interpolating their values along the clipped edge.

Vertices in clip space are still homogeneous coordinates (see Section 2.1.2); the next step is to divide them by the h-coordinate to yield normalized device coordinates. The resulting coordinate triplet is mapped to a 2D plane by the viewport transformation: mapping coordinates in clip space to physical window coordinates.

In the next step, primitives (points, lines, or polygons) are decomposed into smaller units corresponding to pixels in the destination frame buffer. This process is called rasterization. Each of these smaller units generated by rasterization is called a fragment or a pixel. For example, the process of rasterization converts a triangle defined by three vertices into a set of fragments (pixels) covering the triangle area. A fragment has several attributes: window coordinate, depth ($Z-$coordinate), color, texture coordinates, and so on. The value for each of these attributes is determined by interpolation between the values specified or computed at the vertices of the primitive. When they are rasterized, vertices have a primary color and a secondary color. Color values are interpolated between the vertices if smooth shading (Gouraud shading, see Section 2.3.1) is used. Otherwise, the color values for the last vertex of the primitive are used for the entire primitive (flat shading).

After fragments have been generated by rasterization, several fragment operations are performed. One of the most important operations at this stage is texture mapping. The texture coordinates associated with the fragment are used to access the texture memory in the graphics card. Textures can be accessed and applied in several ways specified within the application.

Other fragment operations are fog: modifying the color of the fragment depending on its distance from the viewpoint, and color sum: combining the values of the fragment's primary and secondary colors.

The goal of the rendering pipeline is to take the graphics primitives defined by the application and convert them into pixels to fill in a frame buffer that will be used for display. For a more detailed explanation of the rendering pipeline, you can refer to the book by R. Rost, *OpenGL Shading Language* [46].

What we have described is the fixed functionality that is implemented in hardware in current graphics cards. However, modern hardware also offers the possibility to let the user define many steps of the rendering pipeline.

Programmable Rendering Pipeline

Figure 2.16 shows how most of the operations at the level of vertices and fragments can be replaced by shaders. Operations are specified by programs called shaders, which are compiled and linked at run time and executed by the graphics processing unit (GPU) in modern graphics cards. There are two kinds of shaders: vertex and fragment shaders.

Vertices and their attributes are sent to a vertex shader that is responsible for providing texture coordinates, colors, fog coordinates, and other information. Vertex shaders allow us to define new transformation, lighting, and texture coordinate operations. Vertices can be transformed by the modelview and projection matrices or suffer other nonconventional transformations within a vertex shader. Different lighting models can be implemented in order to generate the vertex colors.

In the case of fragment shaders, they allow for replacing the texturing, color sum, and fog fragment operations.

When using OpenGL, shaders are written in a high level language called GLSL (OpenGL Shading Language) [46]. Direct3D, the 3D graphics component of the DirectX API, uses an analogous language called HLSL (High Level Shading Language).

By the time we were writing this book, DirectX 10 and OpenGL 2.1 were introducing geometry shaders (Shader Model 4.0). This new kind of shader allows us to create new geometry within the shader and perform operations at the level of primitives: triangles, lines, etc. Creating new geometry at run time and manipulating polygons at the GPU frees the CPU for other tasks, increasing the computing power, and opens interesting possibilities for 3D simulations, video games, and other general-purpose applications.

Nowadays, the use of shaders is more and more frequent. Even for pedagogical purposes, shaders are useful for teaching computer graphics because they allow for implementing algorithms and equations in a more direct way [47], for example, implementing Phong illumination as a vertex shader.

In the context of Virtual Reality, using shaders is a must in order to have high-quality images. Modern GPUs are faster than CPUs for stream and parallel processing, and they allow us to generate real-time images that would be impossible otherwise. Common uses of shaders include approximations to global illumination (see references in Section 2.3.2); skinning (displacement of vertices in articulated structures to give the illusion of bones covered by muscles and skin, essential for virtual humans and other animated characters); particle simulation (commonly used to simulate water, dust, etc.); and various effects derived from texture mapping (bump mapping, displacement mapping, environment mapping).

3

Computer Animation

3.1 Introduction

Most virtual worlds are dynamic, they change over time: objects move, rotate, transform themselves; in inhabited virtual worlds, virtual characters live. Object and character motion is an essential part of these virtual worlds. The main goal of computer animation is to synthesize the desired motion effect, which is a mixing of natural phenomena, perception, and imagination. The animator designs the object's dynamic behavior with a mental representation of causality. He or she imagines how it moves, gets out of shape, or reacts when it is pushed, pressed, pulled, or twisted. So the animation system has to provide the user with motion control tools that can translate his or her wishes from his or her own language. Computer animation methods may also help to understand physical laws by adding motion control to data in order to show their evolution over time. Visualization has become an important way of validating new models created by scientists. When the model evolves over time, computer simulation is generally used to obtain the evolution of time, and computer animation is a natural way of visualizing the results obtained from the simulation. Computer animation may be defined as a technique in which the illusion of movement is created by displaying on a screen, or recording on a recording device, a series of individual states of a dynamic scene. Formally, any computer animation sequence may be defined as a set of objects characterized by state variables evolving over time. For example, a human character is normally characterized using its joint angles as state variables.

3.1.1 Animation Types: Real Time and Image by Image

Two types of animation are generally distinguished:

- animation in real time
- animation image by image

For Virtual Reality, we are only interested in real time, where the computer calculates the movements and the transformations sufficiently quickly that the user in front of his or her graphic display can see these movements and transformations. It is also what we can find in video games and flight simulators. Image-by-image computer animation, corresponds to traditional animation. It is initially necessary to calculate the images, record them on videotape (or film), and then visualize them or project at a fast rate (e.g., 25 images/second for video PAL). The calculated images can take a split second to several hours. This is not what we want for Virtual Reality.

To produce a computer animation sequence, the animator has two principal techniques available. The first is to use a model that creates the desired effect; a good example is the growth of a green plant. The second is used when no model is available. In this case, the animator produces "by hand" the real-world motion to be simulated. Until recently, most computer-generated films have been produced using the second approach: traditional computer animation techniques like key-frame animation, or spline interpolation. Then animation languages, scripted systems, and director-oriented systems were developed. In the next generation of animation systems, motion control tends to be performed automatically using artificial intelligence (AI). and robotics techniques. In particular, motion is planned at a task level and computed using physical laws. More recently, researchers have developed models of behavioral animation and simulation of autonomous creatures.

3.1.2 Articulated Bodies and Virtual Characters

An important class of entities that are very often animated are virtual characters, and especially virtual humans. They are articulated figures modeled with multiple layers: a virtual skin is usually attached to an underlying skeleton that animates the whole body. We will discuss in more details virtual characters and virtual humans in Chapter 4. However, we will present in this chapter the concept of skeleton, as most animation methods are applied to skeletons. The skeleton is a hierarchically organized set of joints that depends on the animation requirements, for example, it might be relevant for a medical surgery tool to model each vertebra of the spine, while a simpler decomposition into four joints could be sufficient for a video game character. Of course, it is better to create morphologically correct skeletons, but this can turn out to be quite costly. Real humans have so many degrees of freedom that virtual characters frequently omit some of them.

A skeleton can be described as a hierarchically organized set of joints, with each joint having one or more rotational degrees of freedom (DOF). It also often stores a 4D transformation matrix for representing the length and orientations of the bones, together with joint limits in order to avoid unnatural rotations. Since matrices are always expressed locally, the resulting global posture is the composition of all previous transformation matrices in the hierarchy, starting from the root. For example, the shoulder is a joint with three DOFs, and the elbow joint is its successor in the hierarchy (see Figure 3.1). If the matrix of the shoulder is modified, then the elbow moves, but its local matrix stays the same.

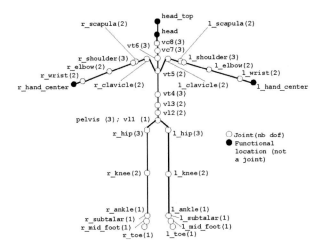

Fig. 3.1: H-ANIM skeleton

In an effort to standardize on a common representation for virtual humans, the Web3D Consortium defined the Humanoid Animation Specification (H-Anim) for VRML and MPEG4. They specify a fixed topology and a naming convention for the articulated structure as well as tools for adding an outer mesh, the skin or cloth.

As shown in Figure 3.1, the skeleton consists of a number of segments (such as the forearm, hand, and foot), which are connected to each other by the joints (such as the elbow, wrist, and ankle). For an application to animate a virtual character, it needs to obtain access to the joints and alter the joint angles. The application may also need to retrieve information about such things as joint limits and segment masses. Animation of the skeleton is performed by modifying 4D matrices associated with the bones, either by synthesizing the motion or with the help of inverse kinematics and key-framing, as we present in the next sections.

3.2 Motion Control Methods

We start from the classification introduced by Thalmann and Thalmann [48] based on the method of controlling motion. A motion control method specifies how an object or an articulated body is animated and may be characterized according to the type of information to which it is privileged in animating the object or the character. For example, in a key-frame system for an articulated body, the privileged information to be manipulated is joint angles. In a forward dynamics-based system, the privileged information is a set of forces and torques; of course, in solving the dynamic equations, joint angles are also obtained in this system, but we consider these a derived information. In fact, any motion control method will eventually have to deal with geometric information (typically joint angles), but only geometric motion control methods are explicitly privileged to this information at the level of animation control.

The nature of privileged information for the motion control of characters falls into three categories: geometric, physical, and behavioral, giving rise to three corresponding categories of motion control methods.

- The first approach corresponds to methods heavily relied on by the animator: motion capture, shape transformation, parametric key-frame animation. Animated objects are locally controlled. Methods are normally driven by geometric data. Typically, the animator provides a lot of geometric data corresponding to a local definition of the motion.
- The second way guarantees a realistic motion by using physical laws, especially dynamic simulation. The problem with this type of animation is controlling the motion produced by simulating the physical laws that govern motion in the real world. The animator should provide physical data corresponding to the complete definition of a motion. The motion is obtained by the dynamic equations of motion relating the forces, torques, constraints, and the mass distribution of objects. As trajectories and velocities are obtained by solving the equations, we may consider actor motions as globally controlled. Functional methods based on biomechanics are also part of this class.
- The third type of animation is called behavioral animation, takes into account the relationship between each object and the other objects. Moreover, the control of animation may be performed at a task level, but we may also consider the animated objects as autonomous creatures. In fact, we will consider as a behavioral motion control method any method that drives the behavior of objects by providing high-level directives indicating a specific behavior without any other stimulus.

3.3 Motion Capture and Performance Animation

Performance animation or motion capture consists of measurement and recording of direct actions of a real person or animal for immediate or delayed analysis and playback. The technique is used today especially in production environments for 3D character animation. It involves mapping measurements onto the motion of the digital character. This mapping can be direct: e.g. human arm motion controlling a character's arm motion, or indirect, mouse movement controlling a character's eye and head direction. Real-time motion capture is very important in Virtual Reality, as it can provide the computer with information on the motion of the user: position and orientation of the limbs, postures, and gestures.

We may distinguish two kinds of systems, optical and magnetic.

3.3.1 Optical Motion Capture Systems

Passive optical systems use markers coated with a retroreflective material to reflect light back that is generated near the cameras lens. The camera's sensitivity can be adjusted, taking advantage of most cameras' narrow range of sensitivity to light so that only the bright markers will be sampled, ignoring skin and fabric. The centroid of the marker is estimated as a position within the 2D image that is captured. The gray-scale value of each pixel can be used to provide subpixel accuracy. Markers are attached to an actor's body and on several cameras focused on performance space. By tracking the positions of markers, one can get locations corresponding to key points in the animated model; for example, we attach markers at joints of a person and record the position of markers from several different directions. Figure 3.2 shows the principles. We then reconstruct the 3D position of each key point at each time. The main advantage of this method is freedom of movement; it does not require any cabling. There is, however, one main problem: occlusion; that is, the lack of data resulting from hidden markers, for example, when the performer lies on his back. Another problem comes with the lack of an automatic way of distinguishing reflectors when they get very close to each other during motion. These problems may be minimized by adding more cameras, but at a higher cost, of course. Most optical systems operate with four or six cameras, but for high-end applications like movies, 16 cameras is usual. A good example of optical system is the VICON^{TM} system.

Active optical systems triangulate positions by illuminating one LED at a time very quickly or multiple LEDs at once, but sophisticated software identifies them by their relative positions, somewhat akin to celestial navigation. Rather than reflecting light back that is generated externally, the markers themselves are powered to emit their own light.

The use of conventional video cameras is still a dream, as it is very difficult to detect automatically the joints in three dimensions and to make a correct correspondence between 3D points on images captured by several cameras. This is an active area of research in computer vision.

3.3.2 Magnetic Position/Orientation Trackers and Systems

The main way of recording positions and orientations is to use magnetic tracking devices like those manufactured by Polhemus^{TM} and Ascension Technology^{TM}. Magnetic systems calculate position and orientation by the relative magnetic flux of three orthogonal coils on both the transmitter and each receiver. The relative intensity of the voltage or current of the three coils

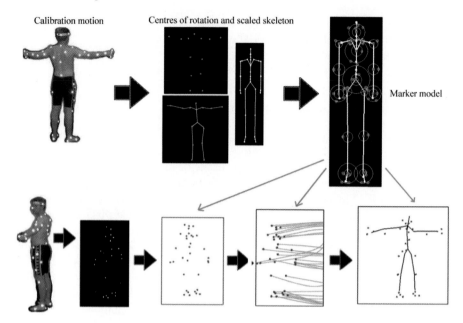

Fig. 3.2: Principles of optical motion capture

allows these systems to calculate both range and orientation by meticulously mapping the tracking volume. The markers are not occluded by nonmetallic objects but are susceptible to magnetic and electrical interference from metal objects in the environment, like rebar[1] (steel reinforcing bars in concrete) or wiring, which affects the magnetic field, and electrical sources such as monitors, lights, cables and computers. The sensor response is nonlinear, especially toward the edges of the capture area. With the magnetic systems, there is a distinction between AC and DC systems: one uses square pulses, the other uses sine wave pulses.

These magnetic sensors are used in Virtual Reality to track the position and orientation of the head in head-mounted displays (see Section 7.2.1), the position and orientation of the listener in audiospace systems (see Section 8.3), or the position and orientation of the hand in data gloves (see Section 9.2). They are also the basis for magnetic motion capture systems as we are describing in this chapter.

For example, Polhemus STAR-TRAK[TM] is a long-range motion capture system that can operate in a wireless mode (totally free of interface cables) or with a thin interconnect cable. The system can operate in any studio space regardless of metal in the environment, directly on the studio floor. ULTRATRAK PRO[TM] is a full-body motion capture system; it

---

[1] http://en.wikipedia.org/wiki/Rebar

is also the first turnkey solution developed specifically for performance animation. ULTRATRAK PRO^{TM} can track a virtually unlimited number of receivers over a large area. FASTRAK^{TM}, an award-winning system is a highly accurate, low-latency 3D motion tracking and digitizing system. FASTRAK^{TM} can track up to four receivers at ranges of up to 10 feet. Multiple FASTRAKs^{TM} can be multiplexed for applications that require more than four receivers. Ascension^{TM} Technologies manufactures several different types of trackers including the MotionStar^{TM} Turnkey, the MotionStar^{TM} wireless, and the Flock of Birds^{TM}. MotionStar^{TM} wireless was the first magnetic tracker to shed its cables and set the performer free. Motion data for each performer is now transmitted through the air to a base station for remote processing. MotionStar^{TM} turnkey is a motion capture tracker for character animation. It captures the motions of up to 120 receivers simultaneously over a long range without metallic distortion. Each receiver is tracked up to 144 times per second to capture and filter fast complex motions with instantaneous feedback. The system utilizes a single rack-mounted chassis for each set of 20 receivers. Flock of Birds^{TM} is a modular tracker with six degrees of freedom for simultaneously tracking the position and orientation of one or more receivers (targets) over a specified range of 4 feet. Motions are tracked to accuracies of 0.5 and 0.07 inch at rates up to 144Hz. The Flock employs pulsed DC magnetic fields to minimize the distorting effects of nearby metals. Due to simultaneous tracking, fast update rates and minimal lag occur even when multiple targets are tracked. The Flock is designed for head and hand tracking in VR games, simulations, animations, and visualizations.

Magnetic motion capture systems require the real actor to wear a set of magnetic sensors (see Figure 3.3), as defined earlier, which are capable of measuring their spatial relationship to a centrally located magnetic transmitter. The position and orientation of each sensor are then used to drive an animated character. One problem is the need to synchronize receivers. The data stream from the receivers to a host computer consists of 3D positions and orientations for each receiver. Since the sensor output has six degrees of freedom, useful results can be obtained with two-thirds the number of markers required in optical systems; one on the upper arm and one on the lower arm for elbow position and angle. For complete human body motion, eleven sensors are generally needed: one on the head, one on each upper arm, one on each hand, one in the center of the chest, one on the lower back, one on each ankle, and one on each foot. The most common way to calculate the rest of the necessary information, is to use inverse kinematics (see Section 3.5). The wiring from the sensors tends to preclude extreme performance movements, but, as already seen, there are wireless sensors on the market. The capture volumes for magnetic systems are dramatically smaller than for optical systems.

3.3.3 Motion Capture Advantages and Disadvantages

The motion capture approach offers the following advantages:

Fig. 3.3: Motion capture using magnetic sensors

- It works in real time
- The amount of work does not vary with the complexity or length of the performance
- Complex movement and realistic physical interactions such as secondary animation, weight, and exchange of forces can be more easily re-created in a physically accurate manner
- Motion capture allows one actor to play multiple roles within a single film.

Unfortunately, the motion capture approach has the following drawbacks:

- Specific hardware and special programs are required to obtain and process the data
- Cost of software and equipment and personnel required can be prohibitive
- Motion capture systems may have specific requirements for the space in which they are operated
- Applying motion capture to quadruped characters can be difficult
- Technology can become obsolete every few years as better software and techniques are invented
- Results are limited to what can be performed within the capture volume without extra editing of the data
- Movement that does not follow the laws of physics generally cannot be represented
- If the computer model has different proportions from the capture subject, artifacts may occur. For example, if a cartoon character has large, over-sized hands, these may intersect strangely with any other body part when the human actor brings them too close to his body. In the same way, feet

may enter the floor if characters' legs are longer than the human actors'
legs

- Motion capture does not bring any really new concept to animation
  methodology. For any new motion, it is necessary to record the reality
  again. Moreover, motion capture is not appropriate, especially in real-time
  simulation activities, where the situation and actions of people cannot be
  predicted ahead of time, and in dangerous situations, where one cannot
  involve a human actor

3.4 Key-Frame Animation

3.4.1 Shape Interpolation and Parametric Keyframe Animation

Key-frame animation consists of the automatic generation of intermediate
frames, called in-betweens, based on a set of key-frames supplied by the animator. There are two fundamental approaches to key-frame:

1. The in-betweens are obtained by shape interpolation. This technique was
   introduced by Burtnyk and Wein [49]. It plays a major role in film production and has been improved continuously by using more and more
   sophisticated mathematical tools [50],[51]. This method makes it possible to transform one geometrical form into another during an animation.
   Figure 3.4 shows the principle. There is a serious problem for the image-
   based key-frame: the motion can be distorted due to the interpolation.
   The problem becomes complicated when the two drawings do not have
   the same number of vertices. In this case, it is initially necessary to carry
   out a preprocessing step to equalize the number of vertices in the two
   drawings.
2. A way of producing better images is to interpolate parameters of the
   model instead of the object itself. This technique is called parametric
   key-frame animation by Parke [52] and Steketee and Badler [53] and key
   transformation animation by Zeltzer [54]. The parameters are normally
   spatial parameters, physical parameters and visualization parameters that
   decide the models' behavior.

Parametric key-frame animation is considered a direct kinematics method
in motion control when the interpolated parameters are defined in the joint
space of the articulated figure. Efficient and numerically well-behaving methods exist for the transformation of position and velocity from joint space to
Cartesian space.

In both key-frame methods, linear interpolation produces undesirable effects, such as lack of smoothness in motion, discontinuities in the speed of
motion, and distortions in rotations. For these reasons, spline interpolation
methods are used. Splines can be described mathematically as piecewise approximations of cubic polynomial functions. Two kinds of splines are very

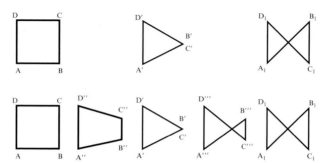

Fig. 3.4: Interpolation between two drawings: (top) an interpolation with 50%; (bottom) interpolations with 25%, 50%, and 100%

popular: interpolating splines with C1 continuity at knots, and approximating splines with C2 continuity at knots. For animation, the most interesting splines are the interpolating splines: cardinal splines, Catmull-Rom splines, and Kochanek-Bartels [55] splines (see Section 3.4.2).

3.4.2 Kochanek-Bartels Spline Interpolation

This method consists of interpolating splines with three parameters for local control: tension, continuity, and bias. Consider a list of points P_i and the parameter t along the spline to be determined. A point V is obtained from each value of t from only the two nearest given points along the curve (one behind P_i, one in front of P_{i+1}). But the tangent vectors $\overrightarrow{D_i}$ and $\overrightarrow{D_{i+1}}$ at these two points are also necessary. This means that we have:

$$V = THC^T$$

where T is the matrix $[t^3\ t^2\ t\ 1]$, H is the Hermite matrix, and C is the matrix $[P_i\ P_{i+1}\ \overrightarrow{D_i}\ \overrightarrow{D_{i+1}}]$. The Hermite matrix is given by:

$$H = \begin{bmatrix} 2 & -2 & 1 & 1 \\ -3 & 3 & -2 & -1 \\ 0 & 0 & 1 & 0 \\ 1 & 0 & 0 & 0 \end{bmatrix}$$

This equation shows that the tangent vector is the average of the source chord $P_i - P_{i-1}$ and the destination chord $P_{i+1} - P_i$. Similarly, the source derivative (tangent vector) $\overrightarrow{DS_i}$ and the destination derivative (tangent vector) $\overrightarrow{DD_i}$ may be considered at any point P_i.

Using these derivatives, Kochanek and Bartels propose the use of three parameters to control the splines: tension, continuity, and bias.

The tension parameter t controls how sharply the curve bends at a point P_i. As shown in Figure 3.5a, in certain cases a wider, more exaggerated curve may be desired, while in other cases the desired path may be much tighter.

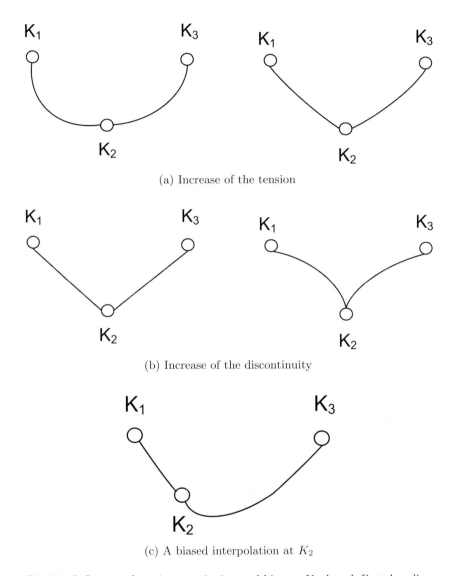

(a) Increase of the tension

(b) Increase of the discontinuity

(c) A biased interpolation at K_2

Fig. 3.5: Influence of tension, continuity, and bias on Kochanek-Bartels spline

The continuity c of the spline at a point P_i is controlled by the parameter c. Continuity in the direction and speed of motion is not always desirable.

Animating a bouncing ball, for example, requires the introduction of a discontinuity in the motion of the point of impact, as shown in Figure 3.5b.

The direction of the path as it passes through a point P_i is controlled by the bias parameter b. This feature allows the animator to have a trajectory anticipate or overshoot a key position by a certain amount, as shown in Figure 3.5c.

Equations combining the three parameters may be obtained:

$$\overrightarrow{DSi} = 0.5[(1-t)(1+c)(1-b)(P_{i+1} - P_i) + (1-t)(1-c)(1+b)(P_i - P_{i-1})]$$

$$\overrightarrow{DDi} = 0.5[(1-t)(1-c)(1-b)(P_{i+1} - P_i) + (1-t)(1+c)(1+b)(P_i - P_{i-1})]$$

A spline is then generated using $V = THC^T$ with $\overrightarrow{DD_i}$ and $\overrightarrow{DS_i}$ instead of $\overrightarrow{D-i}$ and $\overrightarrow{D_{i+1}}$.

3.5 Inverse Kinematics

Formally, the direct kinematics problem consists in finding the position of endpoint positions (e.g., hand, foot) with respect to a fixed-reference coordinate system as a function of time without regard to the forces or moments that cause the motion. Efficient and numerically well-behaved methods exist for the transformation of position and velocity from joint space (joint angles) to Cartesian coordinates (end of the limb).

The inverse kinematics problem is the opposite of the direct kinematics problem (see Figure 3.6). This is the determination of the joint variables given the position and the orientation of the end of the manipulator, or end effector, with respect to the reference coordinate system. It can be solved by various methods, such as inverse transform, screw algebra, dual matrices, dual quaternian, iterative, and geometric approaches. More details of each method can be found in [56]. Inversion is possible if the dimensions of joint space and Cartesian space are the same. However, a general articulated structure may contain more DOFs in joint space, which are highly redundant in accomplishing tasks. The inversion is not always possible. The solution is the first-order approximation of the system: to linearize the direct geometric model. As a consequence of the linearization, the solution's validity of inverse kinematics is limited to the neighborhood of the current state and, as such, any desired motion has to comply with the hypothesis of small movements.

The position and orientation vector of the end effector in Cartesian space are called the main task (or behavior). If its dimension m (usually six: three rotations and three translations) is less than the dimension n of the joint space, the $(n - m)$ vectors in joint space are projected to the null vector in Cartesian space by the linear transformation J. They do not modify the achievement of the main task. The $(n - m)$ vector in Cartesian space is called the secondary task (or behavior). The discrete form of the general solution provided by inverse kinematics is:

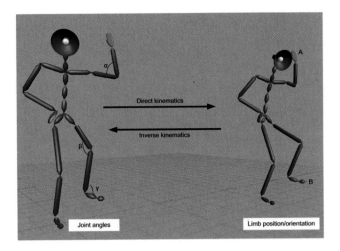

Fig. 3.6: Direct and inverse kinematics

$$\Delta q = J_+ \Delta x + (I - JJ_+)\Delta z$$

Where Δq is the unknown vector in the joint variation space of dimension n; Δx describes the main task as a variation of the end effector position and orientation in Cartesian space; the dimension m of the main task is usually less than or equal to the dimension n of the joint space; J is the Jacobian matrix of the linear transformation, representing the differential behavior of the controlled system over the dimensions specified by the main task; J_+ is the unique pseudo-inverse of J providing the minimum norm solution, which realizes the main task; I is the identity matrix of the joint variation space $(n*n)(I - J_+J)$, is a projection operator on the null space of the linear transformation J; any element belonging to this joint variation subspace is mapped by J into the null vector in the Cartesian variation space; Δz describes a secondary task in the joint variation space. This task is partially realized via the projection on the null space. In other words, the second part of the equation does not modify the achievement of the main task for any value of Δz. Usually Δz is calculated to minimize a cost function. If the main task belongs to the image space of J, then the null space is $(n - m)$ dimensional in the joint variation space. This information is fundamental to evaluate the potentiality of the secondary task and clearly leads to a tradeoff between realization of main and secondary tasks.

We can summarize the steps using inverse kinematics as shown in algorithm 1:

The so-called Jacobian of the system is the matrix gathering the first-order variations. It is inverted in order to obtain the joint variation realizing a desired variation of the end effector. A more detailed explanation of these steps is given in [57]. Practically, the problem is to determine a joint configuration

Algorithm 1 Inverse Kinematics Steps

1: Define the main task.
2: Evaluate the potential of the secondary ask.
3: Construct the Jacobian matrix.
4: Invert the Jacobian matrix.
5: Handle the joint limits.
6: Manage singularities.

for which a desired task, usually expressed in Cartesian space, is achieved. For example, the shoulder, elbow and wrist configurations must be determined so that the hand precisely reaches a position in space. The equations that arise from this problem are generally nonlinear and are difficult to solve in general. In addition, a resolution technique must deal with the difficulties described later. For the positioning and animation of articulated figures, the weighting strategy is the most frequent: some typical examples are given for posture manipulation [58], [59] and to achieve smooth solution blending [60], [61].

3.6 Motion Retargeting

As we saw in Section 3.2, there is a lot of interest in recording motion using motion capture systems (magnetic or optical), then trying to alterate such a motion to create this individuality. This process is tedious, and there is no reliable method at this stage. Even if it is fairly easy to correct one posture by modifying its angular parameters (with an inverse kinematics engine, for instance), it becomes a difficult task to perform this over the whole motion sequence while ensuring that some spatial constraints are respected over a certain time range and that no discontinuities arise. When one tries to adapt a captured motion to a different character, the constraints are usually violated, leading to problems such as the feet going into the ground or a hand unable to reach an object that the character should grab. The problem of adaptation and adjustment is usually referred to as the motion retargeting problem. Witkin and Popovic [62] proposed a technique for editing motions by modifying the motion curves through warping functions and produced some of the first interesting results. In a more recent paper [63], they extended their method to handle physical elements, such as mass and gravity, and described how to use characters with different numbers of degrees of freedom. Their algorithm is based on reducing the character to an abstract character that is much simpler and only contains the degrees of freedom that are useful for a particular animation. The edition and modification are then computed on this simplified character and mapped again onto the end-user skeleton. Bruderlin and Williams [64] have described some basic facilities to change the animation by modifying the motion parameter curves. The user can define a particular posture at time t, and the system is then responsible for smoothly blending the motion around t. They also introduced the notion of a motion displacement map, which is an offset added to each motion curve. The motion retargeting problem term was brought up by Michael Gleicher [65]. He designed a space-time constraint solver, into which every constraint is added, leading to a big optimization problem. He mainly focused on optimizing his solver to avoid enormous computation time, and he achieved very good results. Given a captured motion associated to its performer skeleton, Monzani et al. [66] decompose the problem of retargeting the motion to the end-user skeleton into two steps:

1. Compute the intermediate skeleton matrices by orienting the intermediate skeleton bones to reflect the performer skeleton posture (motion converter).
2. Set the end-user skeleton matrices to the local values of the corresponding intermediate skeleton matrices.

The first task is to convert the motion from one hierarchy to a different one. An intermediate skeleton model is introduced to solve this, implying three more subtasks: manually set at the beginning the correspondences between the two hierarchies, create the intermediate skeleton, and convert the movement. The resulting motion is then corrected and Cartesian constraints are enforced using inverse kinematics. When considering motion conversion between different skeletons, one quickly notices that it is very difficult to directly map the performer skeleton values onto the end-user skeleton, due to their different proportions, hierarchies, and axis systems. This raised the idea of having an intermediate skeleton: depending on the performer skeleton posture, its bones are reoriented to match the same directions. It is then easy to map the intermediate skeleton values onto the end-user skeleton (see Figure 3.7).

Bindiganavale and Badler [67] also addressed the motion retargeting problem, introducing new elements: using the zero-crossing of the second derivative to detect significant changes in the motion, visual attention tracking (and the way to handle the gaze direction), and applying inverse kinematics to enforce constraints, by defining six subchains (the two arms and legs, the spine, and the neck). Finally, Lee and Shin [68] used in their system a coarse-to-fine hierarchy of B-splines to interpolate the solutions computed by their inverse kinematics solver. They also reduced the complexity of the IK problem by analytically handling the degrees of freedom for the four human limbs. Lim and Thalmann [69] have addressed an issue of solving customers' problems when applying evolutionary computation. Rather than the seemingly more impressive approach of wow-it-all-evolved-from-nothing, tinkering with existing models can be a more pragmatic approach. Using interactive evolution, they experimentally validate this point on setting parameters of a human walk model for computer animation while previous applications are mostly about evolving motion controllers of far simpler creatures from scratch. More recently, Glardon et al. [70] have proposed a novel approach to generate new

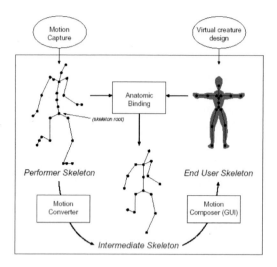

Fig. 3.7: Use of an intermediate skeleton for motion retargeting

generic human walking patterns using motion-captured data, leading to a real-time engine intended for virtual human animation. The method based on PCA (principal component analysis) is described in Section 4.3.2.

3.7 Procedural Animation

Procedural animation corresponds to the creation of a motion by a procedure describing specifically the motion. Procedural animation should be used when the motion can be described by an algorithm or a formula. For example, consider the case of a clock based on the pendulum law:

$$\alpha = A \; \sin(\omega t + \phi)$$

A typical animation sequence may be produced using a program, as shown in algorithm 2:

The generation of motion using a procedure is not really a method; it is more a framework. There are so many possibilities to express motion using procedures or laws that the possible algorithms are unlimited. Two important cases are when the laws are physical laws and when they are behavioral; these two cases will be presented in the next two sections.

Algorithm 2 Procedural Animation

$create\ CLOCK(...)$
for $FRAME = 1$ to $NBFRAMES$ **do**
  $TIME = TIME + 1/25$
  $ANGLE = A * SIN(OMEGA * TIME + PHI)$
  $modify(CLOCK, ANGLE)$
  $draw\ CLOCK$
  $record\ CLOCK$
  $erase\ CLOCK$
end for

3.8 Physics-Based Animation

A great deal of work exists on the dynamics of articulated bodies [71], and efficient direct dynamics algorithms have been developed in robotics for structures with many degrees of freedom [72]. In computer animation, these algorithms have been applied to the dynamic simulation of the human body [73]. Given a set of external forces (like gravity or wind) and internal forces (due to muscles) or joint torques, these algorithms compute the motion of the articulated body according to the laws of rigid body dynamics. Impressive animations of passive structures like falling bodies on stairs can be generated in this way with little input from the animator. Figure 3.8 shows an example of animation generated using dynamics. In fact, an important issue that arises in this direct or forward dynamics is how to control the model. Mathematically, forward dynamics translates into differential equations, which are typically posed as an initial-value problem; the user has little control other than setting up the initial configuration. This is opposite to key-frames, where the animator has full control. Control of physics-based models remains an open research issue.

More generally, it is unpractical for an animator to specify a temporally coordinate sequence of force/torque activation to generate a desired active behavior. This is the inverse dynamics problem, which has been addressed for walking in [74]. Figure 3.9 shows the relation between forward and inverse dynamics. Impressive results have also been achieved by Hodgins et al. [75] with the simulation of dynamic human activities such as running and jumping. Some controller architectures have also been proposed by Lazlo et al. [76] to generate a wide range of gaits and to combine elementary behaviors [77]. The use of constraints to avoid the direct specification of torques has also been researched; for example, in the computer graphics community, the satisfaction of space-time constraints has been proposed by Witkin and Kass [78] with the minimization of an objective function such as the total energy expenditure.

Fig. 3.8: Dynamics-based motion [48]

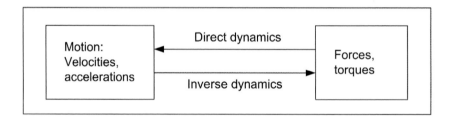

Fig. 3.9: Direct and inverse dynamics

3.9 Behavioral Animation

A common way of describing behavior is by scripting, where the interaction must be described step by step. This approach provides full control and flexibility; however, if used alone, it does require programming of every possible outcome of an interaction, which may not be practical for larger systems. An interesting solution to this problem is to use scripting in a complementary role to other methods of specifying behavior. For example, the lower-level details (usually related to animation since behavior and animation cannot be fully separated) can be scripted, whereas a higher-level module can carry out reasoning. Specially designed or general-purpose interpreted programming languages can be used. If a general-purpose programming language is used, some extensions may need to be implemented to simplify the process of writing scripts for nonprogrammers (e.g., designers).

Behaviors can also be specified based on rules. Rule-based systems are rather simplistic, and rules essentially correspond to if-then statements. For example, the Improv system [79] combines scripting and rule-based behavior, trying to tackle the problems of animation and behavior simultaneously. It consists of an animation engine, used for the motion generation aspects, and a behavior engine, used for describing the decision-making process through rules. State machines are also widely used for specifying behaviors as they have useful graphical representations. In fact, in most cases, even if scripting is used, there will be a state machine implemented. The disadvantage is that implementing complex systems with state machines requires a lot of states and transitions, so a state machine can easily become difficult to maintain.

Vosinakis and Panayiotopoulos have introduced the task definition language [80]. This work aims at filling the gap between higher-level decision processes and agent interaction with the environment. This language supports complex high-level task descriptions through a combination of parallel, sequential, or conditionally executed built-in functions. The main advantage of this language is that it enables tasks to be reused by different agents in different environments.

Reynolds [81] introduced a distributed behavioral model simulating flocks of birds, herds of land animals and fish schools. For birds, the simulated flock is an elaboration of a particle system with the simulated birds being the particles. A flock is assumed to be the result of the interaction between the behaviors of individual birds. Working independently, the birds try to both stick together and avoid collisions with one another and with other objects in their environment. In a module of behavioral animation, positions, velocities and orientations of the actors are known from the system at any time. The animator may control several global parameters; such as weight of the obstacle-avoidance component, weight of the convergence to the goal, weight of the centering of the group, maximum velocity, maximum acceleration, and minimum distance between actors. The animator provides data about the leader trajectory and the behavior of other birds relative to the leader. Wilhelms and Van Gelder[82] propose a system based on a network of sensors and effectors. Ridsdale [83] proposes a method that guides lower-level motor skills from a connectionist model of skill memory, implemented as collections of trained neural networks. Another approach for behavioral animation is based on timed and parameterized L-systems [84] with conditional and pseudo-stochastic productions. With this production-based approach a user may create any realistic or abstract shape, play with fascinating tree structures, and generate any concept of growth and life development in the resulting animation. Figure 3.10 shows an example. More advanced research in behavioral animation can be found in autonomous characters, which is detailed further in Section 4.6, as well as crowd simulation in Section 4.7.

Fig. 3.10: L-system-based environment

Part II

Virtual Worlds

4

Virtual Characters

4.1 Virtual Humans in Virtual Environments

As we already explained, Virtual Reality (VR) refers to a technology that is capable of shifting a subject into a different environment without physically moving him or her. Immersion is a key issue in VR systems, as it is central to the paradigm in which the user becomes part of the simulated world, rather than the simulated world being a feature of the user's own world. Presence is the psychological sense of "being there" in the environment based on the technologically founded immersive base. However, any given immersive system does not necessarily always lead to presence for all people. The problem is that immersion is too often considered a hardware problem. The use of an HMD or a CAVE is supposed to provide immersion and increase the sense of presence. But how can we believe we are in a world when there is no inhabitant even when immersed? We may think about virtual worlds inhabited by a virtual character society, where virtual humans will co-operate, negotiate, make friends, communicate, group and ungroup, depending on their likes, moods, emotions, goals, fears, and so on. We may also think about a virtual world inhabited by animals or fictitious creatures. This chapter is dedicated to virtual characters and their role in virtual worlds.

In the case of virtual humans, one important point in the simulation is the believability of the individual virtual humans; they should behave like real humans, including having capabilities such as perception, language understanding, and generation, emotions, goal-driven behavior, reactivity to the environment including with other virtual humans, memory, inference, appearance of thought and personalities, interpersonal interactions, and social skills. To be believable an actor has to be affected by what takes place around it and needs to engage in social behaviors with other actors and the user. Therefore, the behavioral model of an actor needs to be versatile enough to allow a change of behavior, the emotional state of the actor must be reflected and must affect its behavior, andthe interpersonal relationships with the other actors must be taken into account and possibly bring the actor to engage in social interactions. These actors should be able to act freely and emotionally. Ideally, they should be conscious and unpredictable. But we are far from such an ideal situation.

In this chapter, we will discuss the representation of the skin of the virtual character in Section 4.2. Concerning the motion control of the skeleton, we will not explain again the general motion control methods described in Chapter 3, but we will present two actions which are specific to Virtual Humans: locomotion (Section 4.3) and object manipulation (Section 4.4). In Section 4.5, we survey methods to animate the characters face. The concept of Autonomous Virtual Character is the key concept of Section 4.6, while crowd simulation is briefly summarized in Section 4.7.

4.2 Character Skinning

Many different approaches have been proposed to connect a deformable skin to its underlying skeleton. They can be roughly subdivided into three main categories: skeleton-based deformations, data-driven methods, and physics-based approaches. However, we will emphasize the two first categories, because they are more appropriate to real-time deformations needed for VR.

4.2.1 Skeleton-Based Deformations

The skeleton-driven deformation, a classical method for basic skin deformation is probably the most widely used technique in 3D character animation. In research literature, an early version was introduced in 1987 by Magnenat-Thalmann and Thalmann [85], who introduced the concept of joint-dependent local deformation (JDL) with operators to smoothly deform the skin surface (see Figure 4.1); the method was also extended to handle hand deformations [86]. This technique has been given various names, such as subspace deformation (SSD), linear blend skinning, or smooth skinning. This method works first by assigning a set of joints $1, ..., n$ with weights to each vertex v of the character. The deformation of a vertex v_0 is then computed by a weighted combination of the transformation T_j of the influencing joint j with the following function:

$$S(v_0) = \left(\sum_{j=0}^{n} w_j T_j \right) v_0 \qquad (4.1)$$

The skeletal deformation makes use of an initial neutral pose. While this method provides fast results and is compact in memory, its drawbacks are the undesirable deformation artifacts in case of important variation of joint angles among the influencing joints.

Fig. 4.1: JLD deformations: early version of skeleton-based deformation from the movie "Rendez-vous à Montréal" By Nadia Magnenat-Thalmann and Daniel Thalmann [85]

The method has been extended [87] to address a crucial issue related to linear blending skinning: setting the appropriate vertex weight values. An interesting extension of SSD-based approaches is the multiweighting approach [88], which assigns each vertex one weight for each coefficient of each influencing joints transformation matrix instead of a single weight per influencing joint. It therefore defines a new deformation function with a high-dimensional input space: 12 weights/vertex/bone, to provide the resulting skinning approach with an increased flexibility to control and transform each skin vertex. As it would be almost impossible to define the multiweight values interactively, an automated process automatically estimates the set of values. The multiweights can be derived from a set of example poses. This initial set of poses can be produced from any variety of sources. Each bone must also be assigned with an influence map, which defines its influence over the surface vertices. The influence maps are user-defined. The user must also provide a scaling parameter to control the smoothness of the deformation solution and avoid overfitting, when large weights deform skin badly on a new pose. The training poses are then used as examples to estimate the multiweight vectors using a statistical analysis (principal component analysis) and a modified least square optimization method. The weights computed from the set of training poses generalize to other postures.

More complex models include intermediate layers to improve and refine the control of the skin. For example, an intermediate muscle layer is introduced between the flexible skin and the rigid skeleton [89]. This intermediate structure is made of free-form deformation (FFD) control boxes attached to the skeleton. The control box shapes are parameterized with the joint angles of the skeleton. Two main deformation operators are applied to the control boxes, the first controls the bending of the mesh around the joint, and the second mimics the muscle behavior by inflating the skin along the bones to replicate the muscle contraction effect. Another approach [90] combines implicit surfaces and B-spline patches. In this method, the implicit surfaces are ellipsoidal metaballs that represent the gross shape of bone, muscle, and fat tissue. The motion/deformation of each primitive with respect to underlying joints is specified via a graphical interface. A skin of fixed topology is extracted by casting rays from the skeleton segments in a star-shaped manner and using the intersection points as control points of B-spline patches. Figure 4.2 shows an example.

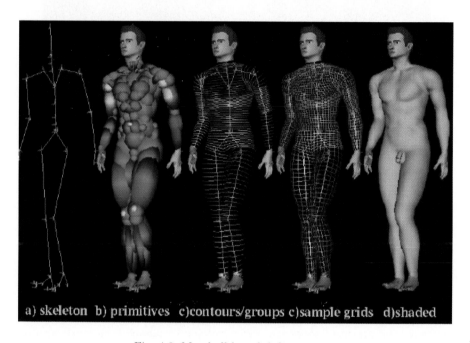

a) skeleton b) primitives c)contours/groups c)sample grids d)shaded

Fig. 4.2: Metaball-based deformations

Character skinning has also been investigated to simulate anatomy and reproduce as closely as possible the anatomical behavior of characters [91], [82]. Anatomy-based modeling considers that using flexible surfaces at joints and along the limbs is an oversimplification and thus adopts a similar approach as artistic anatomy, assuming that the skin surface changes may be more accurately represented as the result of the behavior of the underlying anatomical structures such as muscles, fat, and connective tissues. Complex volumes are used to approximate the real shape of muscles with tendon attachments to the bones.

Various approaches have been investigated.

- Passive muscles, where geometric or physics-based deformations are used to adjust the shape of the muscle to the current posture of the skeleton
- Active muscles, where biomechanical physics-based deformation models are used to simulate the dynamic behavior of muscles

Muscle elongation and contraction (see equation 4.2) are used to activate the skeleton joints and produce motions [91]:

$$r = (1 - t)\, r_n + kt r_n = (1 - t + kt)\, r_n \tag{4.2}$$

where k is a tension-control parameter, t a tension parameter, r the ratio of the width and height of the muscle, and r_n this ratio in a fully relaxed state.

An interesting approach [92] introduces the idea of abstracting muscles by an action line (a polyline in practice), representing the force produced by the muscle on the bones, and a surface mesh deformed by an equivalent mass-spring mesh. In order to smooth out mesh discontinuities, they employ special springs termed angular springs that tend to restore the initial curvature of the surface at each vertex. However, angular springs cannot deal with local inversions of the curvature. Another method [93] also uses an action line and a muscle mesh. The action line, represented by a polyline with any number of vertices, is moved for each posture using a predefined behavior and a simple physically based simulation. It is then used as a skeleton for the surface mesh, and the deformations are produced in a usual way. Each vertex of the muscle mesh is parameterized by one or two underlying action lines so that the deformations of the muscle shape are driven by the associated action lines. It therefore reduces the 3D nature of the elasticity problem to one dimension for fusiform muscles (one action line) and two dimensions for flat muscles (several action lines). Each action line is approximated by a polyline associated with a 1D mass-spring-damper system. The muscle insertion and origin are anchored to the skeleton joints in order to estimate the action line deformations from skeleton motions. Collision avoidance between components is handled with repulsive force fields.

4.2.2 Data-Driven Methods

Several attempts have been made to overcome the limitation of geometric skin deformation by using examples of varying postures and blending them during animation. Aimed mostly at real-time applications, these example-based methods essentially seek solutions to efficiently leverage realistic shapes that come from the captured skin shape of real people, physically based simulation results, or sculpted by skilled designers. Data-driven methods have recently arisen with the growth of 3D acquisition devices, particularly with full-body

3D scanners. These acquisition devices allow us to get reliable and accurate data from complex shapes like the human body. The basic idea of these approaches is to use real data that cover the space of shape variation of the character to train a deformable model. The underlying hypothesis is that it is possible to generalize from a set of individuals by, for example, applying statistical analysis to the training set. This family of methods initially started by modeling static shape variations (morphology) such as the human face [94] and has been further applied to address dynamic shape variations (poses) such as deformable human bodies. We have now reached the stage where both types of variations (morphologies and poses) are simultaneously handled.

The recent approach named Skinning Mesh Animations (SMAs) [95], presents an original skin example-based scheme. The main difference is that it does not require a predefined skeleton. The method takes as inputs a set of deformed meshes representing the pseudo-articulated deformable shape in different poses. It then automatically estimates statistically relevant bones based on the hypothesis that clustering triangles with analogous rotation sequences indicates the near rigid structure of the mesh animation. It further determines bone transformations, bone-vertex influence sets, and vertex weight values for producing skinned animations that approximate the original deformable animation. The skinning approximation is particularly suited for shapes with a sufficient near-rigid structure and does not apply well for highly deformable shapes. SMAs support hardware rendering and pose editing.

4.2.3 Physics-Based Approaches

Various approaches have been proposed to introduce more realism by introducing dynamic-based deformations [96]. For example, it could be based on the introduction of a framework for skeleton driven animation of elastically deformable characters [97]. The proposed framework is somehow similar to FFD-based animation approaches as it embeds the object in a control lattice, but it uses continuum elasticity and FEM to compute the dynamics of the object being deformed. Bones of the control skeleton are restricted to lying along the edges of the control lattice, so that the skeleton can be considered a constraint in the dynamic system.

4.3 Locomotion

4.3.1 Locomotion Generation

Walking has global and specific characteristics. From a global point of view, every human walking has comparable joint angle variations. However, close up, we notice that individual walk characteristics are overlaid to the global walking gait. We will take as an example the walking engine described in [98].

Walking is defined as a motion in which the center of gravity alternatively balances from the right to the left side. It has the following characteristics:

- at any time, at least one foot is in contact with the floor, the single support duration (ds);
- there exists a short instant during the walk cycle, where both feet are in contact with the floor, the double support duration (dds);
- it is a periodic motion that has to be normalized in order to adapt to different anatomies.

The joint angle variations are synthesized by a set of periodic motions which we briefly describe here:

- sinus functions with varying amplitudes and frequencies for the humanoid's global translations (vertical, lateral, and frontal) and the humanoid's pelvic motions (forward/backward, left/right, and torsion);
- periodic functions based on control points and interpolating hermite splines. They are applied to the hip flexion, knee flexion, ankle flexion, chest torsion, shoulder flexion, and elbow flexion.

More generally, many works have been dedicated to the locomotion of virtual humans [99], [100]. The key-framing technique allows an animator to specify key postures at specific key times. Using appropriate software (e.g., Autodesk's 3ds Max or Maya), skilled designers can control the motion in detail. However, this technique is quite labor-intensive, as any motion parameter change entails the animators to modify every key-frame. Kinematics approaches generate motions from parameters such as position feet or speed value [101], [102]. Motions are generated by giving a predefined set of foot positions (footprints) and timing information. These data are generally computed by a motion planning technique, which has to be as interactive as possible to be comfortable for animators.

Dynamics approaches aim to describe a motion by applying physics laws. For example, it is possible to use control algorithms based on finite state-machine to describe a particular motion and proportional derivative servos to compute the forces [103]. However, even if these methods produce physically correct animations, the configuration of their algorithms remains difficult. It is not easy to determine the influence of each parameter on the resulting motions. Many methods based on empirical data and bio-mechanical observations are able to generate walking [104] or running patterns [105], reactive to given user parameters. Other similar approaches take into account the environment, to walk on uneven or sloped terrains [106] or to climb stairs [107]. Despite their real-time capability, all these methods lack realism, as the legs' motion is considered symmetrical, for example.

Another class of animation techniques reuses original motion capture data. Treated as a time-varying signal, a new motion can be generated by modifying its frequency bands [64] or its Fourier coefficients [108]. Other methods [109], [110] define each motion by B-spline coefficients. New motions are then computed by setting weights on the various original motions and performing interpolations using polynomial and RBF (radial basis function) functions.

The Kovar and Gleicher [111] method wraps input motions into a data structure that ensures consistent time warping, root alignment, and constraint matching.

We will explain in more details in the next section the method introduced by Glardon et al. [112], which applies **PCA (principal component analysis)** on a motion-capture database composed of various walking and running cycles. The generation of new parameterized motions is performed by interpolation and extrapolation into a hierarchical structure of PCA spaces.

4.3.2 PCA-Based Locomotion

A method from statistics, PCA [113] has recently become attractive in animation synthesis. It is used either to compress the data [114] or to emphasize similarities between input data [94], [115] in order to generate motion according to control parameters such as age or gender. In this section we introduce a model allowing efficient generation of a whole locomotion sequence only at each high-level parameter update. To illustrate our methodology, we use two examples of locomotion: walking and running.

The first step consists in creating a motion database; for example, we use an optical motion-capture system and a treadmill to record five subjects differing in age and gender (two women and three men). The physical parameter speed of the various sequences varies from 3.0 km/h to 7.0 km/h, by increments of 0.5 km/h in the case of walking, and from 6.0 km/h to 12.0 km/h, by increments of 1.0 km/h for running. The sequences were then segmented into cycles (one cycle includes two steps, starting at right heel strike), and four of them have been selected. These cycles are aligned to an identical locomotion direction, converted to joint angle space (represented by axis angles, according to the standard H-ANIM skeleton [116]), and finally normalized so that each sequence is represented by the same number of samples. In addition, a standing (neutral) position sequence of each subject has been inserted to represent the speed value 0 km/h. Consequently, the database is composed of 180 walking cycles and 140 running cycles.

In practice, a person posture, or a body pose, in a given key-frame can be defined by the position and orientation of a root node and a vector of joint angles. A motion can then be represented by an angular motion vector μ, which is a set of such joint angle vectors measured at regularly sampled intervals. Computing the entire locomotion sequence is time-consuming; the PCA technique [113] is applied, drastically reducing the dimension of the input motion-capture data space. The resulting space, referred to as the main PCA, is computed with the input motion matrix M composed of all motion vectors μ from our database with k subjects. To center this space with respect to the whole data set, we define μ_0 as an average vector of all n motion vectors. The basis vectors describing this space are the m first orthogonal PCs (principal components) necessary to compute an approximation of the original data. Let $\alpha = (\alpha_1, \alpha_2, ..., \alpha_m)$ be a coefficient vector and $E = (e_1, e_2, ..., e_m)$ a vector

matrix of the first PCs (or eigenvectors) of M, a motion θ can be expressed
as:

$$\theta \cong \theta_0 + \sum_{i=1}^{m} \alpha_i e_i = \theta_0 E \tag{4.3}$$

As mentioned, the purpose of this PCA is to reduce the dimensionality of
the input data, a very important aspect for real-time purposes. To generate a
new and entire motion, a blending technique could be applied on various α,
according to three high-level parameters: personification vector p, where p_i is
the weight for the i subject; type of locomotion T (walk or run); and speed
S. In theory, a linear interpolation between coefficient vectors is performed,
while original data are nonlinear (axis angle). This ambiguity can be solved
by applying the method presented in [117]. However, in practice, the method
here is intended for locomotion, where the different motions show small variations between postures, mostly in the sagittal plane, therefore allowing linear
interpolation.

Unfortunately, blending is not appropriate for motion extrapolation. As
the goal of a locomotion engine is to propose extrapolation of physical parameters, speed in our example, an alternative technique has to be applied. A
complete method proposes a hierarchical structure of PCA spaces that first
help to classify the motions and second allows a linear least square in a very
low dimension, instead of in the main PCA space.

Data are then retargeted to different human sizes from those captured,
and there is a process, based on motion analysis, to unwrap the normalized
data. To produce animation adaptable to any kind of virtual human, the
generalization of the heterogeneous input data we used is an important aspect.
Indeed we captured various subjects, not only with differences in the style of
motion, but also, and more importantly, with differences in size.

First, all 3D positions (i.e., the humanoid root joint) of the motion vectors are divided by the leg length H of the captured subject. Murray [118]
has shown that all the leg relative angles in the sagittal plane (hip, knee,
ankle) show very similar trajectories for all adult men for the same value of
normalized speed V, obtained by dividing the walking velocity v (in m/s) by
the hip joint height H (i.e., the leg length in meters). We can generalize this
statement to the running motion, too. The normalization of the input data is
performed at the speed control level, as the end user has to additionally give
the leg length parameter H of the human he wants to animate. Every input
locomotion sequence and each generated sequence contain a fixed number of
frames, due to the normalization step performed during preprocessing. The
time warp induced is handled using a walking cycle frequency function f that
links a given normalized speed to a cycle frequency [119] called the Inman
law. We adapted this law to our observations, performed on a treadmill, and
extended it to the case of running motion. We fit the data to an approximation
function of the form axb, similar to the Inman law. The resulting frequency
functions are described by the equation:

$$f(V) = 0.85V^{0.4} \tag{4.4}$$

for walking motions and by:

$$f(V) = 1.07V^{0.24} \tag{4.5}$$

for running motions.

Therefore, the animation engine is able to continuously vary the speed and compute the "phase update" as in the walking engine in [104], where the phase varies between $[0...1]$ and the phase update is computed with the following equation:

$$\Delta\varphi = \Delta t f(V) \tag{4.6}$$

where Δt is the elapsed time between two updates and V the normalized speed. The phase $\Delta\varphi$ multiplied by the number of frames in the normalized sequences returns the frame to display.

Finally, the goal of the method is to allow the end user to set some high-level parameters: a personification vector p composed of weights assigned to each subject, the type of locomotion T, the speed S, and the human size H (i.e., the leg size). Figure 4.3 shows an example.

Fig. 4.3: Walking generated using PCA

4.4 Virtual Human-Object interaction

4.4.1 Feature Modeling and Smart Objects

Making virtual characters, especially virtual humans, capable of manipulating objects usually requires solutions to closely related issues on two fronts: the specification of object behavior and its reflection through animation. The former usually takes place on a more abstract level, whereas the latter is mainly concerned with generation of valid and believable motion for humans and objects. There are works in the literature that have addressed both, together or separately.

The human hand is a complicated articulated structure with 27 bones. Not only must the movements of these joints be calculated, but also the reaching motion of the arm and the body needs to be considered. For real-time performance in a VR system with many agents, fast collision-detection and inverse kinematics algorithms [120] will be necessary in most cases. The calculation of the hand and body postures is not the only difficulty in grasping: realistic grasping also requires significant input about the semantics of the object. Even if the geometric and physical constraints permit, sometimes an object is simply not grasped that way. For example, a door handle must not be grasped from the neck section if the goal is to turn it. A fully automatic grasping algorithm that only takes the geometry of the object into account cannot always come up with solutions that are satisfactory in this sense. Fortunately, the grasping problem for virtual characters is easier than its robotics counterpart. Simply put, we do not have to be as accurate and physical constraints are much less of a problem. The main criterion is that the grasp must look realistic. In fact, the apparent physical realities of a virtual environment can be very different from those of the real world, with very different constraints being imposed. For example, we can imagine a virtual human holding an object that is several times his size and weight in air, while grasping it at a small site on the edge. This does not conflict with the previous examples addressing the reality issue, as for an autonomous virtual human in a virtual setting this is more a question of what he intends to do with the object (semantics) than the actual physics of grasping.

On the behavior front, virtual human-object interaction techniques were first specifically addressed in the object specific reasoner (OSR) [121]. The primary aim of this work is to bridge the gap between high-level AI planners and the low-level actions for objects, based on the observation that objects can be categorized with respect to how they are to be manipulated. There is little consideration given to interaction with more complex objects, although there are examples that employ object grasping. The closely related work on parameterized action representation [122] addresses the issue of natural language processing for virtual human-object interactions. Natural language usually describes actions at a high level, leaving out many crucial details. A PAR describes an action by specifying conditions and execution steps. Components of a natural language instruction are mapped to the parameters of a PAR, which is linked to the motion generators.

Feature modeling is an interesting approach to modeling objects for manipulation. In feature modeling, object models contain more than geometric information, for example, the function of some part of the object or its semantics. For example, in a CAD/CAM application, the definition of an object may contain instructions of how a certain part of the object is to be assembled.

The *smart objects* paradigm has been introduced as a feature modeling approach for interactions of virtual humans with virtual objects [123], [124]. In essence, smart objects provide not only the geometric information necessary for drawing them on the screen, but also semantic information useful for manipulation purposes. The smart objects paradigm is based on extending objects (shapes) with additional information on their semantics. Its focus is on autonomous virtual humans within virtual environments. The semantic information that a smart object carries is mainly about the behavior of the object when an interaction occurs between the object and a virtual human. By "behavior", we mean the changes in the appearance and state of an object as a result of the interaction (i.e., a virtual human opening a door). Attributes are the primary means of specifying information on how a virtual human manipulates its environment. They convey various kinds of information (e.g., where and how to approach to manipulate the object or to position the hands to grasp it), animation sequences (e.g., a door opening), and general nongeometric information associated with the object (e.g., weight or material properties). The semantic information in the smart object is used by the virtual characters to perform actions on/or with the object, such as grasping it, moving it, and operating it (e.g., a machine or an elevator).

Figure 4.4 shows how to define a smart object (here a CD-ROM) and how a virtual character can then use it.

Furthermore, the smart objects paradigm is focused on behavioral animation and virtual human actor-object interactions, where predefined interaction plans and finite state machines are strongly bound to the objects. This imposes a limitation on situations where direct or indirect interactions between agents and multiple objects, or simply multiple objects, are required. Recent work in [125] applied the smart objects approach to implementing "attentive" agents. Attention points and face descriptors are specified on objects in the modeling phase, which are then used by a gaze manager to automatically generate gaze behaviors for an agent when he needs to look at an object. Three low level gaze functions are used: glance, look, and stare.

4.4.2 Grasping

Grasping is perhaps the most important and complicated motion that manipulation of objects involves. The difficulty comes not only from properly "wrapping" the fingers around the object but also from the fact that the

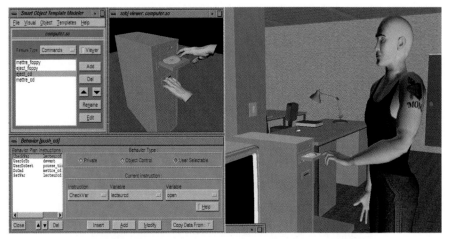

(a) Definition of smart object   (b) Visualization

Fig. 4.4: Defining and using smart objects

grasp must be suitable for the intended manipulation. In [126], a classification of the hand postures commonly used for grasping in manufacturing tasks is given. One of the earlier works on grasping that uses this classification to automatically generate grasping motions is the approach described in [127].

This approach is based on three steps:

- Heuristic grasping decision. Based on a grasp taxonomy, Mas and Thalmann [128] proposed a completely automatic grasping system for synthetic actors. In particular, the system can decide to use a pinch when the object is too small to be grasped by more than two fingers or to use a two-handed grasp when the object is too large. Figure 4.5 shows the taxonomy.

- Inverse kinematics to find the final arm posture. Inverse kinematics is also commonly used for creation of reaching motions for articulated structures [129], [120], [130], but it is still difficult to obtain realistic full-body postures without substantial tweaking. On the other hand, database-driven methods [131] cope better with full body postures. These methods are based on capturing motions for reaching inside a discrete and fixed volumetric grid around the actor. The reaching motion for a specific position is obtained through interpolation of the motions assigned to the neighboring cells.

- Multisensor hand. Huang et al. [132] approach is adapted from the use of proximity sensors in robotics [133], the sensor-actuator networks [134], and their own work on human grasping. In their work the sphere multisensors have both touch and length sensor properties, and have been found very efficient for synthetic actor grasping problem. Multisensors are considered as a group of objects attached to the articulated figure. A sensor is activated for any collision with other objects or sensors. Here we select sphere sensors for their efficiency in collision detection. Figures 4.6a and 4.6b show the multisensors and Figure 4.6c a cube grasped.

Fig. 4.5: Grasping taxonomy

In case of large objects, such as furniture, grasping simultaneously involves two or more persons. Therefore, we focused on a multiagent grasp action for encumbering objects (see Figure 4.6d). As the object's weight and geometry is distributed over several hand support points of different agents, the heuristic motion planning schemes have to be different from the ones for an object grasp performed by a single individual. For example, a large object might be grasped frontally by the first agent and from behind by the second agent (see Figure 4.7).

The humanoid is the active agent, the balloon the passive agent. We can reverse the role of active and passive agent, for example, the balloon can be active and the human passive (see Figure 4.8). The choice of the active and passive agents depends on which agent is supposed to control the other one: is the human carrying the balloon or is the balloon lifting the human into the air? By extension, any agent can be active and passive at the same time, for example, a box attaches to a balloon and is attached to a humanoid.

Another approach used in the Jack system [135], [136] that is based on Cutkosy's grasp classification [126] is described in [137]. This approach uses specialized controllers for each different type of grasp to close the fingers. It uses parallel transition networks (PaT-Nets) [138] to control each finger. Transitions in the PaT-Nets are triggered by collisions between the fingers and the object. Different PaT-Nets are used to simulate different grasp types; the differing responses of the different PaT-Nets actually define how the grasp is to take place.

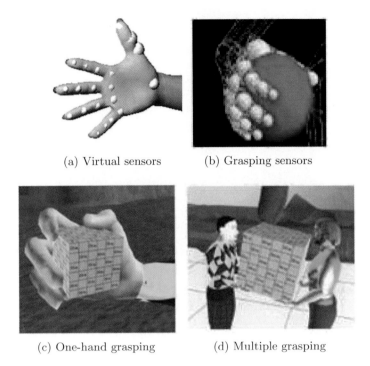

(a) Virtual sensors   (b) Grasping sensors

(c) One-hand grasping   (d) Multiple grasping

Fig. 4.6: Grasping

A very recent approach in [139] takes the interactions between the fingers and the object into account by means of dynamics simulation. This work proposes passive and active controllers for the hand. The passive controller is constructed to attract the hand posture toward a naturally comfortable pose and to force it to remain within joint limits. The active controller is used for the actual grasping and drives the hand toward a pose that is a blend of two out of a total of six setpoints that are automatically extracted from motion-capture examples. The authors demonstrate that the method can be used for manipulation of simple objects by interactively switching between set points for the active controller. This work looks at the problem of grasping from an interesting angle since properly modeling physical interactions between the fingers and the object is important. However, the method is limited to executing grasps that are in the library of examples. Furthermore, the amount of control one can exercise on the grasping may not be enough if a specific and meaningful object manipulation sequence is to be realized.

Knowledge about the presence of elongated features is relevant in the context of animation for the definition of posture and grasping motion for virtual humans. While tubular or elongated features can be quite easily defined during

Fig. 4.7: Multi-agent carrying

the design processes, their automatic extraction from unstructured 3D meshes
is not a trivial task. Moreover, geometric parameters such as tube axis or Section size should be made readily available to the animation tool. Among the
many methods for shape analysis, skeleton extraction techniques are the most
suitable for identifying tubular features. Topology-based skeletons, for example, code a given shape by storing the evolution of the level sets of a mapping
function defined on its boundary. A geometric skeleton is usually associated
with this coding, defined by the barycenters of the contours.

Ciger et al. [140] introduces a new grasping framework, which brings
together a tubular feature-classification algorithm, a hand grasp posture-
generation algorithm, and an animation framework for human-object interactions. This unique combination is capable of handling grasping tasks within
the proper context of virtual human object manipulation. This is very important because how an object is to be grasped depends strongly on how it is be
used. The method has the advantage that it can work with relatively complex objects, where manual approximation with simple geometrical primitives
may not be possible or practical. Furthermore, the method supports many
intuitive parameters for controlling the grasping posture, such as the finger
spread or the thumb configuration. Since the grasp parameters are specified
as ranges, it is possible to generate a different posture each time a virtual

(a)   (b)

Fig. 4.8: Is the human carrying the balloon or is the balloon lifting the human into the air?

human attempts to grasp an object, depending on the current configuration of the virtual human.

The algorithm to detect tubular features is called Plumber, and it is a specialized shape-classification method for triangle meshes. The Plumber method analyzes the shape of an object by studying how the intersection of spheres centered at the mesh vertices evolve while the sphere radius changes. For example, for a thin limb, the curve of intersection between the mesh and a sphere will be simply connected for a small radius and then will rapidly split into two components when the radius increases and becomes greater than the tube size. A detailed description of the shape-analysis technique, which uses the intersecting sphere, and of the Plumber method can be found in [141], [142]. The algorithm segments a surface into connected components that are either body parts or elongated features, that is, handle-like and protrusion-like features, together with their concave counterparts, narrow tunnels and wells. The segmentation can be done at single or multiscale and produces a shape graph that codes how the tubular components are attached to the main body parts. Moreover, each tubular feature is represented by its skeletal line and an average cross-sectional radius.

Grasping is perhaps the most important part of a manipulation sequence, but it is not alone. A full sequence can consist of walking to and reaching for the object, looking at it, grasping it multiple times, and keeping the hands constrained to the object while it is moving. Therefore, the smart objects are required to provide a full manipulation sequence, putting the grasping action into the proper context.

4.4.3 Motion Planning

An issue commonly encountered in virtual character animation is the problem of collisions with the environment. This problem is common to locomotion and object manipulation. Most animation algorithms (e.g., inverse kinematics) operate only on the virtual character and do not take the environment into account. When these motions are played, collisions between the virtual human and the scene may occur, detracting from the believability of the virtual environment. If care is taken during the design stage, the probability of collisions happening can be reduced; however, it is not possible to completely eliminate them, especially if we are not able to directly control what is happening in the virtual environment (e.g., if virtual characters are present).

In the field of robotics, researchers have been working on motion-planning methods for robots to avoid collisions [143]. These methods can be applied to virtual characters, but a virtual character is an articulated structure with many degrees of freedom; therefore the dimensionality of the search space is very high. Methods based on probabilistic roadmaps [144], [145] are particularly suitable for structures of this complexity. A probabilistic roadmap is a data structure (graph) that is used to capture the connectivity of the search space. Nodes in the roadmap correspond to randomly sampled configurations of the robot (e.g., joint angles) and an edge between two nodes in the roadmap means that the robot is able to move between corresponding configurations by means of a local planner. Among these, visibility-based roadmap [146] construction techniques aim at reducing the number of nodes while the rapidly exploring random trees (RRT) [145], [147] focus on sufficiently exploring the configuration space at the expense of increasing the number of nodes.

The latest trend in motion planning for virtual characters is the use of motion capture data together with roadmap techniques. In [102], the authors attempt to solve the problem of biped locomotion by using randomly sampled feet positions to construct the roadmap, which is augmented afterward with a posture transition graph. Nodes in the roadmap are connected using data from input motion clips. In [148], motion-planning algorithms based on probabilistic roadmaps are used to control 22 degrees of freedom (DOFs) of human-like characters in interactive applications. The main purpose is the automatic synthesis of collision-free reaching motions for both arms, with automatic column control and leg flexion. Generated motions are collision-free, in equilibrium, and respect articulation range limits. In order to deal with the high (22) dimension of the configuration space, the random distribution of configurations is biased to favor postures most useful for reaching and grasping. Figure 4.9 shows examples. In addition, there are extensions to interactively generate object manipulation sequences: a probabilistic inverse kinematics solver for proposing goal postures matching predesigned grasps;

dynamic update of roadmaps when obstacles change position; online planning of object location transfer; and an automatic stepping control to enlarge the character's reachable space. The work in [149] also focuses on the problem of object manipulation. The path of the object to be moved is computed using the RRT algorithm. An inverse kinematics algorithm generates poses that match the object position and orientation. Using soft constraints, it also biases the poses towards those in a posture database. As commonly seen with many virtual humans motion planning methods, some postprocessing steps are used to increase the realism of the generated motions. The authors aim to reduce the dimensionality of the configuration space by planning only for the position and orientation of the object being manipulated.

Fig. 4.9: Reaching examples

Most existing work targeting motion planning for virtual humans assumes that the virtual environment is static. However, if motion planning is to be used for object manipulation, then it is important to consider dynamics of the environment. Possible changes in the workspace can be included as additional dimensions in the configuration space, but a large number of dimensions is undesirable since it will reduce planning performance. To avoid this, dynamic roadmaps (DRM) can be used. For example, the work of Kallmann in [150] proposes a method to construct a dynamic roadmap [151] on top of an RRT planner, for application to a humanoid robot.

4.5 Facial Animation

The goal of facial animation systems has always been to obtain a high degree of realism using optimum-resolution facial mesh models and effective deformation techniques. Various muscle-based facial models with appropriate parameterized animation systems have been effectively developed for facial animation [52], [152], [153]. The Facial Action Coding System [154] defines high-level parameters for facial animation, on which several other systems are based. FACS defines fundamental basic actions known as Action Units (AUs). Each AU describes the contraction of one facial muscle or a group of related muscles. Thus, FACS was derived by analysis of the anatomical basis for facial movements. There are 46 action units. This repertoire of action units can be regarded as a "kit" for creating and compositing facial expressions. FACS is however, limited to those muscles that can be controlled voluntarily. Most facial animation systems typically follow these following steps:

1. Define an animation structure on a facial model by parameterization.
2. Define "building blocks" or basic units of the animation in terms of these parameters, for example, static expressions and visemes (visual counterparts of phonemes).
3. Use these building blocks as key-frames and define various interpolation and blending functions on the parameters to generate words and sentences from visemes and emotions (see an example singing in Figure 4.10) from expressions. The interpolation and blending functions contribute to the realism for a desired animation effect.
4. Generate the mesh animation from the interpolated or blended key-frames. Given the tools of parameterized face modeling and deformation, the most challenging task in facial animation is the design of realistic facial expressions and visemes.

The complexity of the key-frame based facial animation system increases when we incorporate natural effects such as co-articulation for speech animation and blending between a variety of facial expressions during speech. The use of speech synthesis systems and the subsequent application of co-articulation to the available temporized phoneme information is a widely accepted approach [155]. Coarticulation is a phenomenon observed during fluent speech, in which facial movements corresponding to one phonetic or visemic segment are influenced by those corresponding to the neighboring segments. Two main approaches taken for co-articulation are by Pelachaud [156] and Cohen and Massaro [157]. Both these approaches are based on the classification

Fig. 4.10: A singing facial expression

of phoneme groups and their observed interaction during speech pronunciation. Pelachaud arranged the phoneme groups according to the deformability and context dependence in order to decide the influence of the visemes on each other. Muscle contraction and relaxation times were also considered and the Facial Action Units were controlled accordingly.

For facial animation, the MPEG-4 standard is particularly important. The Facial Definition Parameter (FDP) set and the Facial Animation Parameter (FAP) set are designed to encode facial shape; animation of faces thus reproduces expressions, emotions, and speech pronunciation. The FDPs are defined by the locations of the feature points and are used to customize a given face model to a particular face. Figure 4.11 shows the FDPs. They contain 3D feature points such as mouth corners and contours, eye corners, and eyebrow centers. FAPs are based on the study of minimal facial actions and are closely related to muscle actions. Each FAP value is simply the displacement of a particular feature point from its neutral position expressed in terms of the Facial Animation Parameter Units (FAPU). The FAPUs correspond to fractions of distances between key facial features (e.g. the distance between the eyes). For example, the MPEG-4-based facial animation engine [158] for animating 3D facial models works in real time and is capable of displaying a variety of facial expressions, including speech pronunciation with the help of 66 low-level Facial Animation Parameters.

Recently, the efforts in the field of phoneme extraction have resulted in software systems capable of extracting phonemes from synthetic as well as natural speech and generating lip-synchronized speech animation from these phonemes, thus creating a complete talking-head system. It is possible to mix emotions with speech in a natural way, thus imparting to the virtual character emotional behavior. The ongoing efforts are concentrated on imparting "emotional" autonomy to the virtual face, enabling a dialogue between the real and the virtual humans with natural emotional responses. Kshirsagar and Magnenat-Thalmann [159] use a statistical analysis of the facial feature point movements. As the data are captured for fluent speech, the analysis reflects the dynamics of the facial movements related to speech production. The results of the analysis were successfully applied for more realistic speech animation. Also, this approach makes possible an easy blending between various facial expressions and speech. The use of MPEG-4 feature points for data capture and facial animation allows a restriction of the quantity of data being processed, at the same time offering more flexibility with respect to the facial model. A system incorporating a personality model [160] for an emotional autonomous virtual human has also been developed.

4.6 Autonomous Characters

4.6.1 Why Autonomous Virtual Characters?

Virtual characters are not just for movies and games. In the future, they can be at the heart of the simulation of activities for a variety of purposes, including education and training, treatment of psychological problems, and emergency preparedness. Imagine the following scenarios:

- A user is being trained to perform some complex task, such as repairing a copy machine. He uses an interactive user manual, where an autonomous character plays an expert, showing him how to proceed. At every stage, the user is able to see what to do next, even when mistakes are made.
- A therapist is helping a patient overcome a fear of public speaking. To overcome this fear, the patient has to perform while immersed in a virtual environment consisting of a seminar room and a virtual audience, which can react to the user in an autonomous way. The therapist can choose the type of virtual audience (for instance, one that is aggressive or sexist) that will result in a more effective treatment for the patient.
- A user is learning basic life support (BLS) procedures. She is immersed in a virtual setting and discovers a victim lying on the ground. She has to give him BLS through her proxy, a virtual assistant. The user navigates the scene, assesses the situation, and makes decisions by issuing natural voice commands. The virtual assistant waits for commands and executes the actions. If the user's commands are correct, the victim recovers. In cases where the user provides incorrect commands, the virtual assistant may refuse to do harm to the victim; in such situations, the virtual assistant may prompt the user for retrial, or may suggest an alternative possibility. Figure 4.12 shows the scene.

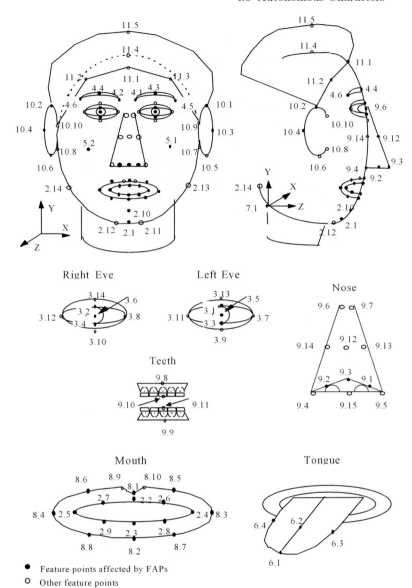

Fig. 4.11: FDP feature points

To be able to accomplish such tasks, virtual characters should be able to act on their own. This means that they should be autonomous virtual characters (AVCs).

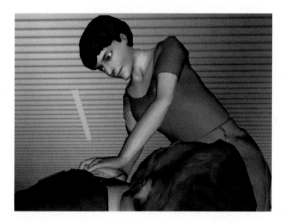

Fig. 4.12: Virtual assistant for basic life support

4.6.2 Properties of Autonomous Virtual Characters

Autonomy is generally the quality or state of being self-governing. Rather than acting from a script, an AVC is aware of its changing virtual environment, making its own decisions in real time in a coherent and effective way. An AVC should appear to be spontaneous and unpredictable, making the audience believe that the character is really alive and has its own will.

To be autonomous, an AVC must be able to perceive its environment and decide what to do to reach an intended goal. The decisions are then transformed into motor control actions, which are animated so that the behavior is believable. Therefore, an AVC's behavior consists of always repeating the following sequence: perception of the environment, action selection, and reaction.

The problem with designing AVCs is determining how to decide on the appropriate actions at each point in time, to work toward satisfaction of the current goal, which represents the AVC's most urgent need. At the same time, there is a need to pay attention to the demands and opportunities coming from the environment, without neglecting, in the long term, the satisfaction of other active needs.

There are four properties that determine how AVCs make their decisions: perception, adaptation and intelligence, memory, and emotions.

Perception: Perception of the elements in the environment is essential for AVCs, as it gives them an awareness of what is changing. An AVC continuously modifies its environment, which, in turn, influences its perceptions. Therefore, sensorial information drastically influences AVC behavior. This means that we cannot build believable AVCs without considering the way they perceive the world and each other. It is tempting to simulate perception by directly retrieving the location of each perceived object straight from the environment. To realize believable perception, AVCs should have sensors that simulate the functionality of their organic counterparts, mainly for vision, audition, and tactile sensation. These sensors should be used as a basis for implementing everyday behaviors, such as visually directed locomotion, responses to sounds and utterances, and the handling of objects. What is important is the functionality of a sensor and how it filters the information flow from the environment. It is not necessary or efficient to model sensors with biological accuracy. Therefore, virtual eyes may be represented by a Z-buffered color image representing a character's vision [161]. Each pixel of the vision input has the semantic information giving the object projected on this pixel and numerical information giving the distance to this object. So, it is easy to know, for example, that there is a table just in front at 3 meters. A virtual nose, or other tactile point-like sensors, may be represented by a simple function evaluating the global force field at the sensor's location. The virtual ear of a character may be represented by a function returning the ongoing sound events. With these virtual sensors, AVCs should be able to perceive the virtual world in a way that is very similar to the way they would perceive the real one. In a typical behavioral animation scene, the actor perceives the objects and the other actors in the environment, which provides information on their nature and position. This information is used by the behavioral model to decide the action to take, which results in a motion procedure. The synthetic actor perceives his environment from a small window in which the environment is rendered from his point of view.

Adaptation and intelligence: Adaptation and intelligence define how the character is capable of reasoning about what it perceives, especially when unpredictable events happen. An AVC should constantly choose the best action so that it can survive in its environment and accomplish its goals. As the environment changes, the AVC should be able to react dynamically to new elements, so its beliefs and goals may evolve over time. An AVC determines its next action by reasoning about what it knows to be true at a specific time. Its knowledge is decomposed into its beliefs and internal states, goals, and plans, which specify a sequence of actions required to achieve a specific goal. When simulating large groups or communities of AVCs, it is possible to use bottom-up solutions that use artificial life techniques, rather than top-down, plan-based approaches, such as those that are common in artificial intelligence. This allows new, unplanned behaviors to emerge.

Memory: It is necessary for an AVC to have a memory so that similar behaviors can be selected when predictable elements reappear. Memory plays an important role in the modeling of autonomy, as actions are often decided based on memories. But imagine an AVC in a room containing 100 different objects. Which objects can be considered memorized by the virtual character? It is tempting to decide that whenever an object is seen by the AVC, it should be stored in its memory. But if you consider humans, nobody is able to remember every single object in a room. Therefore, the memory of a realistic AVC should not be perfect either. Noser et al. [162] proposed the use of an octree as the internal representation of the environment seen by an actor because it can represent the visual memory of an actor in a 3D environment with static and dynamic objects.

Emotions: The believability of an AVC is made possible by the emergence of emotions clearly expressed at the right moment. An emotion is an emotive reaction to a perception that induces a character to assume a physical response, facial expression, or gesture or to select a specific behavior. The apparent emotions of an AVC and the way it reacts are what give it the appearance of a living being with needs and desires. Without them, an actor would just look like an automaton. Apart from making them appear more realistic, AVC's visible emotions can provide designers with a direct way of influencing the user's emotional state. To allow AVCs to respond emotionally to a situation, they could be equipped with a computational model of emotional behavior. Emotionally related behavior, such as facial expressions and posture, can be coupled with this computational model, which can be used to influence their actions. The development of a good computational model is a challenge.

4.6.3 Behaviors for Autonomous Virtual Characters

The four properties just discussed are very important in creating believable autonomous characters and should greatly contribute to their behavior. Behaviors can range from very simple, like reflexes, to very complex, although it is not really clear what a complex behavior is. We could find in daily life many examples of simple but complex situations. Let's take two examples.

1. Suppose a pedestrian walking along a boardwalk suddenly perceives another pedestrian coming exactly on the same line. What to do? This is a common problem that we solve without explaing the strategy; this is dependent on psychological factors.
2. How to make people eating realistic? Some specific behaviors have to be taken into account, like eating a T-bone steak. In this case people generally (when they are right-handed) use the right hand for the knife and the left for the fork when they cut their steak, but then they switch the fork into their right hand to eat.

Reflexes

The simplest spontaneous behavior in human beings produced by external stimuli is the reflex. Reflexes are unconscious movements regulated by the nervous system. They can be considered the basis of movements or even as the root of human movement. We can also consider reactions produced by reflexes as primitive responses that protect our body from danger and help us adjust to our surroundings. The movement performed during a reaction depends on many factors. The most evident factors are the physical characteristics:

gender, age, body constitution, etc. For example, aged people have uncertain or slow reactions. Other less evident factors are the internal or psychological parameters of the person such as personality and emotional state. Consider a person who has been frightened; if she is highly neurotic she might shout out very loudly as a reactive response.

A typical example where people react to a stimulus is when a ball is thrown to them [163]. The reactive behavior controller algorithm tracks the position of the objects all the time. In this case the object is a ball that has an initial position and initial velocity. When the Euclidean distance between the object and the character is less that the attention distance, we can say that the character can see the object. At this point the perception algorithm will compute a projection of the trajectory of the ball to know if the ball can be reached by the arms of the character. If the object is reachable, the character starts reacting. The emotional state produced in a person by a specific event could influence the kind of movement he may perform. If the character is afraid of a stimulus, he will contract the body; if he is surprised he will do an expansive movement, and so on. In this kind of movement, we are able to modify some characteristics such as amplitude or velocity, which are also factors that influence the variation of movements. Therefore, the inputs of the reactive behavior controller are the individual descriptors and the properties of the stimuli. The algorithm chooses which kind of behavior the character will perform. The first part of the algorithm chooses a movement according to the gender and age. Having the movement type defined, we can know from the ontology that "intercept reaction" implies putting the hands in the stimuli, "protect" implies raising the lower part of the arms, and "avoid" implies an inclination of the column. The second part of the algorithm provides other configurations of simple movements that will integrate the final one. It defines the recruiting level for the spine inclination according to the level of danger of the stimuli. And finally, according to the emotional state we add other movements, where we suppose that a person who is afraid may contract the body (e.g., flex the knees); and a person that is surprised will perform a broad movement (e.g. extend the arms). In Figure 4.13, we present some results of combinations of movements by changing individual parameters and parameters of the stimuli.

Motivations

Motivation is also a key cause of action, and we will consider basic motivations as essential to model life in the virtual world, providing a true virtual life. We adapt basic actor motivations and needs to urban situations, where most actions involve interactions with the environment, especially manipulation of objects in natural situations like eating or drinking. We focus on common life situations, where the actor senses and explores his environment and following an action-selection mechanism determines the suitable actions to take. For this, we can consider a mechanism of action selection based on a free-flow

Fig. 4.13: Reflex reactions to a ball

hierarchy associated with a hierarchical classifier [164]. The hierarchy of our model will contain four levels (depicted in Figure 4.14).

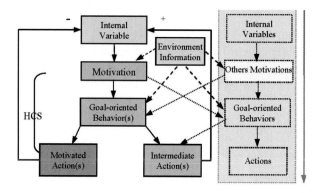

Fig. 4.14: Simplified motivational model of action selection for virtual humans

The free-flow hierarchy [165] permits us to take into account different types of motivations and information coming from the environment perception. The key idea is that, during the propagation of the activity in the hierarchy, no choices are made before the lowest level in the hierarchy represented by the actions is reached. The hierarchical classifier [166] provides a good solution to model complex hierarchies by reducing the search domain of the problem, and using rules with weights. Also, we can easily make behavioral sequences (composed of a sequence of actions). As a result, the virtual character can move to a specific place to perform a physiological action and satisfy the motivations no matter where it is. In other words, the main role of the action-selection mechanism is to maintain the internal variables under the threshold by choosing the correct actions. Actions involving interactions are preferably chosen because they are defined to be directly beneficial for the virtual human. Otherwise, the virtual human is instructed to walk and reach the place where the motivation can be satisfied. During the simulation, the model is fed with parameters describing the current state of the actor concerning each of the motivations, and by flowing inside the hierarchical structure, will correctly trigger the concerned actions. After an action is selected as a response to satisfy one of the actors motivations, the state parameter of the internal variable is adapted accordingly. An example is shown in Figure 4.15.

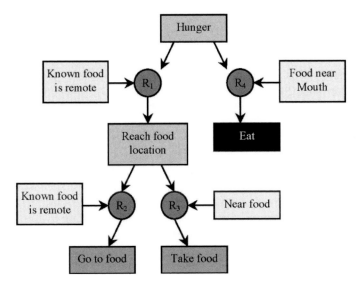

Fig. 4.15: Virtual life simulation: by default, the virtual human is working, waiting for a motivation (for instance, drinking) to be activated. The food is kept into the kitchen, as seen in the background

Social Behavior

To model human society, it is important to consider motivations and social behavior. Interesting implications of introducing communication abilities for agents could be in modeling emergent collective behavior. Emergent crowds (see next section) can be formed based on transfer of both emotional states and behaviors, for example, by verbal and nonverbal communication between physically close agents. In order to realistically simulate how humans interact in a specific social context, it is necessary to precisely model the type of relationship they have and specify how it affects their interpersonal behavior. Sociologists have identified several dimensions that are important to provide for the simulation of any group behavior: 1) power (dominance and submissiveness of the agents), 2) attraction (friendliness and unfriendliness), 3) instrumental control (hierarchical rank), and 4) emotional expressiveness. For the development of the agents' behavior in an organizational context, taking into account the hierarchical relationship is, of course, crucial, but the importance of the more informal dimensions should not be underestimated.

The agents behavior within a group is highly dependent on their location in the sociometric structures but also on their own social identity. This social characterization should be done using social-statistical variables: 1) culture, 2) gender and 3) age, taking into account the agents' roles within the group. A distinction between 4) task roles (e.g., function) and 5) socio-emotional roles (e.g., confident) is often used. An additional 6) status rating (prestige) can also be introduced. Social interactions require us to reproduce verbal communication. In such a graphical environment, interagent communication would be more than just an exchange of messages. We need to create models for sound propagation, which should be suitable for verbal communication.

To increase the believability of behaviors resulting from emotions we include nonverbal communication elements. A nonverbal communication is concerned with postures and their indications of what people are feeling. Postures are the means to communicate and are defined by a specific position of the arms, legs, and angles of the body. It is also essential to notice that the effects of nonverbal communication, though unconscious, are nevertheless important. For example, two persons communicating with each other (see Figure 4.16) and rejecting a third one. The first two persons are standing in an open triangle formation commonly used for friendly conversation. It leaves a potential opening for a third person to join them. Such a person attempts to join the group, but the first two respond by rejecting him. One raises his left arm, forming a barrier. The other deliberately avoids making eye contact with the newcomer. They have formed a closed formation, suppressing any possibility for a new person to join them. The newcomer feels rejected and leaves unhappily.

4.7 Crowd Simulation

Real-time crowds bring different challenges compared to the systems, either involving a small number of interacting characters (for example, the majority of contemporary computer games) or nonreal-time applications (as crowds in movies or visualizations of crowd evacuations after offline model computations). In comparison with single-agent simulations, the main conceptual difference is the need for efficient variety of management at every level, whether it is visualization, motion control, animation, or sound rendering. As everyday experiences hint, virtual humans comprising a crowd should look different, move different, react different, sound different, and so forth. Even if we assume that perfect simulation of a single virtual human is possible, creating

Fig. 4.16: Intercommunication

a simulation involving multiple such humans would be a difficult and tedious task. Methods easing control of many characters are needed; however, such methods should still preserve ability to control individual agents. For an extended study of crowd simulation, see [99].

In comparison with nonreal-time simulations, the main technical challenge is increased demand on computational resources, whether it is general processing power, graphics performance, or memory space. One of the foremost constraining factors for real-time crowd simulations is crowd rendering. Fast and scalable methods to compute behavior, that can take into account inputs not known in advance and render large and varied crowds are needed. While nonreal-time simulations are able to take advantage of knowing a full run of the simulated scenario (and therefore, for example, can run iteratively over several possible options selecting the globally best solution), real-time simulations have to react to the situation as it unfolds in the moment.

Animating crowds [167] is challenging in both character animation and virtual city modeling. Though different textures and colors may be used, the similarity of the virtual people would be soon detected even by nonexperts, for example, if everybody walks the same in this virtual city! It is, hence, useful to have a fast and intuitive way of generating motions with different personalities depending on gender, age, emotions, etc. from an example motion, say, a genuine walking motion. The problem is basically to generate variety among a finite set of motion requests and then to apply it to either an individual or a member of a crowd. It also needs very good tools to tune the motion [168].

Bouvier et al. [169], [170] used a combination of particle systems and transition networks to model human crowds in visualization of urban spaces; lower level enables people to avoid obstacles using attraction and repulsion forces analogous to physical electric forces. Higher-level behavior is modeled by transition networks, with transitions depending on timing, visiting of certain points, changes of local densities, and global events. Brogan and Hodgins [171] simulated group behavior for systems with significant dynamics. They presented an algorithm for controlling the movements of creatures traveling as a group. The algorithm has two steps: first a perception model determines the creatures and obstacles visible to each individual and then a placement algorithm determines the desired position for each individual given the locations and velocities of perceived creatures and obstacles. Simulated systems included groups of legged robots, bicycle riders, and point-mass systems.

Musse and Thalmann's [167] proposed solution addresses two main issues: crowd structure and crowd behavior. Considering crowd structure, the approach deals with a hierarchy composed of crowd, groups and agents, where the groups are the most complex structure containing the information to be distributed among the individuals. Concerning crowd behavior, the virtual agents are endowed with different levels of autonomy. They can act according to an innate and scripted crowd behavior (programmed behavior), react as a function of triggered events (reactive or autonomous behavior), or be guided by an interactive process during simulation (guided behavior) [172]. Figure 4.17 shows a crowd guided by a leader.

Fig. 4.17: Crowd simulation

For emergent crowds, Ulicny and Thalmann [173] proposed a behavior model based on a combination of rules and finite state machines [174] for controlling agent's behavior using a layered approach. The first layer deals with the selection of higher-level complex behavior appropriate to the agent's situation, the second layer implements these behaviors using low-level actions provided by the virtual human [175]. At the higher level, rules select complex behaviors (such as flee) according to the agent's state (constituted by attributes) and the state of the virtual environment (conveyed by events). In rules, it is specified for whom (e.g., particular agent or agents in a particular group) and when the rule is applicable (e.g., at a defined time, after receiving the event, or when some attribute reaches a specified value), and what is the consequence of rule firing (e.g., change of the agent's high-level behavior or attribute). At the lower level, complex behaviors are implemented by hierarchical finite state machines.

In terms of rendering, the goal of a real-time crowd visualizer [176] is to render a large number of entities according to the current simulation state, which provides the position, orientation, and velocity for each individual. System constraints are believability, real-time updates (25 frames per second), and a number of digital actors ranging in the tens of thousands. Also actors are made believable by varying their appearance (textures and colors) and animation; we may also add accessories like hats, glasses, or mobile phones (see Figure 4.18). Their graphical representation is derived from a template, which holds all the possible variations. Thus, with only a limited set of such templates, we can achieve a varied crowd, leading to considerable time savings for designers. A template is defined as:

- a set of three meshes with decreasing complexity (LODs),
- a set of textures in gray scale (except for the skin) identifying color modulation areas (pants, shirt, hair, etc.),
- a skeleton (kinematic structure), and
- a corresponding animation database as skeletal orientations (here 1000 different walk cycles generated using a motion-blending-based locomotion engine).

Each human in the visualization system is called an instance and is derived from a template. Individualization comes from assigning a specific gray-scale texture and a color combination for each identifiable region. Instances have individualized walk velocities and are animated by blending the available walk animations.

The rendering pipeline advances consecutively in four steps. The first consists in culling, that is, determining visibility, and choosing the rendering fidelity for each simulated human. Three fidelities are defined: dynamic meshes, static meshes, and impostors.

The next step of the pipeline is the rendering of dynamic meshes, which are the most detailed fidelity capable to interpolate animations based on skeletal postures. According to the current instance state (linear and angular walk velocities and time), animations are retrieved from the database and interpolated, yielding a smooth animation, with continuous variations of velocities,

Fig. 4.18: Crowd simulation

and no foot-sliding. The resulting skeletal posture is sent to a hardware vertex shader and fragment shader deforming and rendering the human on the graphics card.

Then static meshes (also called baked or predeformed) constitute the second rendering fidelity, which keeps a pretransformed set of animations using the lowest-resolution mesh of the deformed mesh in the previous step. Precomputing deformations allows substantial gains in speed but constrains the animation variety and smoothness.

The final rendering fidelity is the billboard model that, compared to previous approaches, uses a simplified scheme of sampling and lighting. World aligned billboards are used, with the assumption that the camera will never hover directly above the crowd. Thus, only sampled images around the waist level of the character are needed. For example, the templates are sampled at 20 different angles, for each of the 25 key-frames composing a walk animation. When constructing the resulting texture, the bounding box of each sampled frame is detected to pack them tightly together. When rendering billboarded pedestrians, cylindrical lighting is applied: each vertex normal is set to point in the positive $Z-$ direction, plus a small offset on the $X-$ axis so that it points slightly outside the frame. We then interpolate the light intensity for each pixel in the fragment shader. Figure 4.18 shows a crowd with the three fidelities.

If we consider real crowds, they are formed by thousands of individuals that move in a bounded environment. Each pedestrian has individual goals in space that he wants to reach, avoiding obstacles. People perceive their environment and use this information to choose the shortest path in time and space that leads to their goal. Emergent behaviors can also be observed in crowds. For example, in places where the space is small and very crowded, people form lanes to maximize their speed. Also, when dangerous events such as fires occur, pedestrians tend to react in very chaotic ways to escape. Planning crowd motion in real time is a very expensive task, which is often decoupled into two distinct parts: path planning and obstacle avoidance. Path planning consists in finding the best way to reach a goal. Obstacles can either be other pedestrians or objects that comprise the environment. The path selection criteria are the avoidance of congested zones and minimization of distance and travel time. Path planning must also offer a variety of paths to spread pedestrians in the whole scene. Avoidance, on the other hand, must inhibit collisions of pedestrians with obstacles. For real-time simulations, such methods need to be efficient as well as believable. Multiple motion-planning approaches for crowds have been introduced. As of today, several fast path planning solutions exist. Avoidance, however, remains a very expensive task. Agent-based methods offer realistic pedestrian motion planning, especially when coupled with global navigation. This approach gives the possibility to add individual and cognitive behaviors for each agent but becomes too expensive for a large number of pedestrians. Potential field approaches [177] handle long- and short-term avoidance. Long-term avoidance predicts possible collisions and inhibits them. Short-term avoidance intervenes when long-term avoidance alone cannot prevent collisions. These methods offer less-believable results than agent-based approaches, because they do not provide the possibility to individualize each pedestrian. However, this characteristic also entails much lower computational costs.

Recently, a hybrid architecture [178] has been proposed to handle realistic crowd motion planning in real time. In order to obtain high performance, the approach is scalable. The authors divide the scene into multiple regions of varying interest, defined at initialization and modifiable at run time. According to its level of interest, each region is ruled by a different motion planning algorithm. Zones that attract the attention of the user exploit accurate methods, while computation time is saved by applying less expensive algorithms in other regions. The architecture also ensures that no visible disturbance is generated when switching from an algorithm to another. The results show that it is possible to simulate up to 10,000 pedestrians in real time with a large variety of goals. Moreover, the possibility of introducing and interactively modifying the regions of interest in a scene offers a way for the user to select the desired performance and to distribute the computation time accordingly.

A simulation of pedestrians taking advantage of this architecture is illustrated in Figure 4.19.

Fig. 4.19: Pedestrians using a hybrid motion planning architecture to reach their goal and avoid each other

5

Architecture of Virtual Reality Systems

The creation of VR systems to support virtual environments (VE) is a challenging problem requiring diverse areas of expertise, ranging from networks to psychology. Developing VEs is a very expensive task in terms of time and financial and human resources. VEs can be applied in a broad range of areas, such as scientific visualization, socializing, training, psychological therapy, and gaming (for more details, see the "Applications" part of this book). Such a diversity of applications produces a set of requirements that make it very difficult, if not impossible, to build a single system that fits all needs. The result has been the creation of monolithic systems that are highly optimized to a particular application, with very limited reusability of components for other purposes.

According to Oliveira et al. [179], the problem of lack of reusability is due to the current trend in the VE community: developing a new VE system for each different application. The "reinventing the wheel" and "not invented here" syndromes limit the innovation and delay the use of VEs in wider areas for the general public.

Monolithic systems such as DIVE [180], MASSIVE [181], NPSNET [182], SPLINE [183], and dVS/dVISE [184], among others, proliferated in the past due to the lack of system flexibility for a particular application [179]. The introduction of more modular architectures led to the emergence of toolkits such as WorldToolkit [185], Avocado [186], VR Juggler [187], VHD++ [188], and Virtools (http://www.virtools.com). These software suites have different degrees of flexibility. Frameworks like VHD++ differ from others due to its specialized skills in a particular domain, such as virtual humans simulation technologies. All of them are based on a hierarchical representation of the virtual environment: a scene graph.

5.1 Scene Graph-Based Systems

A scene graph is an abstract logical access structure, a "tree." It is used to represent objects comprising the environment (scene data) and the relationships between them. The scene graph consists of parent nodes, child nodes, and data objects. The parent nodes, also called group nodes, organize and, in some cases, control how to interpret their descendants. Group nodes serve as the glue that holds a scene graph together. Child nodes can be either group nodes or leaf nodes. Leaf nodes have no children. They encode the core semantic elements of a scene graph, for example, what to draw (geometry), what to play (audio), how to illuminate objects (lights), or what code to execute (behavior). Leaf nodes refer to data objects. These objects are not scene graph nodes, but they contain the data that leaf nodes require, such as the geometry to draw or the sound sample to play.

Scene graphs should not be confused with data structures used to do visibility culling or collision queries such as octrees, BSP, ABT, KdT. Scene graphs are used to connect game rules, physics, animation, and AI systems to the graphics engine.

Popular implementations of scene graph programming interfaces (APIs) include: Cosmo3D (SGI), Vega Scene Graph,[1] Java3D,[2] OpenSceneGraph,[3] and OpenGL Performer[4]. All of them were designed for creating real-time visual simulations and other performance-oriented 3D graphics applications.

OpenGL Performer is a commercial toolkit that evolved from Open Inventor, which is corrently an open-source project.[5] Open Inventor is considered the archetypical example of a scene graph library. It presents an object-oriented programming model based on a 3D scene database (scene graph) that provides a higher layer of programming for OpenGL.

Java 3D gained popularity as the main scene graph-based API for developing 3D applications with Java. It is frequently used for developing Web-based applications enhanced with real-time 3D graphics [189],[190],[191]. It is also a very representative example of a scene graph-based 3D toolkit.

Scene graph implementations are based on a hierarchical spatial representation of the objects in the scene, for example, a terrain contains a house, and inside the house there is a person holding a hammer in her right hand.

Usually, the semantic information that is encoded in the scene graph corresponds mainly to visualization aspects, geometry to draw, and associated effects such as a sound sample. Only elemental relationships between objects can be specified, for example, smart objects [192] (simple tools and objects such as a hammer or a drawer) that contain information describing how they

---

[1] http://www.presagis.com
[2] http://java3d.dev.java.net
[3] http://www.openscenegraph.org
[4] http://www.sgi.com/products/software/performer
[5] http://oss.sgi.com/projects/inventor

can be grasped by a virtual human and a predetermined behavior to perform (see Section 4.4.1).

Efforts aimed at enhancing the adaptability and reusability of VE applications and entities within them have focused on designing software component frameworks to manage the resources and building blocks of a VE system. Such is the case of the Java Adaptive Dynamic Environment (JADE) [179], which permits dynamic runtime management of all components and resources of a VE system. While this kind of initiative is successful in terms of providing reusability, and interoperability at the level of the code source, they do not address the fundamental problem of reusing the virtual entities that participate in the VE application. The use of scene graphs as hierarchical spatial representations is not questioned. As a result, source code implementing animation, visualization, and interaction algorithms can be reused to some extent. But the knowledge associated with a virtual entity remains difficult to reuse. In [193] Gutiérrez proposed the "semantic virtual environments" approach, which considers virtual entities as complex items with different types of data and knowledge associated with them.

5.2 Semantic Virtual Environments

The main idea behind semantic virtual environments (SVE) [193] is that a higher-level semantic representation of virtual environments can enhance the reusability and adaptation capabilities of the virtual entities participating in a VE. The semantics-based representation that is proposed builds on the concept of a scene graph, with the difference that it does not focus on visual or spatial relationships between entities but on higher-level semantics.

The SVE approach is based on the semantics of the virtual entities and not on their geometry, as is the case in most of the VE applications. A semantic model provides a way to specify alternative geometric representations for each entity and a range of functionalities. The entities are called digital items and can be not only virtual objects to be rendered as part of the scene, but also independent user interfaces and controls for animation or interaction.

A semantic model of a virtual environment can be defined keeping in mind that the main attribute of a virtual entity (objects or characters) is its 3D shape. Virtual environments are geometry-based applications. However, depending on the context, the shape of the entity can change. Moreover, there are contexts in which multiple shapes representing the same virtual entity must be manipulated and synchronized. For instance, when displaying a virtual character on a large projection screen, we require information for rendering a high-resolution (hi-res) 3D shape. Nevertheless, the hi-res shape could be controlled by the user interactions performed through a different representation, either a simplified shape or an abstract manipulator: a menu, a slider, or any other GUI control. Using independent representations for each case is costly in terms of data synchronization. The semantic model encapsulates the set of geometric and/or abstract representations belonging to each virtual entity and associates descriptors to inform the rendering and interface systems about how to handle each object.

Figure 5.1 shows a general class diagram of the semantic model for the VE and the tools that can be used to control and interact with it.

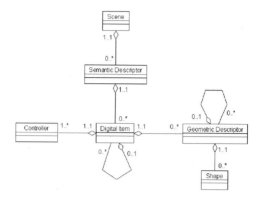

Fig. 5.1: Semantic representation of an interactive virtual environment

The scene is the main container of the VE model; it has references to the digital items contained in the VE. It is the data repository used by digital items and other software tools such as viewers or interaction devices.

A semantic descriptor provides human- and machine-readable information about a particular digital item (we also call them virtual entities). They are the entry points for the scene controller to choose the correct geometry and interface to present. The semantic descriptor is the placeholder for any information describing how the digital item is to be used and how it is related to other items in the scene.

The geometric descriptor of a digital item specifies the type of shape associated with the entity: a deformable mesh, an articulated body (joints and segments), and the like. For instance, hierarchical structures for skeleton-based animation can be defined by the geometric descriptors, such as H-Anim,[6] the standard specification of a hierarchical structure for humanoid character animation. Moreover, alternative skeletons with different levels of detail on the number of joints and/or the complexity of the segments (3D shapes associated with each joint) can be specified as well.

Handling alternative geometric representations for each virtual entity in the environment is not enough to provide a complete representation of a virtual world. The model reflects also the relations between entities. The semantic

---

[6] http://www.h-anim.org

descriptors characterize each object or character in the scene and constitute a scene graph that can be used for both rendering and extracting the underlying information about its contents. Digital items can contain other items or be related to each other in different ways, for example, entities that move together or that trigger events on other entities, the model is general enough to express a variety of relations.

A digital item can be controlled in a variety of ways: interactive controls (requiring user input), autonomous animation controllers (implementation of algorithms to synthesize some kind of behavior or animation), etc. A controller specifies the interaction possibilities: predefined object behaviors that react to human intervention and the way to provide access (interfaces) to them. For instance, an interactive control can describe the animation to open and close a door and expose the parameters controlling this behavior. This information can be used to implement a variety of interfaces to access the same parameter: 3D manipulators or 2D GUI controls. Usually, digital items in a VE are animated in either an autonomous or an event-triggered way.

The virtual entities contained in a scene can be controlled and displayed in several ways. Different viewers and interfaces can be used depending on the devices available and the information associated with each virtual object or character. For example, a single virtual character can be rendered as a hi-res 3D model in an OpenGL-based viewer or a simplified version can be displayed in a PDA screen, provided that the character's descriptor contains alternative representations associated with it. The character can be controlled through a 3D manipulator or a 2D GUI control. All the previous cited information can be stored in the corresponding semantic descriptor. This model has been successfully applied in the development of VR applications with adaptive multimodal interfaces. The work presented in [194] uses a graphic interface to design real-time multimodal interfaces to interact within a virtual world. For example, virtual characters can be controlled either through an optical gesture recognition system, which detects face gestures, or by means of a PDA, in a similar way as with the "mobile animator" [195] (see Section 7.2.3).

5.3 Generic System Architecture for VR Systems

In addition to the SVE approach explained earlier, other researchers and developers have designed system architectures for VR systems. The main goal is to maximize the reusability of software and data while maximizing the variety of VR applications that can be developed.

Steinicke et al. [196] have proposed a generic architecture for VR systems composed of three main layers: application, graphics, and rendering.

The application layer is dedicated to create the VR user interface. Various GUI (graphical user interface) toolkits can be used for this purpose, such as Qt,[7] Gtk,[8] wxWidgets.[9]

The graphics layer deals with 3D models (graphics objects) managed through a scene graph and controlled by behavior graphs, which can describe event-dependent and time-dependent behavior in the virtual scene. Both graphs are contained in a canvas, which can be the equivalent of the scene container of the SVE model (Section 5.2).

The rendering layer allows us to plug adapters for different rendering technologies, such as OpenGL, global illumination software (see Section 2.3.2) like RenderMan[10], or POVRay.[11]

An additional component in the architecture is used to control VR devices such as trackers or data gloves. In many cases, those devices are controlled by their own separate computer. In this case, data exchange between the device controller and the main application is usually done through the network (e.g., using UDP or TCP sockets). Network connections also serve to share data describing the virtual environment among several users, making it possible to create distributed and multiuser virtual environments.

5.4 Distributed Virtual Environments

This Section is based on the definitions provided by Lee et al. in [197] and [198].

A distributed virtual environment (DVE) is a software system that allows users in a network to interact with each other by sharing a common view of their states. As users are geographically distributed over large networks like the Internet and the number of users increases, scalability is a key aspect to consider for real-time interaction.

In [199], Molet et al. present an application of a distribued virtual enviroment called *Cybertennis* (see Figure 5.2). This was done for the Telecom conference in Geneva in 1997, to illustrate the concept of DVE. Two users, one in Lausanne and one in Geneva (40 miles away), were playing tennis together on a virtual moon, and the virtual clone of *Marilyn Monroe* was acting as referee.

The approaches for improving scalability of DVE can be classified into the following categories: communication architecture, interest management, concurrency control, data replication, and load distribution.

---

[7] http://trolltech.com/products/qt
[8] http://www.gtk.org
[9] http://www.wxwidgets.org/
[10] https://renderman.pixar.com
[11] http://www.povray.org/

Fig. 5.2: Cybertennis in Telecom Interactive 97, by MIRALab, University of Geneva and EPFL VRlab [199]

5.4.1 Communication Architecture

Depending on how the communication is coordinated, the communication architecture can be characterized as follows: client-server, peer-to-peer, or peer-to-server.

In the client-server model, all messages are sent to a server and then the server distributes them to all or some of the users according to synchronization requirements. As the number of participants in a virtual world increases, the server becomes a bottleneck. Even if additional servers are used, the delay due to additional communication overhead in servers is inevitable.

The peer-to-peer model allows users to directly exchange messages. However, each user has to assume all the responsibility of message filtering and synchronization.

The peer-to-server model exploits the benefits of the two other models. Consistency management is done by a server and communication among users is performed using multicast.

5.4.2 Interest Management

Computing power and rendering speed are rapidly increasing; however, network resources still remain very expensive compared with computational resources. To overcome the limitations of the network resources, various relevance-filtering mechanisms are used. Interest-management strategies exploit the fact that users do not need to receive all update messages related to the whole world. Instead, they receive only messages in which they are interested. Two methods can be used, depending on the fidelity of the message filtering: dividing the virtual world into several regions (usually done offline), or localizing the area of interest of the participants in real time.

As proposed by Benford et al. [200], the awareness level between two objects A and B can be defined by four strength values: A's focus on B, A's nimbus to B, B's focus on A and B's nimbus to A. If A's and B's aurae don't have common components (i.e., there is no adequate aura intersection), these values are null. Focus describes the observers' allocation of attention. The concept of nimbus describes the observed object's manifestation or observability. The observer's awareness of the observed is then some combination of the observed's nimbus and the observer's focus. Aura is defined as the subspace that effectively bounds the presence of an object within a given medium. Aura, focus, and nimbus may all be multivalued functions, may have arbitrary extents and shapes, and are medium specific. Figure 5.3 illustrates these concepts.

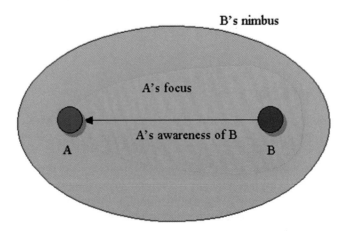

Fig. 5.3: The aura nimbus approach for interest management in collaborative worlds

5.4.3 Concurrency Control

Shared information in DVEs is often replicated at each user's site to provide acceptable interactive performance, especially where users are geographically distributed over large networks like the Internet.

Replication enables users to locally access and update data. On the other hand, the cost of replication is to maintain synchronization among replicas in the presence of multiple concurrent updates, which eventually lead to inconsistent views among users. As communication delay increases, the probability of conflicts between operations does as much. Therefore, concurrency control is required to maintain synchronization among replicas. Approaches to concurrency control have been broadly categorized into pessimistic, optimistic and prediction schemes.

The pessimistic scheme blocks a user until a lock request for an object is granted and then allows him to manipulate the object. It is simple and guarantees absolute consistency. However, interactive performance can be deteriorated by high communication delays due to an increased number of users.

The optimistic scheme allows users to update objects without conflict checks with others and thus to interact with objects more naturally. However, when conflicts occur, a repair must be done. This increases the system complexity and produces strange effects when undoing and redoing previous actions on user interfaces.

When using the prediction-based concurrency control, the owner of an object predicts the next owner before users request ownership of the object. The prediction is calculated on the basis of the position, orientation, and navigation speed of the users.

5.4.4 Data Replication

In order to support real-time interaction, it is common to replicate virtual world data from the server at the client. Each client then updates its replicated data by local changes or notification of remote changes. The initial download delay increases proportionally to the size of the virtual world. To reduce the transmission overhead, several on-demand transmission (partial-replication) techniques are proposed. Instead of downloading all of the virtual world objects, only the required objects are copied. Other approaches use compression of geometry and image data.

A key aspect in partial replication is how to efficiently replicate the required data, in order to minimize the artifacts (incomplete scenes) due to unavailable data. Two schemes are used together: prioritized transfer of objects and caching and prefetching techniques.

The prioritized transfer of objects filters objects within a user's viewing range and transmits only the objects that provide high fidelity to the user using level of details (LODs) or multiresolution techniques. This maximizes the graphical fidelity of world objects as well as interactive performance by mediating the graphical detail and the transmission overhead of the objects.

Caching and prefetching make the demanded data immediately available in a timely manner by exploiting the locality of data. This approach exploits the spatial relationship based on the distance between a user and objects. It is based on the observation that the nearer the object lies to the user, the more probability it has to be accessed again.

5.4.5 Load Distribution

Another approach for enhancing scalability is the multiple-server architecture, adopted in several DVE systems and in many commercial multiplayer network games such as Second Life (http://www.secondlife.com/) or Lineage II (www.lineage2.com). Partitioning a virtual world into multiple regions and distributing the responsibilities for managing the regions across multiple servers can significantly reduce the workloads of individual servers. This enables a system to support more concurrent users and a larger virtual environment.

However, nonuniform distribution of users over the virtual environment would incur a workload imbalance among servers. Some servers would handle more crowded regions than others and suffer from heavy workload and produce low interactive performance.

To avoid such degradation of interactive performance, dynamic load distribution schemes have been introduced: overloaded servers transfer their excessive workloads to less-loaded ones. There are three main approaches: local, global, and adaptive dynamic load distribution.

In the local approach, an overloaded server performs load distribution locally with only its neighboring servers, whose regions are adjacent to that of the overloaded server.

The local approach incurs less overhead than the global approach because an overloaded server requires the information only on its neighboring servers and incurs a small amount of user migrations. However, in the case of a highly skewed workload imbalance (most overloaded servers are neighbored with each other rather than dispersed) an overloaded server cannot give its excessive workload to its neighboring servers because they are also heavily loaded.

The global approach can balance the workloads evenly even in a highly skewed case because all the servers perform load distribution together with the global information. A central coordinator repartitions the whole virtual environment using a graph-partitioning algorithm. However, the repartitioning overhead and the required amount of user migrations increase sharply as do the size of a virtual environment and the number of servers in the system.

In the adaptive approach, an overloaded server balances its workload with a set of servers (beyond its neighboring servers) according to their workload status.

6

Mixed Realities

6.1 Augmented Reality and Augmented Virtuality

In Chapter 1 we introduced the concept of *reality continuum* (Section 1.4) as a way to classify variants of Virtual Reality. Such classification depends on the proportion of virtual imagery with respect to a real-world scene that is displayed in an application. We can distinguish three main categories: *Virtual Reality* (VR), in which only virtual images are used; *augmented reality* (AR), where computer graphics are superimposed over images of the real world; and augmented virtuality (AV), where imaged portions of the real world are integrated within a virtual world. The term *mixed realities* (MR) is used to refer to either augmented reality or augmented virtuality, since both of them combine elements from real and virtual worlds.

All the VR techniques, algorithms, interaction devices, and so on, that are described in this book can also be applied in both AR and AV applications. In addition, an important component should be incorporated: a tracking mechanism. Tracking is usually done applying computer-vision and image-processing techniques to data acquired using a video camera. The objective of tracking is to detect relevant objects in the real-world; acquire their position, orientation, contour, and other visual features, and use this information to "attach" computer-generated images to real objects or portions of the scene.

If an MR application is to operate in real time, where computer-generated graphics are superimposed on live images of the surrounding world, all the MR processes must be able to keep pace with the captured image frame rate. Knowing what is present in the real world and where is a vital component for the effective operation of many MR systems. This description can be used to aid virtual object placement, occlusion culling, collision detection, or many other visual or simulated effects. Building up and reconstructing this real-world description in real time is the main challenge faced by MR systems. Different tracking algorithms and techniques have been developed to solve this problem.

6.2 Tracking Techniques

This Section is based on the survey of 3D tracking methods presented in [10]. In addition to computer vision, other techniques can be used to achieve 3D tracking. Mechanical trackers, such as those based on exoskeletons (see Section 9.4.3), are accurate enough, although they constrain the user to a limited working space. Magnetic trackers, like those used for motion capture (see Section 3.3) are vulnerable to distortions by metallic structures in the environment, and limit the range of displacements. Ultrasonic trackers, such as the Polhemus Isotrac, suffer from noise and tend to be inaccurate at long ranges because of variations in the ambient temperature. Inertial trackers drift with time.

Computer vision has the potential to yield noninvasive, accurate, and low-cost solutions. Different methods with variable degrees of accuracy and robustness can be applied.

6.2.1 Markers-Based Tracking

A popular tracking method for augmented reality applications is adding fiducials, such as LEDs or special markers, to the scene or target object to ease the registration task. This assumes that one or more fiducials are visible at all times. Otherwise, the registration cannot be done. A drawback of this method is that it is not always possible to place fiducials. In fact, AR end users do not like them because they are visible in the scene and it is not always possible to modify the environment before running the application.

The addition in the scene of fiducials, also called landmarks or markers, greatly helps accomplish two main tasks: extracting information from the image and estimating the pose of the tracked objects. Markers constitute image features that are easy to extract. They also provide reliable, easy to exploit measurements for the pose estimation.

There are two types of fiducials: "point fiducials," which give one-point correspondence between the scene and the image and "planar fiducials." To obtain more information from each point fiducial, it is possible to turn it into a planar shape with identifiable corners. A single planar fiducial provides all six spatial constraints needed to define a coordinate frame (position and orientation).

Point fiducials are commonly circular markers because the appearance of circular patterns is relatively invariant under perspective distortion, facilitating their detection. To facilitate their identification, the markers can be arranged in a distinctive geometric pattern. This is the technique used by most optical motion capture systems (see Section 3.3.1).

Planar rectangular fiducials have gained popularity because they yield a robust, low-cost solution for real-time 3D tracking. The ARToolkit software library uses this approach. ARToolkit markers have a black border on a white background to facilitate the detection (see Figure 6.1). An inner pattern allows identification of the different markers. The image is first thresholded, and the system looks for connected regions of black pixels. Regions whose outline contour can be fitted by four line segments are kept. Then each region is corrected to remove the perspective distortion and compare it by template matching with the known patterns.

Fig. 6.1: Markers-based tracking using ARToolkit

The whole process, including marker detection and pose estimation, can run at 30 frames per second. The 3D tracking system does not require any manual initialization, and is robust to fiducial occlusion. Under good lighting conditions, the recovered pose is accurate enough for AR applications.

ARToolkit can be a good solution for 3D tracking if it is possible to add markers to the scene. Due to its low CPU requirements, similar marker-based applications have been implemented on mobile devices such as PDAs and mobile phones [201], see also ARToolkitPlus.[1]

6.2.2 Marker-Less Tracking

In some applications, it is either undesirable or very difficult to add markers to the scene, for example, outdoor environments or unknown environments. In such cases it is necessary to rely on naturally present object features such as edges, corners, or texture. However, this increases the complexity of the tracking algorithm.

Finding and following feature points or edges can be difficult because they are hard to detect, and in many cases there are not enough of them on typical objects. Total or even partial occlusion of the tracked objects typically results in tracking failure. The camera can easily move too fast so that the images are motion-blurred; the lighting during a shot can change significantly; reflections and specularities may confuse the tracker. It should also be considered that

---

[1] http://studierstube.icg.tu-graz.ac.at

an object may drastically change its aspect due to displacement, for example, changes in perspective or appearance of hidden parts when changing the point of view. In such cases, the features to be followed always change, and the tracker must deal with features coming in and out of the picture.

3D knowledge is often used to ease the task of marker-less tracking algorithms. The 3D knowledge can come in the form of a CAD model, a set of planar parts, or even a rough 3D model such as an ellipsoid.

Two kinds of approaches can be distinguished, depending on the nature of the image features being used: edge-based methods and methods that rely on information provided by pixels inside the object's projection (optical flow, template matching, or interest-point correspondences).

Edge-Based Methods

Edge-based methods try to match the projections of the edges of the target object to an area of high image gradient.

Most of the early tracking approaches were edge-based. These methods are both computationally efficient and relatively easy to implement. They are also naturally stable in lighting changes, even for specular materials.

One strategy consists in looking for strong gradients in the image around a first estimation of the object pose without explicitly extracting the contours. This is fast and general. Another strategy is to first extract image contours, such as straight line segments, and to fit the model outlines to these image contours. The loss in generality can be compensated by a gain in robustness.

In the following example (see Figure 6.2), we can see an application of edge-based tracking methods for creating a checkers game with a virtual character.

Optical Flow-Based Methods

Optical flow is the apparent motion of the image projection of a physical point in an image sequence, where the velocity at each pixel location is computed under the assumption that projection's intensity remains constant. The optical flow can be computed using the Lucas-Kanade method [202].

Template Matching

The Lucas-Kanade algorithm [203],[202] was originally designed to compute the optical flow at some image locations, but it can be used for a more general purpose; to register a 2D template to an image under a family of deformations. It does not necessarily rely on local features such as edges or interest points, but on global region tracking, which means using the whole pattern of the object to be tracked. Such a method can be useful to treat complex objects that are difficult to model using local features. Although it can be computationally expensive, it has been shown that under some conditions, it can be effectively formulated.

Fig. 6.2: Playing checkers with a virtual human

Interest-Point Methods

Interest-point methods use localized features instead of global ones; this has several advantages. In the same way as edge-based methods, they rely on matching individual features across images and are able to cope with partial occlusions or matching errors. Illumination invariance is also simple to achieve. But unlike edge-based methods, they do not get confused by background clutter and they exploit more of the image information, which tends to make them more robust. They are similar in some ways to optical-flow approaches, but they allow faster motions since no small interframe motion assumption is made. A representative example of this kind of method is the face-tracking system described by Vacchetti et. al. in [204]; their tracking algorithm uses interest points and one reference image (initialization phase).

Tracking without 3D Knowledge

Using a 3D model as reference for the tracking algorithm increases its reliability, but it can be too expensive or inconvenient to have a model in some applications. If no 3D knowledge is available, different image features should be exploited.

It is possible to simultaneously estimate both camera motion and scene geometry without a 3D reference model. The recovered trajectory and 3D structure are expressed in an arbitrary coordinate system, for example, the one corresponding to the initial camera position. This problem is known as simultaneous localization and mapping (SLAM). SLAM is a common problem for the self-localization of a moving robot. Some approaches rely on projective properties that provide constraints on camera motion and 3D point locations from 2D correspondences. A representative example is the work presented by Nister et al. [205].

6.3 Mixed Reality Tool Kits

The most popular solution for rapid development of augmented reality applications is the ARToolkit[2] or some of its variants, such as the ARToolkitPlus for mobile devices cited earlier.

ARToolkit was originally developed by Dr. Hirokazu Kato, and its ongoing development is being supported by the Human Interface Technology Laboratory (HIT Lab) at the University of Washington; the HIT Lab NZ at the University of Canterbury, New Zealand, and ARToolworks, Inc. in Seattle. ARToolkit is made available freely for noncommercial use under the GNU general public license.

An alternative to ARToolkit is the Mixed Reality Toolkit, or MRT,[3] which can be rapidly applied over live video streams or still images to reconstruct and register 3D shapes. The toolkit consists of a small library of C++ classes and may be freely downloaded and used in accordance with the GNU lesser general public license.

---

[2] http://www.hitl.washington.edu/artoolkit
[3] http://www.cs.ucl.ac.uk/staff/r.freeman/index.htm

Part III

Perceiving Virtual Worlds

7

Vision

Historically, one of the first human senses that was addressed in Virtual Reality applications was vision. The first computer-generated images were produced in the 1950s. Some of the first images generated by an electronic – analog– machine were created by Ben Laposky. This mathematician and artist from Iowa produced images by manipulating electronic beams displayed across the fluorescent face of an oscilloscope's cathode-ray tube. Laposky called his oscillographic artworks "oscillons" and "electronic abstractions."[1] The history of Virtual Reality presented in Chapter 1 shows that the first VR systems like Sutherland's ultimate display or Heilig's Sensorama were based on graphical displays.

As will be discussed in the following chapters, vision is not necessarily the most relevant of human senses, but it is recognized as the primary source of information about the outside world. Vision is commonly used to double check the accuracy of other senses, for example, we direct our sight toward unexpected sources of sound, such as an ambulance siren, to verify their location and evaluate potential danger. The human vision system allows us to recognize shapes in a three-dimensional space with different colors and light intensities.

In Chapter 2 we covered in detail the mathematical and computational foundations for computer graphics generation. Chapter 3 explained how to put such graphics in motion. This chapter describes the technologies that are currently used to display the graphical aspect of a virtual world.

7.1 Graphical Display Technologies

7.1.1 Cathode-Ray Tubes

The cathode-ray tube (CRT) was invented by German physicist Karl Ferdinand Braun in 1879. The "cathode" is a heated filament (electron gun) in a

---

[1] http://www.dam.org/laposky/index.htm

vacuum created inside a glass "tube." The "ray" is a stream of electrons that naturally pour off a heated cathode into the vacuum. The stream of electrons is focused by a focusing anode into a tight beam and then accelerated by an accelerating anode. This beam of electrons flies through the vacuum in the tube and hits the flat screen at the other end of the tube. This screen is coated with phosphor,[2] which glows when struck by the beam.

The tube is wrapped in coils of wire used to steer the electron beam. These coils are able to create magnetic fields inside the tube, and the electron beam responds to the fields. Two set of coils create magnetic fields that move the electron beam vertically and horizontally. By controlling the voltages in the coils, the electron beam can be positioned at any point on the screen.

In a CRT, phosphor coats the inside of the screen. When the electron beam strikes the phosphor, it makes the screen glow. In a black-and-white screen, there is one phosphor that glows white when struck. In a color screen, there are three phosphors arranged as dots or stripes that emit red, green and blue light. There are also three electron beams to illuminate the three different colors together.

CRTs still find adherents in computer gaming because of higher resolution per initial cost and small response time. They are also still popular in the printing and broadcasting industries as well as in the professional video, photography, and graphics fields due to their greater color fidelity and contrast, better resolution when displaying moving images, and better view from angles, although improvements in LCD technology increasingly alleviate these concerns.

7.1.2 Liquid Crystal Displays

Liquid crystals were first discovered in 1888, by Austrian botanist Friedrich Reinitzer. Reinitzer observed that when he melted a cholesterol-like substance (cholesteryl benzoate), it first became a cloudy liquid and then cleared up as its temperature rose. Upon cooling, the liquid turned blue before finally crystallizing. In 1968, RCA made the first experimental LCD.

Liquid crystals are affected by electric current. A particular sort of nematic liquid crystal, called twisted nematics (TN), is naturally twisted. Applying an electric current to these liquid crystals will untwist them to varying degrees, depending on the current's voltage. LCDs use these liquid crystals because they react predictably to electric current in such a way as to control light passage.

If an electric charge is applied to liquid crystal molecules, they untwist. When they straighten out, they change the angle of the light passing through

---

[2] A phosphor is any material that, when exposed to radiation, emits visible light. The radiation might be ultraviolet light or a beam of electrons. Fluorescent colors absorb invisible ultraviolet light and emit visible light at a characteristic color.

them so that it no longer matches the angle of a top polarizing filter. Consequently, no light can pass through that area of the LCD, making it darker than the surrounding areas.

Small and inexpensive LCDs reflect light from external light sources, for example in LCD watches, numbers appear where small electrodes charge the liquid crystals and make the layers untwist so that light does not pass through the polarized film.

Most computer displays are lit with built-in fluorescent tubes above, beside and sometimes behind the LCD. A white diffusion panel behind the LCD redirects and scatters the light evenly to ensure a uniform display. There are two main types of LCDs, passive- and active-matrix displays. Passive-matrix LCDs use a simple grid to supply the charge to a particular pixel on the display. The grid is created with two glass layers called substrates. One substrate is given columns and the other is given rows made from a transparent conductive material, usually indium-tin oxide. The rows or columns are connected to integrated circuits that control when a charge is sent to a particular column or row. The liquid crystal material is inserted between the two glass substrates, and a polarizing film is added to the outer side of each substrate. To turn on a pixel, the integrated circuit sends a charge down the correct column of one substrate and a ground activated on the correct row of the other. The row and column intersect at the designated pixel, and that delivers the voltage to untwist the liquid crystals at that pixel.

Passive-matrix systems have significant drawbacks, notably slow response time and imprecise voltage control. Response time refers to the LCD's ability to refresh the image displayed. Imprecise voltage control makes it difficult to influence only one pixel at a time. When voltage is applied to untwist one pixel, the pixels around it also partially untwist, which makes images appear fuzzy and lacking in contrast.

Active-matrix LCDs depend on thin film transistors (TFT). TFTs are tiny switching transistors and capacitors. They are arranged in a matrix on a glass substrate. To address a particular pixel, the proper row is switched on, and then a charge is sent down the correct column. Since all of the other rows that the column intersects are turned off, only the capacitor at the designated pixel receives a charge. The capacitor is able to hold the charge until the next refresh cycle. The amount of voltage supplied to a crystal determines the amount of light that goes through.

In order to show colors, an LCD requires three subpixels with red, green and blue color filters to create each color pixel. Through the careful control and variation of the voltage applied, the intensity of each subpixel can range over 256 shades. Combining the subpixels produces a possible palette of 16.8 million colors (256^3).

Color displays require a large number of transistors, one per subpixel; a typical LCD with a resolution of 1024×768 pixels uses $2,359,296$ transistors. A problem with one transistor creates a "bad pixel" on the display. It is very likely to have a few bad pixels scattered across the screen, particularly in very large LCDs.

LCDs are found in many devices, including watches, handheld devices, and large computer monitors. Desktop-based applications can use this kind of display due to the limited space required by the screen, the brightness, and the flicker-free[3] image they provide.

Important factors to consider when evaluating an LCD monitor include the following:

- *Resolution*: VR applications usually require high resolutions to produce realistic images. Unlike CRT monitors, LCDs have a native-supported resolution for best display effect.
- *Dot pitch*: The distance between the centers of two adjacent pixels. The smaller the dot pitch size, the less granularity is present, producing a sharper image.
- *Active display area*: The size of an LCD panel measured on the diagonal.
- *Response time*: The minimum time necessary to change a pixel's color or brightness. The faster the response time, the smoother will be the animation.
- *Matrix type* (active or passive): Nowadays, most of the LCDs on the market are active.
- *Viewing angle*: more specifically known as viewing direction. The direction from which the display will look the best. For multiple-user applications, a wider viewing angle is desirable.
- *Color support*: How many types of colors are supported, also known as color gamut.
- *Brightness*: Refers to the emitted luminous intensity on screen and is measured in candelas per square meter (cd/m^2 or nits). A higher cd/m^2 or nit value means higher onscreen brightness. Office applications usually require lower brightness to prevent eye strain due to the long periods the user spends in front of the screen. On the contrary, VR applications benefit from high luminous intensity.
- *Contrast ratio*: The ratio of the intensity of the brightest bright to the darkest dark.
- *Aspect ratio*: The ratio of the width to the height, as is 4:3 (used by most CRTs), 16:9 (common format for films), or 16:10.
- *Input ports*: Most LCD panels still use the traditional analog VGA connector known as the DSUB-15 or HD15 connector. This is the same connector that is used on all CRT monitors and on most PC graphics cards. Modern LCDs and graphics cards use the DVI connector. This is a digital interface that is supposed to allow for a cleaner and brighter picture compared to

---

[3] The constant refreshing of a CRT produces an effect called flickering, which can cause headaches in migraine sufferers and seizures in epileptics, if they are photosensitive. Screen filters are available to reduce these effects. A high refresh rate (above 75 Hz) also helps to prevent these effects.

standard VGA connectors. Some monitors may also come with composite video connectors to allow them to function as a TV screen.

7.1.3 Plasma Displays

The plasma display was invented at the University of Illinois at Urbana-Champaign by Donald L. Bitzer, H. Gene Slottow, and graduate student Robert Willson in 1964 for the PLATO computer system. The original monochrome (orange, green, or yellow) panels enjoyed a surge of popularity in the early 1970s because the displays were rugged and needed neither memory nor circuitry to refresh the images. A long period of sales decline followed in the late 1980s as semiconductor memory made CRT displays cheaper than plasma displays. Plasma's relatively large screen size and thin profile made the displays attractive for high-profile placement, such as in lobbies and stock exchanges.

In 1997, Pioneer started selling the first plasma televisions to the public. Plasma televisions compete with projector screens. Screen sizes have increased since the 21-inch (533 mm) display in 1992. The largest plasma video display in the world was shown at the 2006 Consumer Electronics Show in Las Vegas, a 103-inch (2.616-m) unit manufactured by Matsushita Electrical Industries (Panasonic).

A plasma display panel (PDP) is a type of flat panel display now commonly used for large TV displays (typically above 37 inches or 940 mm). Many tiny cells located between two panels of glass hold an inert mixture of noble gases (neon and xenon). The gas in the cells is electrically turned into a plasma which then excites phosphors to emit light. Each pixel is made up of three fluorescent lights (red, green, and blue).

The central element in fluorescent light is plasma, a gas made up of free-flowing ions (electrically charged atoms) and electrons. Under normal conditions, a gas is mainly made up of uncharged particles. If many free electrons are introduced into the gas by establishing an electrical voltage across it, the free electrons collide with the atoms, knocking loose other electrons. With a missing electron, an atom loses its balance. It has a net positive charge, making it an ion.

To ionize gas in a particular cell, the plasma display's computer charges electrodes that intersect at that cell. This process is done thousands of times in a fraction of a second, charging each cell in turn.

When the intersecting electrodes are charged, an electric current flows through the gas in the cell. The current creates a rapid flow of charged particles, which stimulates the gas atoms to release ultraviolet photons.

The released ultraviolet photons interact with the phosphor material coated on the inside wall of the cell. When an ultraviolet photon hits a phosphor atom in the cell, one of the phosphor's electrons jumps to a higher energy level and the atom heats up. When the electron falls back to its normal level, it releases energy in the form of a visible light photon.

The phosphors in a plasma display give off colored light when they are excited. Every pixel is made up of three separate subpixel cells, each with different colored phosphors. By varying the pulses of current flowing through the different cells, the control system can increase or decrease the intensity of each subpixel color to create hundreds of different combinations of red, green, and blue, producing colors across the entire spectrum.

Plasma display technology makes it possible to produce very wide screens using extremely thin materials. And because each pixel is lit individually, the image is very bright and looks good from almost every angle. The image quality isn't quite up to the standards of the best cathode-ray tube sets, but it certainly meets most people's expectations.

Until quite recently, the superior brightness, faster response time, greater color spectrum, and wider viewing angle of color plasma video displays, when compared with LCD televisions, made them one of the most popular forms of display for HDTV flat panel displays. However, improvements in LCD technology have narrowed the technological gap. The lower weight, falling prices, higher available resolution, and often lower electrical power consumption of LCDs make them competitive against plasma displays in the television set market.

7.2 Virtual Reality Displays

Virtual Reality displays use the technologies described in the previous Section to provide the user with a system to visually explore a virtual world. Based on the number of users that can participate in the VR experience, displays can be roughly classified in two main categories: individual and collective displays. A second classification criterion is the degree of visual immersion. Following this criterion, VR displays range from fully immersive systems that completely isolate the user's field of view from the real world (HMDs) up to handheld displays that provide a small visualization area and are used as auxiliary tools in real world tasks.

7.2.1 Head-Mounted Displays

Most head-mounted displays (HMD) have either one or two (for stereoscopic vision) small displays with lenses and semitransparent mirrors embedded in a helmet, eyeglasses, or visor. The display units are miniaturized and may use CRT, LCDs, liquid crystal on silicon (LCos), or OLED technology.

Many head-mounted displays include speakers or headphones so that it can provide both video and audio output. HMDs almost always include a tracking device so that the point of view displayed in the monitor changes as the user moves her head.

HMDs have the potential to display a different image to each eye. This can be used to show stereoscopic images. An object located at a distance of

9 meters or more is seen from essentially the same perspective by each of the average human eyes, which have an interpupillary distance of between 2.5 and 3 inches. At shorter distances, the perspective from each eye is significantly different and the expense of generating two different images becomes worthwhile.

Humans have a field of view (FOV) of approximately 180°; see Figure 7.1. However, most HMDs offer a more limited FOV, ranging from 25° to 45°.

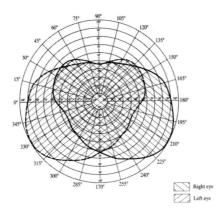

Fig. 7.1: Human field of view

To achieve their full potential, HMDs are used in combination with tracking sensors that detect changes of angle and orientation and even position. When such data are available in the computer controlling the VR application, it can be used to render the images corresponding to the angle of look at a particular time. This allows the user to "look around" a virtual environment simply by moving the head without needing a separate controller to change the viewpoint. Tracking devices can be wired or wireless (radio transmission) and use either magnetic fields or accelerometers to acquire orientation (3 DOF) and even position (6 DOF) in space.

HMD manufacturers include: Fifth Dimension Technologies (5DT), Cybermind, Kaiser Electro-Optics (KEO), Virtual Research Systems, nVision, I-O Display Systems and eMagin. Figure 7.2 shows different types of HMD.

Some HMDs allow to view a computer-generated image superimposed on a real-world view (Figure 7.2 shows monocular and binocular see-through HMDs). This is done by projecting the synthetic image on a semitransparent mirror. This kind of application is referred to as augmented reality.

These devices, also known as see-through HMDs have applications in the maintenance of complex systems as they can provide the technician with

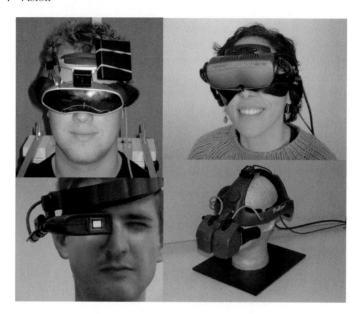

Fig. 7.2: Different types of head-mounted displays

"X-ray vision" by combining computer graphics (e.g., system diagrams) with natural vision.

See-through HMDs also have applications in surgery, as they allow the combination of radiographic data (CAT scans and MRI imaging) with the surgeon's natural view of the operation. Police, soldiers, and firefighters can use see-through HMDs to display tactical information such as maps or thermal imaging data while viewing the real scene.

Conventional HMDs are supposed to provide the most immersive experience to the user by completely isolating her from the real world. This approach has some drawbacks, mainly due to the limitations of current technology. We have already mentioned the reduced field of view, which produces discomfort in many users. The limited resolution (VGA: 640 × 480 or SVGA: 800 × 600) of most HMDs is an additional disadvantage when compared to other VR display technologies, such as fish tank VR (desktop-based VR), large projection screens, or CAVE systems.

HMD systems can be classified as "inside-out" displays that let the user look outward from inside the virtual world. Other technologies, like fish tank, are "outside-in" displays that can be used to look inward from outside the virtual environment.

HMDs can be an appropriate choice for VR applications requiring frequent turns and spatial orientation, such as navigation tasks, for example, when virtual cities or buildings. Virtual environments (VE) presented through HMDs are often explored on foot. The area of the VE that can be explored is limited to the dimensions of the tracking space of the HMD. Some strategies have been proposed to overcome this limitation. In [206] Williams et al. describe a strategy that takes advantage of people's natural ability to spatially update. The authors propose the method of "resetting," which involves manipulating the user's location in physical space to move out of the path of the physical obstruction while maintaining her spatial awareness of the virtual space.

7.2.2 Fish Tank VR

Ware et al. [207] defined "fish tank Virtual Reality" as a system using a high-resolution monitor supplemented with hardware for stereoscopic viewing such as shutter glasses and a head-tracking device for adjusting the perspective transformation to a user's eye position can simulate the appearance of stable 3D objects positioned behind or just in front of the screen.

Stereoscopic view is commonly achieved using LCD shutter glasses. These devices use polarizing filters and take advantage of the property of liquid crystals, which become dark when a voltage is applied but are otherwise transparent. A pair of eyeglasses can be made using this material and connected to a computer video card. The video card alternately darkens over one eye and then the other, in synchronization with the refresh rate of the monitor, while the monitor alternately displays different perspectives for each eye. This is called alternate-frame sequencing. At sufficiently high refresh rates, the viewer's visual system does not notice the flickering; each eye receives a different image, and the stereoscopic effect is achieved.

Fish tank VR systems afford a number of practical advantages over HMDs that make them an attractive alternative. The term "fish tank Virtual Reality" is used to describe such systems because the experience is similar to looking at a fish tank inside which there is a virtual world [208].

As reported by Qi et al. [209], studies reveal that VR display technologies like fish tank allow users to have better performance in terms of response time and accuracy in tasks involving judging the shape, density, conectivity, and other characteristics of objects in a virtual world. This is true in particular for scientific visualization applications that allow users to carefully examine complex structures.

7.2.3 Handheld Displays

One of the first examples of using a mobile device as an interface to a virtual environment is the work of Fitzmaurice et al. [210]. Actually, the authors implemented their own palmtop device.[4] A 4-inch color monitor with an attached 6-DOF input device was used to navigate and interact through the

---

[4] The term palmtop can be considered equivalent to "handheld": a device that can be held in the palm of the hand

virtual world. The small screen was the only "window" into the VE. The experiment showed the feasibility of using a handheld display in a VE and its advantages: user mobility and an intuitive way to interact with the computer.

The work of Watsen, Darken, and Capps [211] was one of the first implementations of a true handheld-based interface to a virtual environment. The authors implemented a 2D interface on a 3Com PalmPilot® to be used while standing inside a CAVE system. Basic scene and object manipulation were done through slider controls on the handheld. While this prototype confirmed the benefits of a mobile interface to VE, the CAVE opposed some problems to the use of a handheld. Being a full-immersion system, the CAVE made it difficult for the user to switch between the surrounding 3D world and the handheld.

More recent research has continuously focused on the implementation of 2D GUIs for basic interaction: camera control and scene management (object picking, navigation through a simplified representation of the 3D environment) [212], [213]. Emphasis has been made on the portability and mobility of the GUI itself. Some other problems starting to be targeted are peer-to-peer communications between handhelds, together with client-server (handheld–main graphic workstation) interactions to control the VE and interact with other users at the same time [214].

In [195] Gutiérrez et al. describe a PDA-based interface for real-time control of virtual characters in multiuser semi-immersive virtual environments using a large rear-projection screen. The "mobile animator" eliminates the display of floating menus and other widgets over the simulation screen and shows the potential of handheld devices as powerful interfaces to VR applications (see Figure 7.3b).

Other authors still consider the PDA a virtual viewer. In the Touch-Space system [215] the PDA is optically tracked and used to display virtual objects superposed on the real world (augmented reality).

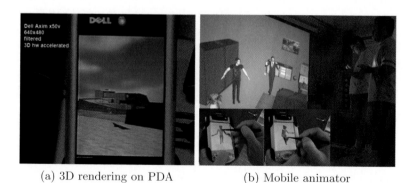

(a) 3D rendering on PDA   (b) Mobile animator

Fig. 7.3: Use of handheld devices in VR applications

Handheld devices represent a real alternative to head-attached devices for mobile applications. Especially consumer devices, such as PDAs and mobile phones, have the potential to bring augmented reality to a mass market. As is the case for PCs, the graphics capabilities of hand-held devices are clearly driven by the game industry. Vendors, such as ATI and nVidia, already offer the first 3D graphics acceleration chips for mobile phones and PDAs (e.g., Dell's Axim, see Figure 7.3a) [216].

7.2.4 Large Projection Screens

This semi-immersive approach consists in positioning one or more users in front of a large rear-projection screen displaying the virtual world. Stereo glasses and 3D surround sound enhance the experience.

This approach has gained popularity due to the possibilities it provides for direct interaction and communication between users. It has been observed that a semi-immersive VE improves the overall user experience [217]. Moreover, this kind of system can be used as a collaborative tool by design and development teams, making the implementation of a VE application more interactive and effective.

Besides flat rear-projection screens, other systems have been designed to produce a more immersive experience, similar to a CAVE system. A representative example is the Allosphere, developed by the University of California, Santa Barbara [218]. This is a large-scale instrument for immersive visualization and simulation. It is one of the world's largest immersive environments. The three-story-high cubical space comprises an anechoic chamber with a spherical display screen, 10 meters in diameter, surrounding from one to thirty users standing on a bridge structure.

The Allosphere is equipped with high-resolution active stereo projectors, a complete 3D sound system with hundreds of speakers, and interaction technology. This system is positioned between CAVE environments, which give fully immersive experiences to a small number of users, and full-dome planetarium style theaters, which have a limited sense of immersion.

7.2.5 CAVE Systems

As mentioned in Chapter 1, the CAVE system was designed by Cruz-Neira et al. in 1992 [2],[219]. The name "CAVE" is both a recursive acronym (CAVE automatic virtual environment) and a reference to "the simile of the cave" found in Plato's *Republic*, in which the philosopher discusses inferring reality (ideal forms) from projections (shadows) on the cave wall [219].

The main idea behind the CAVE project was to create a VR system without the common limitations of previous VR solutions like poor image resolution, inability to share the experience directly with other users, and isolation from the real world. A head-tracking system is used to produce the correct stereo perspective. This allows the user to see her entire environment from the correct viewpoint, thus creating a compelling illusion of reality. Real and virtual objects are blended in the same space and the user can see her body interacting with the environment.

Interest and development of CAVEs and spatially immersive displays (SIDs) have become increasingly significant. Commercial products by Barco (www.barco.com) and VRCO (www.vrco.com) have been created. Despite the amount of development in this direction, both professional and customized solutions are still extremely expensive. Most of the available systems are close to the prototype stage and require very specific care and maintenance.

A variety of software libraries have been developed to produce the individual images required. Some work has been done to adapt popular video games to work in CAVE environments [220].

There are also reduced versions of CAVE systems, with fewer walls or that are even transportable. In [221], Peternier et al. present a tutorial for building a low-cost CAVE with four screens (see Figure 7.4).

Fig. 7.4: A CAVE system with four screens

8

Audition

8.1 The Need for Sound in VR

Sounds are part of our real-life experience and offer rich information about our environment. Sound perceived as coming from different spatial locations as we hear it in everyday life is also known as spatial sound. Spatial sound is a key aspect in producing realistic virtual environments. It has been shown that the combination of sound and graphics enhances the sense of presence [222].

Sound can play different roles in a Virtual Reality system.

Complementary information: sound allows to provide additional and richer information about the simulated environment. Slight echoes and reverberations in the surrounding environment give the brain cues about the direction and distance of objects as well as information about the size of the environment. For example, an office has fewer echoes than a cathedral. The use of sound contributes to enhance the user awareness of the simulated space, for example, sounds coming from parts of the environment beyond the field of view let the user know that "there is more than meets the eye." Sound can convey simulated properties of the entities within the virtual environment, for example, surface features (different sounds produced when touching soft or rough objects), weight, and impact force.

Alternative feedback: sound feedback can enhance user interfaces (e.g. sounds can indicate the reception of user commands or confirm selection of objects). Sound can help people with visual impairments.

Alternative interaction modality: in the form of voice, sound can be an efficient communication channel. Although it is still not completely reliable, speech recognition has been recognized as a convenient input for human-computer interaction in VR (see the VIEW system in Section 1.3). Speech synthesis can be used as an alternative way to provide information to the user within a virtual environment.

8.2 Recording and Reproduction of Spatial Sound

There are three main methods for sound recording: monaural, stereo, and binaural.

A monaural sound recording uses a single microphone. No sense of sound positioning is present in monaural sound.

Stereo sound is recorded with two microphones separated by a certain distance. This gives a sense of the sound position as recorded by the microphones. Sound sources in stereo recordings are often perceived as being positioned inside the listener's head. This is due to the fact that humans do not normally hear sounds in the manner they are recorded in stereo, separated by empty space. When we hear a sound, our head acts as a filter.

Binaural recordings sound more realistic because they are recorded in a way that resembles the human acoustic system. The microphones are embedded in a dummy head. Binaural recordings sound closer to what humans hear in the real world, as the dummy head filters sound in a manner similar to the human head.

8.3 Synthesis of Spatial Sound

Spatial sound synthesis consists in processing sound signals to produce realistic audio, taking into account individual sound signals and parameters describing the sound scene: position and orientation of each source and acoustic characterization of the room or space. Several techniques can be applied, as discussed in the next subsections.

8.3.1 Sound Rendering

Sound rendering is mostly used to generate synchronized soundtracks for animation. This method creates spatial sound by attaching a characteristic sound to each object in the scene. Sound sources can come from sampling or artificial synthesis.

The technique is a pipelined process of four stages:

- generation of each object's characteristic sound (recorded, synthesized, modal analysis collisions)
- sound instantiation and attachment to moving objects within the scene
- calculation of the necessary convolutions to describe the sound source interaction within the acoustic environment
- convolutions are applied to the attached instantiated sound sources

The technique exploits the similarity of light and sound to provide the necessary convolutions. A sound source in space propagates sound waves in all directions. Sound waves can be reflected and refracted due to the acoustic environment. A sound wave interacts with many objects in the environment as it makes its way to the listener. The final sound that the listener hears is the integral of the signals from the multiple simultaneous paths existing between the sound source and the listener.

Sound rendering is very similar to ray-tracing and has a unique approach to handling reverberation. But just as with ray-tracing it is difficult to use in real-time applications.

8.3.2 Head-Related Transfer Function

Between a sound source and your eardrum (the thin membrane that transmits sound from the air to the ossicles inside the middle ear) there are a number of obstructions that cause reflections and absorption of the sound signal. Obstructions include shadowing and boundary effects of the head, reflections off the pinna (visible part of the ear) and shoulders, and resonance in the ear canal. The signal that reaches your eardrum includes all of the effects caused by these components and more.

The combination of these effects depends on the position of the sound source in space and the orientation of the head. The sound arriving at your two ears will be different unless the sound source is on the median plane (plane dividing your body into right and left sides).

If we consider the effect of the body on the sound signal arriving from a given direction and with a given head rotation as a filter, then we can measure the transfer function of that filter. This measurement is called a head-related transfer function or HRTF and consists in recording sounds with tiny probe microphones in the ears of a person. These recordings are then compared with the original sounds to compute the person's HRTF.

The HRTF is a function of four variables: three space coordinates of the sound source and frequency. For sound sources situated at more than one meter, the source is said to be in the far field, and the HRTF falls off inversely with range. Most HRTF measurements are made in the far field, reducing the HRTF to a function of azimuth, elevation and frequency.

Once the HRTF for the left ear and the right ear are calculated, accurate binaural signals can be synthesized from a monaural source. The computations required by the HRTF are so demanding that they currently cannot be performed in real time without special hardware. The Convolvotron[1] is a DSP engine for this purpose. Dimensionality reduction techniques could be applied to accelerate the computation of the HRTF in software, but this is still work in progress [224].

---

[1] Crystal River Engineering and the NASA Ames Research Center designed a special digital signal processing (DSP) engine called the Convolvotron, which computes 128 convolution points in parallel [223].

8.3.3 3D Sound Imaging

The 3D sound imaging technique consists in approximating binaural spatial audio through the interaction of a 3D environment simulation. The following steps are required:

1. Compute line-of-sight information between the virtual user and the sound sources.
2. The sounds emitted by these sources are processed based on their location, using some software DSP algorithms or simple audio effects modules with delay, filter, pan, and reverb capabilities.
3. A headphone set is used to play the final stereo sound sample, according to the user's position.

3D sound imaging is suitable for simple VR systems where a sense of space is more important than high accuracy in the localization of sound sources.

8.3.4 Utilization of Loudspeaker Location

Utilization of loudspeaker location does not attempt to simulate many of the human localization cues[2], instead it focuses on attaching sampled sounds to objects in 3D space. Visual Synthesis Incorporated's Audio Image Sound Cube uses this approach with eight speakers to simulate spatial sound. Two speakers are located in each corner of the cube, one up high and one down low. Pitch and volume of the sampled sounds are used to simulate sound location; volume is distributed through the speakers appropriately to give the perception of a sound source's spatial location.

This technique is less accurate than convolving sound, but it is fast and efficient, making it a good choice for less-expensive real-time spatial sound systems.

8.4 Sound Systems for VR

Virtual Reality applications need an audio rendering pipeline that has to meet several requirements, as explained in [225]:

3D localization: accurate 3D positioning of the virtual sound source. The perceived position of the sound source should match the spatial location of the associated object in the virtual environment.

Acoustics simulation: acoustic room simulation is essential to perceive spatial properties of the virtual environment such as size of the room and reflection properties of the walls.

---

[2] Interaural time difference, head shadow, pinna response, shoulder echo, head movement, reverberation, vision. See [223].

Speed and efficiency: there is a trade-off between accurately simulating the physical properties of spatial sound and the efficient generation of sound in real time. Moreover, realistic virtual environments require a certain number of simultaneous virtual sound sources.

The most important acoustic phenomena can be simulated in software using sound engines. Simplified models of physical properties of spatial sound can produce convincing results.

One of the challenges is to map sound sources at arbitrary virtual positions to a limited number of speakers, whose real position is often constrained by the physical setup of the VR installation.

8.4.1 Sound Hardware

Electroacoustic Playback

Spatial sound can be generated using electroacoustic devices: headphones or loudspeakers. Headphones allow more precise control of the spatial cues because the signals reaching the two ears can be controlled independently. An additional advantage is that there is no indirect sound, such as echoes or reverberation.

Headphones can be more expensive than loudspeakers and may be impractical for applications in which the user does not want to wear a device on the head, as in collaborative virtual environments using a CAVE.

It is more difficult to control the spatial information reaching the listener in a loudspeaker-based system. However, these systems are relatively simple and inexpensive to implement and do not interfere with the user.

Multiple Loudspeaker Systems

The total acoustic signal that reaches each ear is the sum of the signals that can be perceived by that ear coming from each sound source in an environment. Based on this property, spatial auditory cues such as ITD[3] and IID[4] can be modulated by controlling the audio played from multiple speakers situated

---

[3] Depending on the angle between the interaural axis and a sound source, one ear may receive the sound earlier than the other. The resulting interaural time differences (ITDs) are the main cue indicating the laterality (left/right location) of the direct sound [226].

[4] At the high end of the audible frequency range, the head of the listener reflects and diffracts signals so that less acoustic energy reaches the far side of the head (causing an "acoustic head shadow"). Due to the acoustic head shadow, the relative intensity of the sound at the two ears varies with the lateral location of the source. The resulting interaural intensity differences (IIDs) generally increase with source frequency and the angle between the source and the median plane. IIDs are perceptually important for determining source laterality for frequencies above about 2 kHz [226].

around the listener. The signals at the two ears cannot be independently manipulated as is the case with headphones. As a consequence, it is more difficult to control the binaural signal reaching the user, to reproduce the sound that would be perceived in a real scene. However there are methods to specify the signals played from each loudspeaker to simulate spatial auditory cues.

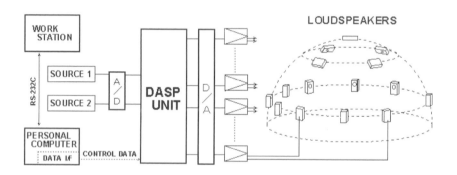

Fig. 8.1: Pioneer sound field control system

The accuracy of spatial sound generation using loudspeakers depends on the number of speakers used. If we put an infinite number of speakers around the listener, spatial sound generation would be reduced to simply playing the desired signal from the loudspeaker at the desired location of the source to achieve a "perfect" reproduction.

Panning between multiple pairs of loudspeakers arrayed in front of and behind the listener is often used to improve spatial sound simulations. These "surround-sound" technologies are popular in the entertainment industry and are implemented via a variety of formats. One of the first surround-sound systems was the one created for the movie "Fantasia," in 1939. "Fantasound" was a three-channel system whose loudspeakers were located in front of the listener at left, middle, and right. Approximately 54 speakers surrounded the audience and carried a mixture of sound from the left and right front speakers. It was not true stereo. Few theaters were ever equipped to play "Fantasound," because it was very expensive.

A representative example of surround-sound systems is the Pioneer Sound Field Control System (PSFC); see Figure 8.1. The PSFC is a DSP-driven hemispherical 14-loudspeaker array. It was installed at the University of Aizu Multimedia Center. The system is able to control an entire sound field, including sound direction, virtual distance, and simulated environment for each source. The PSFC speaker dome is about 14 m in diameter, allowing about 20 users at once to comfortably stand.

Nowadays, one of the most common surround-sound formats is the 5.1 speaker system where speakers are located at the left, middle, and right in front, and left and right behind the listener. The 0.1 speaker is a subwoofer, used to reproduce bass audio frequencies, which are difficult to play with conventional loudspeakers. The middle speaker, located in front of the listener, reproduces most of the speech information. Typical 5.1 Surround formats are Dolby Digital Surround and Digital Theater Systems (DTS).

Newer surround-sound formats include the Dolby Digital Surround EX, a 6.1-speaker system that adds a center speaker behind the listener. Another format is the Sony Dynamic Digital Sound (SDDS) system, which is a 7.1-speaker system adding a left-center and right-center speaker in front of the listener. Surround-sound technologies provide a rudimentary sense of location.

Sound Cards

Most PC systems have sound cards capable of at least stereo playback. In the consumer hardware category we find multichannel sound cards for 5.1, 6.1, and 7.1 surround sound. Some of the main vendors are: Creative,[5] which overtook the OpenAL project in 2003 and is the developer of EAX;[6] Terratec,[7] and Guillemot/Hercules.[8]

Consumer hardware sound cards have limited performance but good native 3D sound engines. Their development is driven by the gaming industry and thus they are continuously updated. Some cards have limited audio quality.

Professional hardware includes special sound cards for custom multichannel sounds, they are mostly DSP boards. Their signal processing capabilities allows for creating custom 3D sound engines. Professional sound

---

[5] http://www.creative.com, http://www.soundblaster.com/

[6] The Environmental Audio eXtensions are a number of digital signal processing presets for audio accessible from the DirectSound API. The latest-version, EAX HD 5.0, supports 128 simultaneous sound sources with up to four effects applied to each source.

[7] http://sounduk.terratec.net/

[8] http://www.hercules.com

cards have very good performance and are mainly used in 3D sound research. Representative vendors include: RME[9] and M-Audio.[10]

8.4.2 Sound Engines

Also known as sound libraries or APIs, sound engines are software components that allow us to interface with the sound card and/or implement 3D sound generation in software. 3D sound engines are the audio counterparts of graphics APIs like OpenGL and Direct3D (the graphics component of Microsoft's DirectX API). Some of the most powerful 3D sound engines are OpenAL, fmod, Miles, and DirectSound.

OpenAL, the Open Audio Library[11] is a free software cross-platform audio API. It is designed for efficient rendering of multichannel 3D positional audio. The library models a collection of audio sources moving in a 3D space that are heard by a single listener somewhere in that space. Its style and conventions are very similar to those of OpenGL.

The fmod music and sound effects system[12] is a library that supports multiple platforms, including game consoles. It is a commercial sound engine that can work with multiple sound file formats, such as MP3.

The Miles Sound System[13] is very popular in the game industry. It is a commercial product that supports multiple platforms and multiple sound file formats.

DirectSound is the audio component of Microsoft's DirectX API. It only supports Windows and the Xbox game console. Most of the video games for the Windows platform use this sound engine.

---

[9] http://www.rme-audio.de

[10] http://www.m-audio.com/

[11] http://www.openal.org/

[12] http://www.fmod.org/

[13] http://www.radgametools.com/miles.htm

9

Touch

9.1 The Need for Touch in VR

In general, VR applications focus on providing visual and auditory feedback and much less on touch or force-feedback. It is easier to develop visual virtual worlds with basic sound effects; it requires less specialized equipment. However, the human haptic system, which involves the tactile and kinesthetic senses, is a very important perception channel. It has been shown that the ability to "touch" virtual objects increases the sense of presence [227].

The term *haptic* comes from the Greek word *haptesthai*, which refers to the sense of touch as the way in which the human body perceives objects and space.

Touch is one of the most important human senses; it can be divided into cutaneous, kinesthetic, and haptic systems. The cutaneous system is composed of mechanoreceptors embedded in the skin. It constitutes the tactile sense, which process any stimulation on the body surface, the skin. The kinesthetic system is composed of receptors located in the muscles, tendons, and joints. It constitutes the kinesthetic sense, which allows us to be aware of our limb positions and movements and muscle tensions. It is also called *proprioception*, from the Latin *proprius*, meaning "one's own."

An example of proprioception is when you touch your nose with closed eyes. To perform such a movement, you rely on the kinesthetic sense to know where your fingertip is relative to your nose. In this and most of the cases, the tactile sense is also involved; the fingertip touches the nose. However, the information that is determinant to the correct execution of the action comes primarily from the kinesthetic sense. Thus, the distinction between tactile and kinesthetic senses is functional and task-dependent [228].

The haptic sensory system can be considered the combination of both cutaneous and kinesthetic systems.

In [229], Robles-De-La-Torre talks about some real-life cases that show how vision cannot fully compensate for the major loss of somesthesis –sense of touch– due to injury or disease. The author discusses the importance of the sense of touch and why haptic feedback enhances virtual environments.

Haptic feedback has different modalities: force, tactile, and proprioceptive feedback. force-feedback integrated in a VR simulation helps the user estimate the hardness, weight, and inertia of virtual objects. Tactile feedback provides a feel of the object's surface contact geometry, smoothness, temperature, etc. Proprioceptive feedback, helps to estimate the relative position of body limbs –body posture within the virtual environment.

9.2 Data Gloves

The hand is one of the main input channels concerning touch. As we have explained, the whole body is able to receive and process haptic feedback, but our hands are the main interface to touch and manipulate our external environment.

One of the first interaction devices created to take advantage of hand gestures was the data glove. See Chapter 1 for additional information on the role that glove-based interfaces play in Virtual Reality applications.

Various sensor technologies are used to capture physical data such as bending of fingers. Often a motion tracker (magnetic or inertial) is attached to capture the global position/rotation data of the glove. These movements are then interpreted by the software that accompanies the glove. Gestures can be categorized into useful information, such as recognizing sign language or other symbolic functions. Some devices, like Immersion's CyberTouch^{TM}(Figure 9.1a) and CyberGrasp^{TM}(Figure 9.1b), can also provide vibrotactile and force-feedback, respectively (see Sections 9.4.1 and 9.4.3. This allows a data glove to also be used as an output device.

9.3 Haptic Rendering

As defined by Salisbury et al. [230], haptic rendering is the process of computing and generating forces in response to user interactions with virtual objects.

We can distinguish two main types of haptic rendering algorithms:

3-DOF haptic rendering: these algorithms consider the paradigm of touching virtual objects with a single contact point, which has only three degrees of freedom (3 DOF); only the position in 3D space can be modified.

6-DOF haptic rendering: these algorithms are designed to render the forces and torques arising from the interaction of two virtual objects. In this case the grasped object has six degrees of freedom: position and orientation in 3D space. The haptic feedback consist of 3D force and torque.

Many everyday-life tasks such as eating with a fork or writing with a pen imply the manipulation of objects in 3D space. In such tasks we feel the interaction with other objects. These kind of activities can be simulated with 6-DOF object manipulation with force-and-torque feedback.

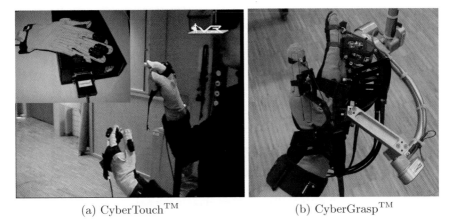

(a) CyberTouch^{TM} (b) CyberGrasp^{TM}

Fig. 9.1: Data gloves for touch and force-feedback

9.3.1 History of Haptic Rendering

Haptic rendering can be traced back to 1965 when Ivan Sutherland proposed a multimodal display that would incorporate haptic feedback into interaction with virtual worlds. By that time, haptic feedback had already been used in flight simulators and master-slave robotic teleoperation. In 1954, at the Argonne National Laboratories, Goertz and Thompson developed the ARM (Argonne Remote Manipulator), an electrical servomechanism that received feedback signals from sensors mounted on a slave robot and applied forces to the master manipulator. The ARM was used in the GROPE project to address the synthesis of force-feedback from simulated interactions (see Section 1.3).

In 1980, Bejczy and Salisbury [231] developed a computer-based Cartesian control for teleoperator systems. Cartesian control was applied to the manipulation of simulated slave robots [232]. The use of tactile feedback in VR was pioneered by several researchers at MIT. Patrick [233] used voice coils (those found in the cone of a loudspeaker) to provide vibrations at the fingertips of a user wearing a Dextrous Hand Master Exoskeleton. The "Sandpaper," developed by Minksy et al. [234], was a tactile joystick that mapped image texels to vibrations, allowing one to feel textures. Burdea et al. [235] at Rutgers University developed a light and portable force-feedback glove called the Rutgers Master. In 1994, Massie and Salisbury [236] designed the PHANTOM® (Personal HAptic iNTerface Mechanism), a stylus-based haptic interface that was later commercialized and has since become one of the most commonly used force-feedback devices (see Figure 9.2. Other commercial force-feedback interfaces are the Impulse Engine, created in 1995 [237] and the CyberGrasp^{TM}glove, which appeared in 1998 and was developed by Virtual Technologies (acquired by Immersion, see Section 1.3). Inexpensive haptic joysticks for video games became available in the late 1990s.

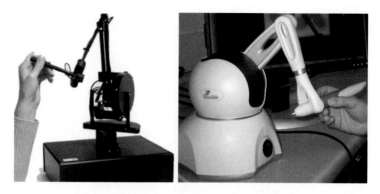

Fig. 9.2: PHANTOM® haptic interfaces

9.4 Haptic Interfaces

Haptic interfaces generate mechanical signals that stimulate human kinesthetic and touch channels. Tactile and kinesthetic channels let us perceive and act in our environment [238]. The objective of haptic interfaces is to facilitate the manipulation of virtual objects by reproducing their physical characteristics. Objects in nature can be roughly classified as inert or active. Inert objects are unanimated; they only dissipate mechanical energy. In the case of active objects, they are animated and they can supply some energy. Thus, there can be two types of haptic interfaces: passive or active.

Passive haptic interfaces can only exert resistance forces against the user's movement. These devices dissipate the mechanical energy (force) exerted by the user during the interaction with virtual objects. This kind of haptic interface is inherently safe because of the passive working of the device. The user will never experience accidental forces or torques exerted by a passive haptic interface because the user is the only energy supplier in the human-machine system. User energy is redirected or dissipated through clutches and brakes. Other passive haptic interfaces utilize variable transmissions to redirect user-supplied energy or to reduce the degrees of freedom of a device so as to follow a specified path.

Active haptic interfaces utilize actuators that are capable of supplying energy. Such actuators can be electric motors, hydraulic systems, piezoelectric, etc. Active systems pose potential stability and safety issues when simulating stiff environments. Hybrid haptic interfaces use both active and passive actuators [239].

Active, passive, and hybrid haptic interfaces can be considered as displays that provide different kinds of stimulation to the human haptic system.

Depending on the type of feedback they provide they can be classified into vibrotactile, tactile, and kinesthetic displays.

9.4.1 Vibrotactile Displays

Vibrotactile displays are composed of a single vibrating component used to encode information in temporal parameters of the vibration signal, such as frequency, amplitude, waveform, or duration. Vibration can be generated by means of solenoids, voice coils, or electric motors like the ones used in mobile phones.

Vibrotactile information has been successfully used in video games, providing touch feedback in handheld controllers. Tactile sensations are used to represent impacts or firing of weapons, or to encode abstract information such as progress bars or tactile "radars."

Current research is focused on encoding more complex information in the vibrotactile signal and on combining this type of feedback with other sensory modalities. For example, in [240] Cardin et al. present a vibrotactile system integrated in the clothes of an aircraft pilot. The device sends vibrotactile feedback to the pilot when the aircraft becomes off-balance. The system also dynamically localizes the position of the actuators in order to ensure accurate feedback independently from the pilot's posture and movements. In [241] the authors developed a vibrotactile system that provides navigation cues (obstacle detection and warning) for visually impaired people. Cassinelli et al. [242] present a vibrotactile interface with similar applications: augmentation of spatial awareness in hazardous working environments, as well as enhanced obstacle awareness for car drivers.

9.4.2 Tactile Displays

Tactile displays can be classified into three types of stimulation: electrotactile, thermal, and mechanical.

Electrotactile displays

Electrotactile (electrocutaneous) displays create touch sensations by passing a small electric current through the skin. Their main advantage is the absence of moving parts, which facilitates their construction, control, and maintenance.

The main problem with this technology is the relatively small difference in the thresholds between signal detection and the onset of pain. In [243], Yamamoto et al. present an application of electrotactile (electrostatic) displays to telepresentation systems.

Thermal Displays

Thermal feedback is a relatively new concept in haptic research. This kind of display can assist in object identification in virtual environments by simulating the thermal cues associated with making contact with materials with different thermal properties. Thermal displays consist of thermal stimulators, thermal sensors, and a temperature-control system that monitors and controls the surface temperature of the thermal display.

A crucial element in developing a thermal display is to characterize the thermal responses that occur on the hand as it makes contact with a material. In most thermal displays the simulation of a virtual material in contact with the skin has been based on empirically derived data of the changes in skin temperature as the hand makes contact with the corresponding real material [244],[245],[239].

The main problems faced by this type of display are the lack of an actuator of suitable bandwidth and the fact that human thermal sensing is relatively little understood.

Mechanical displays

Mechanical displays are used to convey spatial information to the skin. Tactile displays attempt to reproduce the small-scale skin deformations that occur during finger-tip interactions with real objects. The initial interest on this kind of interface was motivated by sensory substitution devices for visually impaired people. Current research also addresses applications in virtual environments, telemedicine, minimally invasive surgery, and virtual training. The most common design approach uses arrays of moving pins or "tactors" that contact the skin to approximate arbitrary shapes [246],[247].

There is a second category of mechanical tactile displays: vibration displays. Vibration displays present shape information by activating patterns of spatially configured transducers at high temporal frequencies (200–250 Hz) of operation. These transducers are much smaller than those used by vibrotactile displays; they can be pins or wires driven by solenoids or piezoelectric actuators. They have been used to convey abstract forms such as letter shapes for sensory substitution applications [248],[249].

A novel mechancial display that provides tactile feedback is the "gravity grabber" developed by Minamizawa et al. [250]. This is a wearable haptic display that applies preassure to the fingerpads to provide the sensation of grasping objects of variable weight. The device is based on the insight that the deformation on fingerpads produces a reliable weight sensation even when the proprioceptive sensation is absent. The wearable haptic display uses dual motors and a belt to produce deformations on the fingerpads of the thumb and index, allowing users to perceive grip force, gravity, and inertia of a virtual object.

9.4.3 Kinesthetic Displays

Kinesthetic feedback can be provided by devices exerting forces to simulate the texture and other high-spatial-frequency details of virtual objects. Various types of force-feedback devices have been designed: single-point interaction, exoskeletons, and haptic surfaces.

Single-Point Force-Feedback

Single-point force-feedback is the most common method for rendering haptic sensations with force-feedback devices. Using this kind of interface, the user is represented in the virtual environment by a single point corresponding to the tip of a probe through which the user interacts with the device. This follows the metaphor of exploring objects remotely through an intermediary link, such as a stick. The PHANTOM® device, a 3-DOF pantograph cited in Section 9.3.1 (Figure 9.2 is one of the best known examples of single point force-feedback devices. Other 3-DOF and 6-DOF pantographs such as the Haptic Master developed by Iwata et al. are described in [251].

Solazzi et al. [252] have developed a haptic interface that combines a fingerpad (tactile) interface and a kinesthetic interface. Kinesthetic feedback is provided by a 3-DOF manipulator. Tactile feedback is obtained by a plate that can contact the fingertip with different orientations, according to the direction of the surface normal of the virtual object being examined. An interesting single-point haptic device is the SPIDAR (SPace Interface Device for Artificial Reality); its development started in 1989 by Sato [253] and has been continuously improved since then. The SPIDAR-G&G [254], one of the latest versions, consists of a pair of string-based 6-DOF haptic devices, named SPIDAR-G. By grasping a special grip on each device, the user can interact with virtual objects using both hands. The grip is used to track hand movement and to grasp or release virtual objects. Each hand has its own workspace and is able to feel different haptic sensations such as contact, weight, or inertia.

Single-point haptic devices can have interesting applications in 2D environments. This is the case of the 2-DOF planar parallel manipulator developed by Solis et al. [255]. This haptic interface is an example of reactive robot technology, cooperative systems that reproduce and simulate human actions. The haptic interface is used to teach people to write Japanese characters. Following the same principle, the interface has been used to assist on design and sketching tasks [256],[257].

Exoskeletons

An exoskeleton is a set of actuators attached to a hand, arm, or body. They have been commonly used in robotics as master-manipulators for teleoperation, for example, the ARM device used in project GROPE (see Section 9.3.1). One of the first examples of a compact exoskeleton suitable for desktop use was developed by Iwata in 1990 [258]. Burdea et al. [235] developed a lightweight portable exoskeleton that uses pneumatic cylinders to apply force to the fingertips. A popular commercial exoskeleton is the CyberGrasp^{TM}, also mentioned in Section 9.3.1. Recent improvements include a new version that allows two-hand interaction, the Haptic Workstation^{TM}, commercialized by Immersion (see Figure 9.3).

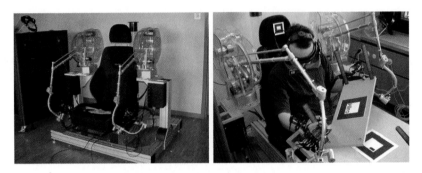

Fig. 9.3: The Haptic Workstation^{TM}

The Haptic Workstation^{TM} combines several peripherals: the CyberGlove^{TM}, CyberGrasp^{TM}, CyberTrack^{TM}, and CyberForce^{TM}. A pair of CyberGlove^{TM}s is used to acquire the hand's posture. On each hand, 22 angles are evaluated, on all phalanges and finger abducts, making it possible to have a good representation of the current hand posture. A pair of CyberGrasp^{TM} exoskeletons of the hand is able to pull each finger separately using wires. This device cannot constrain the user to close his fingers. The CyberGrasp^{TM} can be used to simulate object grasping. The exoskeleton prevents it from closing the fist by applying a force of 10N maximum. Two CyberTracks^{TM}, encapsulated in the CyberForce^{TM} exoskeletons, allow gathering the position and the orientation of the wrist. The precision and the refresh rate (1 kHz) are higher than using a magnetic or optical system. For positioning, the accuracy is around a tenth of a millimeter and around a tenth of a degree for orientation. The CyberForce^{TM} can be used to apply a 3D force of up to 80N on the wrist. This is a 3-DOF device because it cannot be used to constrain hand orientation.

In combination with an HMD, the Haptic Workstation^{TM} has been used in telerehabilitation [195], 3D modeling of organic shapes [259], and teleoperation applications [260].

Other commercial haptic interfaces are the 3-DOF and 6-DOF devices developed by Force Dimension (http://www.forcedimension.com).

One of the most recent advances in exoskeleton developments is the device presented by Frisoli et al. [261]. This is a tendon-driven wearable arm exoskeleton with 5 DOFs. The interface is lightweight and can be used for simulating touch by a hand of large objects. In one of its possible configurations it can be used in combination with a hand exoskeleton that can apply forces on the thumb and index fingers of the right hand. This way it can provide force-feedback on three points: palm, forearm, and the fingers. Bergamasco et al. [262] described the use of a previous version of this exoskeleton in cultural heritage applications using CAVE systems, the "museum of pure form." This type of exoskeleton minimizes the visual interference and maximizes the workspace. Other applications include rehabilitation or simulation of industrial assembly and maintenance operations.

Haptic Surfaces

Haptic surfaces are also known as shape displays. The main idea is to directly create 3D physical shapes out of a modifiable surface. This kind of device moves or deforms to simulate the shapes of virtual objects. One of the first shape displays was FEELEX [263]. This device was composed of a flexible silicon screen, an array of actuators and a projector. The flexible screen was deformed by the actuators in order to simulate the shape of virtual objects. An image of the virtual object was projected onto the surface of the flexible screen and synchronized with the actuators. This configuration allowed the user to touch and feel the projected images with his hands.

Lumen [264] is a 13×13-pixel bitmap display where each pixel can physically move up and down. The display can present 2D images and moving physical shapes that can be touched with the hands. A 2D position sensor lets users input commands and manipulate shapes with their hands.

Haptic surfaces are still rather primitive but in the future could be used to create on-the-fly tangible user interfaces where the components are not physical objects but dynamically created shapes. A review of other shape displays that do not qualify as haptic devices, since they cannot be touched, is presented in [265].

10

Smell and Taste

10.1 The Need for Smells and Tastes in VR

The olfactory nerve is the only sense organ that connects the external world directly to the brain, in particular to the limbic system. The limbic system is composed of structures involved in emotion, motivation, and emotional association with memory. From the evolutionary point of view, the limbic system is one of the oldest structures in the brain and has evolved as part of the olfactory (smell) sense.

It is commonly accepted that smells influence how we act and feel. The sense of smell can stimulate the memorization of concepts or experiences. Odors are well known for their high influence as contextual retrieval cues not only for autobiographic memories, but also for various other types of memory, including visuospatial memories. For example, a recent study has shown that the use of olfactory stimuli for cueing memories during sleep is useful for memory consolidation [266]. Strong correlations have been found between smell and attention, reaction times, mood, and emotional state [267]. The sense of smell was addressed by one of the first Virtual Reality systems, the Sensorama (see Section 1.3). Studies show that olfactory stimuli can enhance the sense of presence by recalling previous experiences and modifying the emotional state of the user.

The sense of taste is the result of a complex interaction between multiple sensory mechanisms: whenever food is placed in the mouth, taste receptors are stimulated. Simultaneously, different types of sensory fiber that monitor several food attributes such as texture, temperature, and odor are activated [268]. Taste perception serves as a primary gatekeeper controlling voluntary ingestion of substances. Humans can distinguish five major taste classes: sweet, sour, bitter, salty, and umami, a savory flavor exemplified by the amino acid glutamate. Each individual has different sensitivity to many different substances. Some of this variation is known to be genetic in origin [269]. Other factors such as age, sex, and exposure to different diets and foods are also known to affect some taste abilities [270]. Recent studies have demonstrated that anxiety or depression are associated with taste disturbances. For instance, altered taste and appetite seen in affective disorders may reflect an actual change in the gustatory system [271].

Whether the sense of taste can be used as an interaction modality in virtual worlds is still an open research question. However, it is clear that this sense plays a very important role in perceiving the real world.

10.2 Smell Interfaces

Smell interfaces are also called olfactory displays. In general, an olfactory display consist of a palette of odorants, a flow-delivery system, and a control algorithm that determines the mixing ratios, concentration, and timing of the stimulus [272].

Olfactory displays have been mainly used to provide alerts and notifications. One of the most frequently cited developments is the work of Kaye [273]. The systems he has developed are used to provide ambient notification information. In the system *inStink*, a spice rack with sensors attached to each spice jar was linked to a set of spray guns at a remote location. Whenever a jar was removed from the rack, the corresponding essential oil was released at the remote location, conveying some kind of sense of presence. It was reported that some scent combinations were rather unpleasant. This is an important issue to consider. Mixing smells is much more complex than mixing colors.

A second system developed by Kaye was *Dollars & Scents*. Two different scents were used to represent the current value of the NASDAQ stock market. The device would emit a mint smell if the market was rising or lemon if it was falling. *Scent Reminder* used the same technology but was integrated in MS Outlook. Scents were released as appointment reminders.

In [274] Washburn and Jones present an overview on olfactory displays for data visualization. Some studies concerning the effects of olfactory cues on the sense of presence are described. In general, the addition of smells to virtual environments increases the perception of realism and presence. Several issues concerning the dissipation, duration, and mixing of scents are reported. Different olfactory displays are described, including some commercial products such as Aromajet (http://www.aromajet.com) and ScentAir (http://www.scentair.com).

In general there are two types of olfactory displays, multiuser and individual. Multiuser olfactory displays are used in special rooms, for example, when using a CAVE system. An example of a multiuser olfactory display is *Scents of Space* (http://www.haque.co.uk/scentsofspace.php). An interactive smell system that allows for 3D placement of fragrances without dispersion. This project demonstrates how smell can be used spatially to create fragrance collages that form soft zones and boundaries that are configurable on the fly. An airflow within the space is generated by an array of fans. Moving air is then controlled by a series of diffusion screens. Computer-controlled fragrance dispensers and careful air control enable parts of the space to be selectively scented without dispersing through the entire space.

Individual olfactory displays include devices such as the one developed by Yanagida et al. [275]. The system uses an air cannon that tracks the user's nose to present smells. This fires a focused vortex of air so that other users do not smell anything. However, the system had some problems, one of the most important was that the temporal duration in which users could detect the smell was too short. The smell would not be perceived if the users exhaled when a scented vortex reached their noses.

The Scent Collar, developed by the Institute for Creative Technologies (http://www.ict.usc.edu) and AnthroTronix (http://www.anthrotronix.com) is another individual olfactory display that fits around a user's neck. It holds four scent cartridges and is controlled by a wireless interface.

A recent application of individual olfactory displays for smell-based interaction is Olfoto [276]. The system is an olfactory photo browsing and searching tool where smells are used to tag photos. The use of olfactory displays in Virtual Reality has not been fully explored. In [273] Kaye overviews some other applications of smell in games and virtual environments. An interesting application of olfactory cues in Virtual Reality is "Friend Park" [277]. The authors paid special attention to providing olfactory cues and proposed the concept of *Aroma Aura*. Two types of smells are used: scent of the environment and scent of the object. The environmental scents provide the smell of a place (aroma aura). This helps users feel like they are in a particular location (sense of presence). The scent of the object gives information about a particular item in the environment.

10.3 Taste interfaces

The sense of taste has never been directly addressed in a Virtual Reality system. This is still an unexplored research area. Very few examples of what we call "taste interfaces" could be found in the scientific literature when we were writing this book.

Food simulator

The "food simulator" developed by Iwata et al. [278] is an interaction device that addresses the sense of taste. This interface could be defined as a "food texture display." The system simulates the action of chewing different kinds of food. The simulator releases flavoring chemicals onto the tongue and plays-back the prerecorded sound of a chewing jawbone corresponding to the food being simulated.

The mechanical part of the simulator that is inserted into the mouth has cloth and rubber covers and is intended to resist the user's bite in a similar way to real food. When someone chews the device, a sensor registers the force of the bite and a motor provides appropriate resistance; see Figure 10.1.

The researchers say their device can be used to design new foods, and may even allow young designers to experience the difficulty older people may face in chewing food.

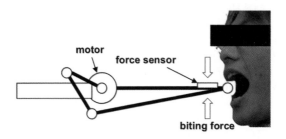

Fig. 10.1: Food simulator

Drink Simulator

The device developed by Hashimoto et al. [279] focuses on providing stimuli to the mouth and lips, simulating the action of drinking. This is a straw-like user interface that simulates the sensations of drinking by reproducing pressure, vibration, and sound.

The system is composed of a disposable straw; a speaker to reproduce pre-recorded sounds of different kinds of food (liquids, solids, gels); and a valve controlled by a solenoid and a servomotor.

Different tests have been conducted to evaluate the effectiveness of the interface for discriminating several kinds of food with an average success between 55% and 72%. The straw-like user interface has been presented in several exhibitions (e.g., ARS Electronica 2005). The researchers affirm that due to the high sensitivity of the mouth and lips, it is possible to develop unique interfaces for interactive arts and entertainment.

Edible User Interfaces

In his master's thesis, B.I. Resner [280] proposed the concept of "edible user interfaces" (EUI), which can be seen as a kind of tangible interface used by animals (e.g., dogs) to communicate with humans by means of computers.

Based on the EUI concept, Maynes-Aminzade [281] has developed two edible interfaces: BeanCounter and TasteScreen. The BeanCounter is a low-resolution gustatory display that dispenses jellybeans according to the use of system resources. Jellybeans drop into a clear chamber when memory is allocated, then fall out into a bowl when the memory is released, enabling programmers to monitor up to six processes. The volume of jellybeans dispensed corresponds to the amount of memory associated with the operation. Besides the fact that jellybeans are edible, in this interface, the sense of taste is not directly exploited. This is more an example of an alternative data visualization system.

The tasteScreen is a USB device that attaches to the top of a flat-panel monitor. The device contains 20 small plastic cartridges filled with flavoring agents that can be mixed together and dripped down the front of the monitor. A user can sample the dispensed flavor by touching his tongue to the computer screen. Certain combinations of flavoring agents re-create a flavor appropriate to the user's task.

While the hygienic aspect of the tasteScreen is questionable, the idea of using the sense of taste to convey information should be explored further.

Part IV

Applications

11

Health Sciences

The areas of health science that have been more frequently addressed by Virtual Reality are surgery, various forms of rehabilitation therapy (psychological, kinesthetic), anatomy, and biomechanics.

11.1 Virtual Surgery

Virtual surgery is an active research subject. Such systems allow physicians to practice and improve their skills in a virtual environment, performing surgery on virtual patients, before entering the operating room (OR). Studies have shown that using VR surgical simulation can significantly improve the performance in the OR [282], in particular for endoscopic and laparoscopic procedures.

Surgery simulation requires real-time computer graphics and haptic interfaces. The main objective of a virtual surgery system is to accurately simulate the behavior of tissues (skin, muscles, internal organs, bones) under cutting operations.

Realistic collisions should be computed to simulate the interaction of surgical instruments with different kinds of tissue. Simulating cutting operations requires surface deformation and other geometric operations. The topology of the 3D shapes representing tissues suffers changes; new geometry should be created during the simulation. The behavior of the tissue should be accurately reproduced. This requires the use of finite element models (FEM) and other free-form surface deformation algorithms [283]. Besides FEM, other methods like the boundary element method (BEM) are used as alternative computational mechanics techniques. BEM differs from FEM in that only the surface is discretized in order to apply boundary conditions to the equations defining the behavior of the body whose surface is being discretized. This reduces the size of the system of equations to be solved and allows for faster calculations. Together with haptic and visual feedback, BEM has been applied to simulate three basic actions performed on virtual deformable objects: prodding, pinching, and cutting. This research is targeted at the development of a neurosurgery simulator [284].

The user interface is a very important element; haptic interfaces, in particular single-point force-feedback devices like the PHANTOM®, are commonly used, as in VR training in gynecologic laparoscopy [285]. Special-purpose haptic interfaces have been developed to simulate the complex interaction involved in endoscopy [286].

Most of the virtual surgery systems are designed to be used for training and planification before real surgery. For example, the EyeSi simulation system [287] used for training surgeons in intraocular surgery. EyeSi immerses the surgeon in an environment of real surgical intruments and virtual tissue deformations provided by interactive 3D graphics.

Other systems are already being used for real-time assistance in the operating room. This is the case of the system for real-time biomechanical simulation for image-guided neurosurgery developed by Warfield et al. [288].

11.2 Virtual Rehabilitation and Therapy

Virtual reality can be used to provide rehabilitation based on physiotherapy (e.g. stroke-based disorders) and also for psychological therapy (phobia treatment).

11.2.1 Physiotherapy

As explained in [289], VR-based rehabilitation involves multiple disciplines, including physical therapy, computer science, psychology, communication. VR systems for rehabilitation integrate haptics and modern sensor technology. The methodology to develop this kind of system includes identification of movement patterns, development of simulated tasks (therapy exercises), and diagnostics (through data acquisition and monitoring). Several research projects address the motor rehabilitation needs of stroke patients (physical therapy) [290],[291], while others focus on the treatment of balance disorders [292].

The VR-based rehabilitation systems are commonly implemented through stereoscopic displays, force-feedback devices (haptic interfaces), and modern sensing techniques that have game-like features and can capture accurate data for further analysis. Diagnostics and evaluation can be made through an artificial intelligence-based model (data mining, dimensionality reduction, etc.) using collected data, and clinical tests have been conducted.

Haptic interfaces such as the "Rutgers ankle" [293] provide 6-DOF resistive forces on the patient's foot, in response to Virtual Reality–based exercises. This kind of physiotherapy for post-stroke rehabilitation has demonstrated to be effective. Results showed that, over six rehabilitation sessions, the patient improved on clinical measures of strength and endurance, which corresponded well with torque and power output increases measured by the Rutgers ankle. There were also substantial improvements in task accuracy and coordination during the simulation and the patient's walking and stair-climbing ability.

 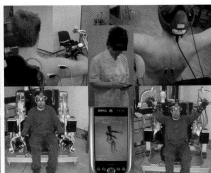

(a) Post-stroke therapy   (b) Shoulder and elbow therapy

Fig. 11.1: VR-based telerehabilitation systems for physiotherapy

The combination of haptic interfaces, Web technologies for data transmission, 3D graphics, and other muldimodal stimuli can be used to develop telerehabilitation systems. The basic concept is to provide the patient with an interface that will allow us to perfom the physiotherapy designed and monitored by a doctor or therapist in a remote location.

Video and audio streaming can be used to keep close contact between patient and therapist regardless of the physical distance. Data transmission over Internet or dedicated networks can be used to control the virtual environment as well as to acquire data for therapy evaluation purposes and progress monitoring. An example of such a system is the telerehabilitation application presented in [195]. A Haptic Workstation^{TM} is used as interface to a virtual environment controlled and monitored by a therapist in a remote location. The patient performs exercises defined by the therapist. A virtual window displaying live video allows the patient to keep visual contact with people in the remote location.

The system illustrated in Figure 11.1a is intended to be used in post-stroke rehabilitation. This kind of therapy helps stroke survivors relearn skills that are lost when part of the brain is damaged. These skills can include coordinating leg or arm movements in order to walk, manipulating objects, or other tasks involved in any complex activity. In this telerehabilitation system, the therapist can design new exercises by means of drawing lines on a PDA; such lines will be transformed into 3D shapes with haptic feedback. The patient will be able to touch and interact with the 3D shapes, relearning arm coordination skills.

A second version of the telerehabilitation system (see Figure 11.1b) has been used for shoulder and elbow therapy. This system provides a better performance monitoring interface (3D character showing the position in real time on a PDA) and has been validated by a physiotherapist with the help of muscular effort measurements acquired by an ElectroMyoGraph (EMG).

11.2.2 Psychological Therapy

Phobias can often be treated effectively by using gradual exposure therapy. Patients are subjected to anxiety-provoking stimuli in a gradual order, from the least difficult stimulus to the most difficult one, attenuating their axiety in a progressive way. Traditionally those stimuli are looked for in actual physical situations (in vivo) or by having the patient imagine the stimulus (in vitro).

Virtual Reality (VR) allows a third option of exposure therapy in a virtual setting that is safer, less embarrassing, and less costly than reproducing the real world situations. An important advantage of VR is that it can create situations that are difficult to find in real life.

Experiments have proven VR to be a useful tool in treating specific phobias such as fear of heights [294], fear of spiders [295], fear of flying [294], claustrophobia [296], and social phobia [297], [298], [299].

For instance, the work of Grillon et al. [297] and Herbelin et al. [298] has focused on the treatment of social phobia and social anxiety: fear of speaking in public. The researchers have developed an exposure-based therapy that consists of immersing patients in a virtual world; the patient should face a group of virtual characters that react to the patient's performance. Different public-speaking situations can be simulated, for example, a job interview, meeting in a bar, speech in an auditory (see Figure 11.2a).

In a preliminary work [300], the authors exposed subjects to a VR situation representing a 3D audience composed of emergent gazes in the dark and surrounding the subject. It was observed that the virtual audience was able to provoke more anxiety in social phobics than in nonphobics. The hypothesis that eye contact is an important factor of social phobia was proposed.

A more recent experiment reported in [297] used an eye-tracking setup integrated in the Virtual Reality exposure system, composed of a large screen with stereoscopic projection (see Figure 11.2b). The virtual audience was rendered in a more realistic way, using animated virtual characters and photo-realistic scenarios. The study attempted to evaluate objectively a specific parameter present in social phobia, namely, eye contact avoidance, by using the eye-tracking system. The results shows a tendency to improve in the subject's feedback to specific assessment scales, which is correlated to the decrease of eye contact avoidance. The presented Virtual Reality exposure therapy protocol could be successfully applied to social therapy. Eye-tracking technology could provide therapists with an objective evaluation of gaze avoidance and

(a) Exposure-based therapy

(b) Eye-tracking setup

Fig. 11.2: VR-based treatment of social phobia

can give tangible feedback to the patients to estimate their progress during gaze behavior exercises.

11.3 Virtual Anatomy

The visible human project (VHP) is one of the most important anatomy-related initiatives that have involved the use of Virtual Reality technologies, in particular, visualization techniques. The VHP was conceived to collect data from human subjects to serve as a guidebook and baseline dataset in modern anatomy research and education [301],[302].

The dynamic 3D model of the inguinal region developed by López-Cano et al. [303] is an illustrative example of the different components of a virtual anatomy system. The interactive 3D model was created for didactic purposes. A geometric model adjusted to real data was created by means of semiautomatic contour segmentation of anatomic units obtained from the visible human project (http://www.nlm.nih.gov/research/visible/) and data generated from classical anatomic information. Contour extraction was based on definition of a set of NURB curves. Realistic rendering allows on-demand visualization of each independent unit of the model. Current implementation enables surface deformation associated with pushing and stretching interaction. This simulator would be a relevant addition to existing tools for anatomical education after clinical validation.

The example cited earlier deals with the modeling of internal organs of a particular region of the body. Virtual anatomy also includes modeling the whole musculoskeletal human system. In [304], Aubel and Thalmann use a multilayered approach for human body modeling and deformation. The model is split into three general anatomical structures: the skeleton, musculature, and skin. Each of these layers is modeled and deformed using fast, procedural, ad hoc methods that are easy to reproduce. The modeling approach is generic enough to handle muscles of varying shape, size, and characteristics and does not break in extreme skeleton poses. The authors have developed an integrated MuscleBuilder system whose main features are easy and quick creation of muscle deformation models and automatic deformation of an over-lying skin. Visually realistic results can be obtained at interactive frame rates. See Figure 11.3a for an example of an interactive 3D model of some muscles and their interaction with the skeleton.

 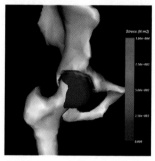

(a) Interactive model of human muscles

(b) Analysis of stress on the hip joint

Fig. 11.3: Virtual model of the musculoskeletal system

Other example of applications of a virtual model of the musculoskeletal system is the work of Maciel et al. [305], [306]. The authors developed a visualization tool for the analysis of stress distribution on the heap joint in pre- and post-operative conditions; see Figure 11.3b.

Recent international research initiatives are focusing on the development of integrated simulation platforms and databases to concentrate current and future knowledge about the human anatomy and physiology. One of those initiatives is the virtual physiological human.

The virtual physiological human (VPH) is a methodological and technolog-ical framework that, once established, will enable investigation of the human body as a single complex system. It is expected that this project will be the basis for personalized (patient-specific) health-care solutions as well as early diagnostics and predictive medicine [307]. The VPH is a European initative based on the international Physiome Project.

The Physiome Project (http://www.physiome.org/) is a worldwide effort of several research groups to define the physiome via database integration and development of integrated quantitative and descriptive models. The physiome describes the physiological dynamics of a normal intact organism. In the con-text of the Physiome Project, it includes integrated models of components of organisms, such as particular organs or cell systems, biochemical, or endocrine systems.

Virtual Reality will play an important role in both the VPH and the Physiome Project. By means of interactive simulation through haptic interfaces and real-time visualization. it will be possible to study and better understand human physiology and its disfunctions. Simulation technologies will allow for *in silico* validation of the effects of drugs, surgical techniques, etc. It will also be possible to design more targeted implants and artificial organs [307].

12

Cultural Heritage

Due to lack of information, the significance of many important sites of cultural interest is often misunderstood by visitors. Learning about the function and relevance of archaeological sites typically involves consultation of specific literature or on-site explanations by tourist guides. A very attractive way to discover and better understand these cultural sites would be to see and visit them at their glory time. For this, travel in time and space would be best, and Virtual Reality is offering it through cultural heritage applications.

In cultural heritage applications, Virtual Reality techniques are used to visually re-create historical elements that have today disappeared in archaeological sites.

This chapter reviews some applications of Virtual Reality and augmented reality in the cultural heritage field. We discuss their benefits to the visitors and/or viewers and the associated technical challenges. We start with archaeological data acquisition and reconstruction. Then, we present projects that allow visiting ancient places with different degrees of realism and interaction. We start with virtual tours of buildings followed by more complex applications, where you could actually meet their inhabitants.

A virtual tour is one of the most traditional applications of VR in the field of cultural heritage. These virtual tours allow the user to walk through, see, and interact with 3D models of old cities or buildings that have historical value. In this Section, we present several tours that are representative of different cultures and technologies.

12.1 Virtual Campeche and Calakmul

Campeche is an old exican city, founded by the Spanish in 1540, located on the Yucatan peninsula. UNESCO declared Campeche as a World Cultural Heritage site in 2001. To protect this city, the king of Spain decided to build during the 16th century a fortress with ramparts. The military sites and the center of the city remain almost intact today.

The project virtual Campeche presented in [308] allows a virtual visit through a Web-based application that runs on standard PCs using a mouse and keyboard as interface. Virtual Campeche was created following a standard approach, used by many cultural heritage projects: data acquisition (orthographic photos of the buildings) and building reconstruction (buildings are modeled in 3D using the post-processed photos as textures).

As the content is supposed to be accessible through the Web, three main techniques are applied to maximize interactivity and system responsiveness: level of detail model of the city, different versions of the same model are used depending on the position of the current viewpoint. Objects far away in the scene are displayed using a low-detail model with fewer polygons, which loads and renders faster. Progressive scene display: the 3D scene is structured into small parts for rapid delivery over the Internet. Potential visibility computation is used to adapt the visual quality of the content according to the available bandwidth for data transmission.

Nearby, in the same Mexican state of Campeche, is an old Maya metropolis called Calakmul, declared a Protected World Heritage Site by UNESCO in 2002. Calakmul is deeply covered by the wild tropical forest. Because of it, visitors endure a 5-hour trip to get to this ancient city. The bountiful vegetation prevents visitors from fully appreciating the complex urban design of the city.

To partially overcome these problems, scientists and archaeologists collaborated to create a digital reproduction (see Figure 12.1) of this Maya archaeological site.

(a) Gobal view of Calakmul at its former glory   (b) Virtual Ramon

Fig. 12.1: Latin American Virtual Reality applications: virtual Calakmul (courtesy of Rocío Ruiz Rodarte, Jesús Savage Carmona and José Larios)

This project is presented in [309] and is composed of three main applications. A physical installation takes advantage of augmented reality techniques to virtually reconstruct funeral chambers and other sites. A virtual intelligent agent with speech recognition capabilities, guides the visitors during their walk through the virtual Calakmul. Finally, it offers interactive re-creations of stelae and death masks.

12.2 Virtual Dunhuang

Dunhuang was an important historical site on the silk road in northwest China close to the Taklamakan desert. It was declared a World Heritage site by UNESCO in 1987. This oasis town is very well known for the Mogao Grottos, which were dug and decorated by the Buddhist monks during the glory time of the silk trade.

Today, the site is composed of almost 550 caves, 3000 statues, and 50000 m^2 of painted murals, which have badly suffered from the Taklamakan climate and visitors. This is one of the reasons why less than 10% of the site is currently open to the public. A virtual environment, for preservation and dissemination of Dunhuang art, was developed in 1999 by the Zheijiang University in Hangzhou (China) and the Fraunhofer-IGD in Darmstadt/Rodstock (Germany).

This project was divided into three main parts: Dunhaung Info Web, Internet-based virtual reality and high-end VR presentation. We describe only the last part, which is presented in [310]. The use of a CAVE system (see Section 7.2.5 for a description of this kind of display device) produces good immersion in a Dunhaung grotto.

As the historical content was aiming to be presented in a CAVE, several technical challenges came to light. First, all museum pieces are illustrated by text describing the age and materials used for sculptures. To avoid disturbing the user while he is immersed in the 3D world, it was decided to provide this information by a virtual voice as if there was a real guide providing explanations. Secondly, a real environment such as a grotto is more complex than a square room, and a mechanism had to be developed to enable free navigation. For that, the researchers developed a "flashlight interaction paradigm," where the user could play the role of the famous archaeologist "Indiana Jones" discovering a lost historical site with his flashlight (see Figure 12.2).

The "virtual Dunhuang" project remains one of the best examples of a fully immersive virtual tour for cultural heritage applications.

12.3 Terracotta Soldiers

A vast field of life-size terracotta statues depicting soldiers, servants, and horses was discovered in China in the 1970s. An estimated total of 6000 pieces based on the real army of the Ch'in emperor. Thanks to the Xian project presented in [311], it is now possible to look at them outside of China.

The Xian project aimed to re-create and give "life" to the terracotta army by using Virtual Reality techniques. As a result, a short movie was presented during the Digital 97 event in Geneva, Switzerland. In it, we first see a scene with the 3D terracotta soldiers inside the earth, exactly where they were found. It is dark with a starry sky. The day is coming, so more and more light is appearing. This suddenly awakes one terracotta soldier. He is extremely

Fig. 12.2: Flashlight interaction in a CAVE (courtesy of Fraunhofer-IGD)

astonished to see the scene around himself. He notices the presence of another soldier near him and his head, which is on the ground. He took the head on the ground and put it on the next soldier's body. This latter starts to live again. They look at each other, and in the same time, all the army is slowly coming to life.

When the historical part still existed, classically we use acquisition technologies such as 3D scanners to create virtual representations of the real models. However, free access to the object of interest is not always easy. Moreover, the data acquired using a scanner are a "point cloud" a set of unconnected 3D points, not a coherent surface (3D mesh), which is required to have an acceptable 3D model. Remeshing operations should be performed, involving hole filling and de-noising algorithms. The meshes obtained are not adapted for Virtual Reality applications: there are too many triangles and no textures.

To overcome the problems mentioned before, Magnenat-Thalmann et al. [311] propose different approaches based on clay sculpting simulation for modeling the faces and meta-balls [90] for modeling the soldiers' bodies.

Despite the judicious choices made during this project, several challenges have been raised. First, the individuality of the soldiers' faces had to be taken into account: all faces are different and the generated face should be adapted to support a facial animation approach [312] based on a hierarchical model (emotions, phrases of speech, head movements).

On the other hand, the goal with the soldiers was to make them realistic enough and with deformation capabilities for animation. The approach used by the research group was to build on top of an animation skeleton a deformable layer based on meta-balls aiming to simulate soft human tissues such as skin and muscles. Finally, clothes were added on the virtual soldiers.

These require an optimized mechanical model to manage collision detection and self-collision. To complete this work, the authors used similar techniques to model and animate the horses that accompanied the terracotta soldiers.

This project is relatively old in terms of the Virtual Reality techniques and technology that were used. However, it clearly points out the main problems that should be faced when creating a film or an interactive virtual world.

12.4 EU-INCO CAHRISMA and ERATO

Can you imagine not only visiting a re-creation of an ancient building but meeting its inhabitants and hearing their sounds with accurate acoustics as if you were in this place a long time ago? This is possible today with advanced real-time 3D rendering techniques and dynamics synthesis of sound. The ERATO project and the earlier CAHRISMA (see Figure 12.3) propose a strong improvement in the believability by integrating **visual** and **acoustical** simulations.

The ERATO project offers virtual simulations of very well known ancient theatres and Odea from the Mediterranean region such as Jerash (Jordan), Aphrodisias [313], Aspendos (Turkey), Aosta (Italy), and Lyon (France). CAHRISMA project created interactive simulation of "Istanbul" mosques (see Figure 12.3a) (Sokullu, Sleymaniye) by the great Ottoman architect Sinan [314]. They were founded by the European Union under the framework of the EU-INCO-MED.[1] The virtual environments include, of course, modeling the ancient environments and their acoustics and simulation of the people and their motion inside the selected spaces.

These projects present two main challenges related to real time: virtual crowd rendering and interactive sound simulation.

The real-time rendering of virtual crowds that composed the audience, requires advanced GPU[2] programming techniques (vertex and pixel shaders) for accelerating the skinning of the virtual characters and the rendering 3D textured meshes, as presented in [315].

Advances in dynamic sound rendering have been made by Rindel et al. [316] during this project. Now it becomes possible to quantify the acoustical properties of the ancient theatres and odea in each condition, leading to valuable information regarding the acoustical consequences and degree of authenticity of permanent restorations and temporary amendments. Musical instruments from the Hellenistic and Roman periods were reproduced, and some music samples were designed to make sound recordings. Based on such recorded samples of authentic-style music/speech the acoustic simulations of the theatres also produced audible sound demonstrations of virtual performances with a high degree of acoustic realism. These sound files were

---

[1] International Research Cooperation with Mediterranean Partner countries
[2] Graphics processing unit

integrated with the visual restorations to form the audio in 3D virtual realizations of performances in the selected venues.

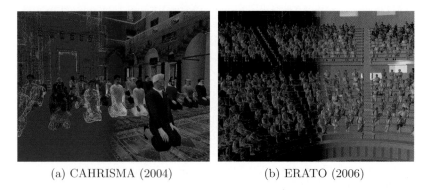

(a) CAHRISMA (2004)   (b) ERATO (2006)

Fig. 12.3: EU-INCO ERATO (2006) and CAHRISMA (2004)

The previous work on the cultural heritage was mainly focusing on the visual realism and not on the user interactivity. In the ERATO and CAHRISMA projects, the research groups propose a unification of graphic and sound models for interactive simulation to obtain authentic and realistic virtual environments. The realism of the experience is enhanced by their inhabitants (virtual crowds).

12.5 EU-IST Archeoguide

Can you imagine visiting ruined buildings in their former glory and walking through them interactively? This is possible today with augmented reality (AR) technologies. The ArcheoGuide project presented in [317] (see Figure 12.4b), allows visitors see not only ruined monuments, but they can also admire and visit the temples in their former glory.

The Aarcheoguide provides a new approach for accessing information at cultural heritage sites in a compelling, user-friendly way through the development of a system based on advanced IT including augmented reality, 3D visualization, mobile computing, and multimodal interaction techniques [318].

The system, described in [319], was tried out in the ancient city of Olympia in Greece. Cultural site visitors were provided with a video through a head-mounted display (HMD), earphone, and mobile computing equipment. A tracking system determines the location of the visitor within the site. Based on the visitor's profile and position, audio and visual information are presented to guide and allow him or her to gain more insight into relevant aspects of the site.

The project introduces new techniques of sensors (global positioning system and image-based recognition of landmarks), aggregation for position, and gaze tracking. To display Virtual Reality through the HMD, the research had to develop an optimized render for mobile platform [320]. The project explores also the multi-modal interfaces using gesture recognition and speech processing. Eficient wireless data transmission between the site server, which contains all archaeological data, and the user has been developed.

(a) EU-IST LifePlus (2005) by MIRALab, University of Geneva, EPFL-VRlab, and 2D3 [322], more details at http://lifeplus.miralab.unige.ch/

(b) EU-IST ArcheoGuide (2002), courtesy of Nicos Ioannidis (INTRACOM)

Fig. 12.4: Augmented reality and cultural heritage

The approach using optical tracking without markers being attached to the surroundings presented in [321] and the wearability of the system made ArcheoGuide an ideal tool for ancient sites that do not allow disturbance of the surroundings.

12.6 EU-IST Lifeplus

Since antiquity, fresco paintings were used as records of both events and lifestyles, and for decorations. Thanks to the technologies developed in the framework of EU-IST LifePLus [322] project, we can bring those frescos to life. We can now meet the inhabitants of ancient Pompeii in the ruined houses and shops (see Figure 12.4a).

The LifePlus project was funded by the European Union under the framework of IST.[3] Its goal was to push the limits of current augmented reality technologies, exploring the processes of narrative design of fictional spaces (e.g. fresco paintings) where users can experience a high degree of realistic interactive immersion.

Based on a captured or real-time video of a real scene, the project enhanced these scenes by allowing the possibility to render realistic 3D simulations of virtual flora and fauna (humans, animals and plants) in real time. According to its key mobile AR technology, visitors were provided with a video see-through HMD (see Figure 12.4a), earphone, and mobile computing equipment. A tracking system determines their location within the site, and audio-visual information is presented to them in context with their exploration, superimposed on their current view of the site. LifePlus extends existing AR systems and provides key new technologies to render lively, real-time animations and simulations of ancient virtual life (3D human groups, animals, and plants).

This project was quite challenging in several domains, and it is certainly one of the more advanced projects in augmented reality applications for cultural heritage purpose.

As with all augmented reality applications, it was mandatory to track the user's gaze for superimposing 3D computer graphics footage of the real world. This has been realized by the aggregation of DGPS[4] technology and marker-less video tracking provided by one of the industrial leaders in the field 2d3.[5]

On the other hand, the project requested the development of real-time "realistic" virtual life, and these are complex tasks. In [323], the authors explain that it is crucial first to have reliable data sources from archaeologists for a scientifically correct and accurate restitution but also to advance the research in the field of real-time: hair simulation, cloth simulation[324], skin rendering, fauna and flora simulation, realistic facial emotion expression and finally artificial-life methods for behavioral animation of the virtual characters.

The integration of these techniques in one application was realized by development of an integrated framework, presented in [188], distributed over two mobile computers. These insures a possible use in ancient sites without disturbing the surroundings.

---

[3] Information Society Technologies
[4] Differential Global Position System
[5] http://www.2d3.com (accessed July, 2007)

13

Other VR Applications

13.1 Vehicle Simulators

It is common practice to develop vehicle simulators based on physical mock-ups. They might be equipped with hydraulic platforms or based on a real car placed in front of large rear-projection screens. The primary application of vehicle simulators is driver training and behavior analysis (see Figure 13.1); they have also been used for virtual prototyping.

Fig. 13.1: A car driving simulator

Most car manufacturers use vehicle simulators as part of product conception. Car simulators allow engineers to test the car before it is built and evaluate ergonomic aspects, interior design and even road behavior.

For virtual prototyping, simulators based on physical reproduction of cabins require substantial time and cost to be manufactured. Therefore, they cannot be reconstructed each time to reflect every part updated on the CAD design. In particular, this difficulty appears when performing ergonomic and visibility evaluations according to changes in the car interior.

Immersive Virtual Reality provides a natural alternative. Virtual prototypes can replace physical mockups for the analysis of design aspects like: layout and packaging efficiency; visibility of instruments, controls, and mirrors; reachability and accessibility; clearances and collisions; human performance; and aesthetics and appeal. The goal is to immerse a person in the virtual car interior, to study the design and interact with the virtual car.

Completely virtual car simulators suitable for analysis activities are still unfeasible due to the limitations of the technology, in particular concerning the haptic feedback. Nevertheless, some prototypes have been developed and tested.

In [325], Kallman et al. present a simulator system built for both training and ergonomics-related tasks. The system can be used in two different configurations: the first is based on a physical mockup of the vehicle, equipped with a force-feedback steering wheel, gearshift, and pedals (see Figure 13.2a); the second configuration is based on a fully virtual control metaphor, allowing one to interact with the vehicle only through the use of motion trackers and data gloves.

(a) Vehicle simulator   (b) Virtual cockpit

Fig. 13.2: Virtual vehicle simulators

Virtual Reality interfaces can also be used to teleoperate real vehicles. An example of this kind of application is presented by Ott et al. in [326]. The authors developed a virtual cockpit with haptic feedback provided by a Haptic Workstation™ Four alternative teleoperation interfaces were implemented. Each interface exploited different aspects of Virtual Reality and haptic technologies: realistic 3D virtual objects, haptic force-feedback, and free arm gestures. Tests with multiple users were conducted to evaluate and identify the best interface in terms of efficiency and subjective user appreciation.

The interface that got the best evaluation was a gesture-based interface that used free arm gestures to drive the vehicle (a small robot). The authors concluded that an efficient interface for direct teleoperation must have rich visual feedback in the form of passive controls such as speedometers and direction indicators. Such visual aids were appreciated by users once they were released from the burden of manipulating the virtual steering wheel and throttle. Force feedback shall be exploited not as a way to simulate tangible objects (interface resembling reality) but to drive the user's movements (gesture-based interface).

The free-form (gesture-based) interface was efficient because it did not require precise manipulations. It reduced the amount of concentration required to drive. The user could direct her attention to the rest of the visuals and use them to improve the driving.

Virtual interfaces resembling real cockpits are usually more intuitive in the sense that users know immediately how they work, from previous real-world experience. Nevertheless, the available hardware can make them less efficient due to problems with the grasping mechanisms and force-feedback inherent to the Haptic Workstation^{TM} Other more advanced haptic interfaces may provide better results.

The work of Salamin et al. [327] is another example of experimentation with virtual cockpits using the Haptic Workstation^{TM} In collaboration with the Renault Trucks Cockpit Studies Department, the authors developed a virtual cockpit with a tangible gearbox. The user was able to grasp and manipulate the gearbox lever and feel the mechanical forces due to the gearbox. Such forces were generated according to the specifications provided by Renault Trucks. Other forces were applied to constrain the user's movements and provide some comfort by partially compensating for the weight of the exoskeleton (a "gravity compensation" mechanism described in [328]). Figure 13.2b shows the virtual cockpit and the virtual representation of the user's hand.

13.2 Manufacturing

Manufacturing comprises some basic classes of engineering tasks. Such tasks can benefit from the application of VR through high-fidelity and interactive visualizations. The simulation of assembly processes requires taking into account several assembly conditions: availability of assembly room, supply of materials and handling of parts and assembly tools. A virtual environment allows one to interactively produce an assembly sequence plan that considers the real production environment. The basic principles of this planning are the structural and geometric construction of the product and all restrictions that arise from the limited assembly space and the restriced accesibility. In [329], Ou et al. present a Web-based manufacturing simulation system based on VRML (Virtual Reality Modeling Language). A more recent work [330] uses X3D, the succesor to VRML as the basis for a distributed virtual manufacturing system for small and medium enterprises. The system allows one to perform collaborative tasks including product design, manufacturing and resource sharing through the Web.

In [331], Salonen et al. present a system that demonstrates the use of augmented reality and multimodal interfaces for assisting human operators during assembly tasks. The system uses a wooden 3D puzzle as a simplified assembly task in a factory. The prototype system uses 3D models generated using CAD-system and translated to STL (the standard for rapid prototyping systems) or VRML. The visualization can be done using a monitor or HMD. A Webcam is used to acquire the images of the user's hands and pieces of the 3D puzzle. The wooden pieces have fiducial markers that can be recognized through image processing, using the Augmented Reality Toolkit (AR-Toolkit, freely available at http://www.hitl.washington.edu/artoolkit/). Once the markers are recognized, the orientation of each part can be computed and 3D images can be superimposed on the real image. The assembly work is described using an XML file describing the marker board file, the models and their identifiers (the markers), and the work phases and parts that belong to each phase. When a work phase is going on, the application visualizes the part that belongs to that work phase and shows the required action. For example, pointing with an arrow to the next part that should be taken and displaying an animation of how to mount this part in the object being assembled. The user can move forward and backward in assembly phases using different modalities: keyboard, speech or gesture commands. The most convenient modalities are speech and gesture user interfaces. The system can be controlled by choosing the appropriate function from a virtual menu using hand gestures.

Fig. 13.3: Augmented reality for operator training

Augmented and mixed reality seem to be excellent tools for manufacturing planning, simulation, and training. In [332], Liverani et al. describe a system for real-time control of human assembling sequences of mechanical components. The development method they propose involves a CAD environment, a hardware system called Personal Active Assistant (PAA), and a set of mixed reality features. The whole scheme is targeted at reducing the gap between engineers and manual operators by means of CAD and mixed reality technologies. The system is based on a CAD assembly module and mixed reality wearable equipment. It can be used to improve several activities in the industrial field, such as operator professional training, optimal assembly sequence seeking, or on-field teleconferencing (suitable for remote collaboration or for full exploitation of concurrent engineering suggestions during design and setup stages). The main characteristic of the PAA is a real-time wireless linkage to a remote server or designer workstation, where project geometric database is stored. The Mixed Reality wearable equipment is a see-through HMD and a head-mounted camera. The user can freely operate in the mixed environment, while the camera can record the human-driven assembly sequence and check the efficiency and correctness via object recognition: an incremental subassembly detection algorithm has been developed to achieve complex dataset monitoring. Conversely, designers or assembly planners can exploit the peculiarities of mixed reality–based assembly: a straightforward interaction with the assembly operator can be obtained by sending vocal advice or displaying superimposed visual information on the real scene.

Another example of the use of augmented reality for operator training in a manufacturing context is the work of Vacchetti et al. [333], partially developed in the framework of the IST STAR European project. The system tracks the 3D camera position by means of a natural feature tracker, which, given a rough CAD model, can deal with complex 3D objects. The tracking algorithm is described in [204]. The tracking method is robust and can handle large camera displacements and aspect changes (see Figure 13.3). The target applications are industrial maintenance, repair, and training. The tracking robustness makes the AR system able to work in real environments such as industrial facilities, not only in the laboratory. Real-time object recognition has been used to augment real scenes with virtual humans and virtual devices that show how to operate various types of industrial equipment.

13.3 Entertainment

Virtual Reality constantly borrows video game technology (advanced rendering algorithms, user interaction paradigms and interfaces) and vice versa; some of the advanced concepts and technologies that were created in research laboratories have found their way into the game industry. VR devices like HMDs, data gloves, and sensors have been used with different degrees of success in video games. In some cases, advanced computer graphics are complemented with highly realistic interfaces to produce a compelling experience; see Figure 13.4. One of the most recent success stories is the case of the Nintendo Wii. The Wii remote game controller, equipped with accelerometers and an infrared sensor that detect its spatial orientation, makes possible the creation of appealing games. VR and human-computer interaction researchers have studied this kind of gesture-based interface before and continue to test novel concepts. Sometimes researchers use commercially available devices. This is the case of Shirai et al. [334], who developed some motion-analysis methods using the Wii remote.

Fig. 13.4: Simulator or advanced video game

A very representative example of VR research applied to the entertainment industry is the case of VR Studio, the Walt Disney Company's center of excellence in real-time graphics and interactive entertainment. The studio was founded in 1992 to explore the potential of Virtual Reality technology for theme park attractions. They have also developed Toontown (http://play.toontown.com), one of the first massively multiplayer online worlds designed for children ages 7 and older.

One of the first VR-based attractions they developed was an interactive system that uses HMDs to immerse multiple users in the movie *Rocketeer*. Another attraction based on the movie *Aladdin* also used an HMD but was a single-user system.

VR Studio was responsible for the development of three of the main DisneyQuest attractions (a theme park that opened in Orlando in 1998):

- Aladdin's Magic Carpet Ride, a four-person race through the world of Aladdin. The players use custom-designed HMDs and climb aboard motorcycle-like vehicles to begin the game.
- Hercules in the Underworld. This attraction uses a five-screen immersive projection theater (IPT). This is similar to a CAVE, but with an hexagonal

shape. The players used 3D glasses and a joystick to navigate through the virtual world.

- Pirates of the Caribbean: Battle for Buccaneer Gold. The game takes place in a four-screen immersive theater built around a ship-themed motion platform. The ship has a real steering wheel and six physical cannons. The players wear stereo glasses and all screens are in stereo.

A historical review of VR Studio describing its research experience is presented by Mine in [217]. One of the most interesting lessons learned reported by Mine is the fact that immersive multiuser (CAVE-like) displays are very effective not only as game interfaces but also as design tools. This kind of display allows one to share experiences and ease communication between participants while examining a prototype or playing a game.

Another important point reported by VR Studio is that the use of physical interfaces helps to immerse users in a VR experience. An example of this is the work of Abaci et al. [335], "Enigma of the Sphinx." This is a VR-based game that uses a large rear-projection screen and a multimodal interface called "Magic Wand." The Magic Wand is a stick equipped with a magnetic tracker. It uses both posture and speech recognition to let the user interact with objects and characters in a virtual world based on ancient Egypt (see Figure 13.5). The VR game was played by several users in a special event; the Magic Wand was an intuitive interface that helped players to get more involved in the virtual world.

Fig. 13.5: "Enigma of the Sphinx" using a multimodal interface: the Magic Wand

The industry of video games has produced highly advanced interactive 3D (I3D) authoring tools and game engines [336]. These software tools are being used not only for developing new games but also all kinds of "serious" applications in the areas of simulation, training and education.

More and more industries and researchers are turning to available game engines and other I3D software issued from the video game industry. There are free (mostly open source) and commercial products, and most of the time they allow one to reduce the costs of development, in terms both of time and financial budget.

Among the most popular and advanced I3D software, we can consider:

- *Unreal game engine* (http://www.unrealtechnology.com), a game development framework that provides a vast array of core technologies (state-of-the-art 3D rendering), content-creation tools, and support infrastructure (e.g., networking functionality for distributed virtual environments).
- *Virtools* (http://www.virtools.com/), a set of tools designed to develop interactive real-time applications for industry and games. It supports the creation of a range of VR applications: online, desktop-based, and large-scale interactive digital mockups.
- *OpenSceneGraph* (http://www.openscenegraph.org), an open source high-performance 3D graphics toolkit. It is used by application developers in fields such as visual simulation, games, Virtual Reality, scientific visualization and modeling. OpenSceneGraphs was written in Standard C++ and OpenGL; it runs on all Windows platforms, OSX, GNU/Linux, IRIX, Solaris, HP-Ux, AIX and FreeBSD operating systems.
- *Quest3D* (http://www.quest3d.com/), a software developer's kit (SDK) that supports various VR devices (inertial and magnetic trackers, data gloves) and provides support for dynamic simulation (Newton physics).

References

1. J.J. LaViola: "A discussion of cybersickness in virtual environments," *SIGCHI Bull.* **32**(1), 47–56 (2000)
2. C. Cruz-Neira, D.J. Sandin, T.A. DeFanti, R.V. Kenyon, J.C. Hart: "The CAVE: Audio visual experience automatic virtual environment," *Commun. ACM* **35**(6), 64–72 (1992)
3. M. Slater, S. Wilbur: "A framework for immersive virtual environments (FIVE): Speculations on the role of presence in virtual environments," *Presence: Teleoperators and Virtual Environments* **6**, 603–16 (1997)
4. M. Krueger: *Artificial Reality II* (Addison-Wesley, Boston, 1991)
5. F.P. Brooks, M. Ouh-Young, J.J. Batter, P.J. Kilpatrick: "Project GROPE: Haptic displays for scientific visualization," in *SIGGRAPH '90: Proceedings of the 17th Annual Conference on Computer Graphics and Interactive Techniques* (ACM Press, New York, 1990) pp. 177–85
6. P. Milgram, H. Takemura, A. Utsumi, F. Kishino: "Augmented Reality: A class of displays on the reality-virtuality continuum," *Proceedings of SPIE, Telemanipulator and Telepresence Technologies* **2351**, 282–92 (1995)
7. R. Martin (Ed.): *Directions in Geometric Computing* (Information Geometers Ltd, Winchester, 1993)
8. W.R. Hamilton: "On quaternions; or on a new system of imaginaries in algebra," *Philosophical Magazine* **XXV**, 10–3 (1844)
9. K. Shoemake: "Animating rotation with quaternion curves," in *SIGGRAPH '85: Proceedings of the 12th Annual Conference on Computer Graphics and Interactive Techniques* (ACM Press, New York, 1985) pp. 245–54
10. V. Lepetit, P. Fua: "Monocular Model-Based 3D Tracking of Rigid Objects: A Survey," *Foundations and Trends in Computer Graphics and Vision* **1**(1), 1–89 (2005)
11. F.S. Grassia: "Practical Parameterization of Rotations Using the Exponential Map," *J. of Graphics Tools* **3**(3), 29–48 (1998)
12. D. Rogers, J.A. Adams: *Mathematical Elements for Computer Graphics* 2nd edn. (McGraw-Hill, New York, 1990)
13. G. Farin: *Handbook of Computer Aided Geometric Design* (Elsevier Science, 2002)
14. M.G. Cox: "The numerical evaluation of B-splines," *J. Inst. Math. Appl.* **10**, 134–49 (1972)

15. C. de Boor: "On Calculation with B-splines," *J. Approx. Theory* **6**, 50–62 (1972)

16. E. Catmull, J. Clark: "Recursively Generated B-Spline Surfaces on Arbitrary Topological Meshes," *Computer Aided Design* **10**(6), 350–5 (1978)

17. L.J. Shiue, I. Jones, J. Peters: "A realtime GPU subdivision kernel," in *SIGGRAPH '05: ACM SIGGRAPH 2005 Papers* (ACM Press, New York, 2005) pp. 1010–5

18. C. Loop, J. Blinn: "Real-time GPU rendering of piecewise algebraic surfaces," in *SIGGRAPH '06: ACM SIGGRAPH 2006 Papers* (ACM Press, New York, 2006) pp. 664–70

19. T. Whitted: "An improved illumination model for shaded display," *Commun. ACM* **23**(6), 343–9 (1980)

20. H. Gouraud: "Continuous Shading of Curved Surface," *IEEE Transactions on Computers* **C-20**(6), 623–9 (1971)

21. B.T. Phong: "Illumination for computer generated pictures," *Commun. ACM* **18**(6), 311–7 (1975)

22. J.T. Kajiya: "The rendering equation," in *SIGGRAPH '86: Proceedings of the 13th Annual Conference on Computer Graphics and Interactive Techniques* (ACM Press, New York, 1986) pp. 143–50

23. J.L. Bentley, J.H. Friedman: "Data Structures for Range Searching," *ACM Comput. Surv.* **11**(4), 397–409 (1979)

24. A.S. Glassner: "Space Subdivision for Fast Ray Tracing," *IEEE Computer Graphics & Applications* **4**(10), 15–22 (1984)

25. T.J. Purcell, I. Buck, W.R. Mark, P. Hanrahan: "Ray tracing on programmable graphics hardware," in *SIGGRAPH '05: ACM SIGGRAPH 2005 Courses* (ACM Press, New York, 2005) p. 268

26. D.R. Horn, J. Sugerman, M. Houston, P. Hanrahan: "Interactive k-d tree GPU raytracing," in *I3D '07: Proceedings of the 2007 symposium on Interactive 3D graphics and games* (ACM Press, New York, 2007) pp. 167–74

27. I. Wald, P. Slusallek: "State-of-the-Art in Interactive Ray-Tracing," in *Proceedings of EUROGRAPHICS 2001* (2001) pp. 21–42

28. H. Friedrich, J. Günther, A. Dietrich, M. Scherbaum, H.P. Seidel, P. Slusallek: "Exploring the use of ray tracing for future games," in *sandbox '06: Proceedings of the 2006 ACM SIGGRAPH symposium on Videogames* (ACM Press, New York, 2006) pp. 41–50

29. C.M. Goral, K.E. Torrance, D.P. Greenberg, B. Battaile: "Modeling the interaction of light between diffuse surfaces," in *SIGGRAPH '84: Proceedings of the 11th Annual Conference on Computer Graphics and Interactive Techniques* (ACM Press, New York, 1984) pp. 213–22

30. P. Guitton, J. Roman, G. Subrenat: "Implementation results and analysis of a parallel progressive radiosity," in *PRS '95: Proceedings of the IEEE symposium on Parallel rendering* (ACM Press, New York, 1995) pp. 31–8

31. F. Sillion, C. Puech: *Radiosity and Global Illumination* (Morgan Kaufmann Publishers, San Francisco, 1994)

32. F. Schöffel: "Online radiosity in interactive virtual reality applications," in *VRST '97: Proceedings of the ACM symposium on Virtual reality software and technology* (ACM Press, New York, 1997) pp. 201–8

33. N.A. Carr, J.D. Hall, J.C. Hart: "GPU algorithms for radiosity and subsurface scattering," in *HWWS '03: Proceedings of the ACM SIGGRAPH/*

EUROGRAPHICS conference on Graphics hardware (Eurographics Association, Aire-la-Ville, Switzerland, Switzerland, 2003) pp. 51–9

34. H.W. Jensen: "Global Illumination using Photon Maps," in *Rendering Techniques'96: 7th. Eurographics Workshop on Rendering* (1996) pp. 21–30
35. H.W. Jensen: *Realistic Image Synthesis Using Photon Mapping* (AK Peters, Ltd, Natick, MA, 2001)
36. H.W. Jensen: "A practical guide to global illumination using ray tracing and photon mapping," in *SIGGRAPH '04: ACM SIGGRAPH 2004 Course Notes* (ACM Press, New York, 2004) p. 20
37. T.J. Purcell, C. Donner, M. Cammarano, H.W. Jensen, P. Hanrahan: "Photon mapping on programmable graphics hardware," in *HWWS '03: Proceedings of the ACM SIGGRAPH/EUROGRAPHICS conference on Graphics hardware* (Eurographics Association, Aire-la-Ville, Switzerland, Switzerland, 2003) pp. 41–50
38. P. Haeberli, M. Segal: "Texture Mapping as a Fundamental Drawing Primitive," in *Proceedings of the 4th Eurographics Workshop on Rendering* (1993) pp. 259–66
39. J.F. Blinn, M.E. Newell: "Texture and reflection in computer generated images," *Commun. ACM* **19**(10), 542–7 (1976)
40. F. Policarpo, M.M. Oliveira, J.L.D. Comba: "Real-time relief mapping on arbitrary polygonal surfaces," in *I3D '05: Proceedings of the 2005 symposium on Interactive 3D graphics and games* (ACM Press, New York, 2005) pp. 155–62
41. F. Policarpo, M.M. Oliveira: "Relief mapping of non-height-field surface details," in *I3D '06: Proceedings of the 2006 symposium on Interactive 3D graphics and games* (ACM Press, New York, 2006) pp. 55–62
42. J.F. Blinn: "Simulation of wrinkled surfaces," in *SIGGRAPH '78: Proceedings of the 5th Annual Conference on Computer Graphics and Interactive Techniques* (ACM Press, New York, 1978) pp. 286–92
43. R.L. Cook: "Shade trees," in *SIGGRAPH '84: Proceedings of the 11th Annual Conference on Computer Graphics and Interactive Techniques* (ACM Press, New York, 1984) pp. 223–31
44. S. Gumhold, T. Hüttner: "Multiresolution rendering with displacement mapping," in *HWWS '99: Proceedings of the ACM SIGGRAPH/EUROGRAPHICS workshop on Graphics hardware* (ACM Press, New York, 1999) pp. 55–66
45. L. Wang, X. Wang, X. Tong, S. Lin, S. Hu, B. Guo, H.Y. Shum: "View-dependent displacement mapping," in *SIGGRAPH '03: ACM SIGGRAPH 2003 Papers* (ACM Press, New York, 2003) pp. 334–9
46. R. Rost: *OpenGL Shading Language* (Addison-Wesley, Boston, 2006)
47. J.O. Talton, D. Fitzpatrick: "Teaching graphics with the openGL shading language," in *SIGCSE '07: Proceedings of the 38th SIGCSE technical symposium on Computer science education* (ACM Press, New York, 2007) pp. 259–63
48. N.M. Thalmann, D. Thalmann: "Complex Models for Animating Synthetic Actors," *IEEE Computer Graphics and Applications* **11**(5), 32–44 (1991)
49. N. Burtnyk., M. Wein: "Computer-generated key-frame animation," *J. Soc Motion Television Engineers* pp. 149–53 (1980)
50. E. Catmull: "The Problems of Computer-Assisted Animation," in *SIGGRAPH '78: Proceedings of the SIGGRAPH '78 conference* (1978) pp. 348–53

51. W. Reeves: "Inbetweening For Computer Animation Utilizing Moving Point Constraints," in *SIGGRAPH '81: Proceedings of the SIGGRAPH '81 conference* (1981) pp. 263–9

52. F. Parke: "Parameterized Models for Facial Animation," *IEEE Computer Graphics and Applications* **2**(9), 61–8 (1982)

53. S. Steketee, N. Badler: "Parametric Keyframe Interpolation In Incorporating Kinetic Adjustment and Phrasing Control," in *SIGGRAPH '85: Proceedings of the SIGGRAPH '85 conference* (1985) pp. 255–62

54. D. Zeltzer: "Representation of complex animated figures," in *Proceedings of the Graphics Interface82 conference* (1982) pp. 205–21

55. D. Kochanek, R. Bartels: "Interpolating Splines with Local Tension, Continuity, and Bias Control," in *SIGGRAPH '84: Proceedings of the SIGGRAPH '84 conference* (1984) pp. 33–41

56. K. Fu, Gonzalez, C.S. G.Lee: *Robotics, Control, Sensing, Vision, and Intelligence* (McGraw-Hill, 1987) pp. 52–76

57. R. Boulic, R. Mas: *Interactive Computer Animation* (Prentice Hall, 1996) Chap. Hierarchical Kinematic Behaviors for Complex Articulated Figure

58. N. Badler, K. Manoochehri, G. Walters: "Articulated Figure Positioning by Multiple Constraints," *IEEE Computer Graphics & Applications* **7**(6), 28–38 (1987)

59. J. Zhao, N. Badler: "Inverse Kinematics Positioning using Nonlinear Programming for Highly Articulated Figures," *ACM Transactions on Graphics* **13**(4), 313–36 (1994)

60. C. Philips, J. Zhao, N. Badler: "Interactive Real-Time Articulated Figure Manipulation Using Multiple Kinematic Constraints," in *SIGGRAPH '91: Proceedings of the SIGGRAPH '91 conference* (1991) pp. 245–50

61. C. Phillips, N. Badler: "Interactive Behaviors for Bipedal Articulated Figures," in *SIGGRAPH '91: Proceedings of the SIGGRAPH '91 conference* (1991) pp. 359–62

62. A.Witkin, Z.Popovic: "Motion warping," in *SIGGRAPH '95: Proceedings of the SIGGRAPH '95 conference* (1995) pp. 105–8

63. Z.Popovic, A.Witkin: "Physically based motion transformation," in *SIGGRAPH '99: Proceedings of the SIGGRAPH '99 conference* (1999) pp. 11–20

64. A. Bruderlin, L.Williams: "Motion signal processing," in *SIGGRAPH '95: Proceedings of the SIGGRAPH '95 conference* (1995) pp. 97–104

65. M.Gleicher: "Retargeting motion to new characters," in *SIGGRAPH '98: Proceedings of the SIGGRAPH '98 conference* (1998) pp. 33–42

66. J.S. Monzani, P. Baerlocher, R. Boulic, D. Thalmann: "Using an Intermediate Skeleton and Inverse Kinematics for Motion Retargeting," in *EUROGRAPHICS'00: Proceedings of the EUROGRAPHICS'00 conference* (2000) pp. 11–9

67. R.Bindiganavale, N.I. Badler: *Modeling and Motion Capture Techniques for Virtual Environments* (Springer : Lecture Notes in Artificial Intelligence, 1998) Chap. Motion abstraction and mapping with spatial constraints, pp. 70–82

68. J. Lee, S.Y. Shin: "A hierarchical approach to interactive motion editing for human-like figures," in *SIGGRAPH '99: Proceedings of the 26th Annual Conference on Computer Graphics and Interactive Techniques* (ACM Press/Addison-Wesley Publishing Co., New York, 1999) pp. 39–48

69. I.S.Lim, D. Thalmann: "Solve Customers' Problems: Interactive Evolution for Tinkering with Computer Animation," in *SAC2000: Proceedings of the ACM Symposium on Applied Computing* (2000) pp. 404–7

70. P. Glardon, R. Boulic, D. Thalmann: "PCA-based Walking Engine using Motion Capture Data," in *CGI04: Proceedings of Computer Graphics International 2004* (2004) pp. 292–8

71. R. Huston: *Multibody dynamics* (Butterworth-Heinemann, Stoneham, 1990)

72. R. Featherstone: *Robot Dynamics Algorithms* (Kluwer Academic Publishers, 1986)

73. M.M. Kenna, D. Zeltzer: "Dynamic Simulation of a Complex Human Figure Model with Low Level Behavior Control," *Presence* **5**(4), 431–56 (1996)

74. H. Ko, N. Badler: "Animating Human Locomotion with Inverse Dynamics," *IEEE Computer Graphics and Applications* **16**, 50–9 (1996)

75. J. Hodgins, W. Wooten, D. Brogan, J. OBrien: "Animating Human Athletics," in *SIGGRAPH '95: Proceedings of the SIGGRAPH '95 conference* (1995) pp. 71–8

76. J. Lazlo, M.V.D. Panne, E. Fiume: "Limit Cycle Control and its Application to the Animation of Balancing and Walking," in *SIGGRAPH '96: Proceedings of the SIGGRAPH '96 conference* (1996) pp. 155–62

77. P. Faloutsos, M. van de Panne, D. Terzopoulos: "Composable Controllers for Physics-based Character Animation," in *SIGGRAPH '01: Proceedings of the SIGGRAPH '01 conference* (2001) pp. 251–60

78. A. Witkin., M. Kass: "Spacetime Constraints," in *SIGGRAPH '88: Proceedings of the SIGGRAPH '88 conference* (1988) pp. 159–68

79. K. Perlin, A. Goldberg: "Improv: A system for scripting interactive actors in virtual worlds," in *SIGGRAPH '96: Proceedings of the SIGGRAPH '96 conference* (1996) pp. 205–16

80. S. Vosinakis, T. Panayiotopoulos: "A task definition language for virtual agents," in *WSCG 2003: J. of WSCG* Vol. 11 (2003) pp. 512–9

81. C. Reynolds: "Flocks and Herds and Schools: A Distributed Behavioral Model," in *SIGGRAPH '87: Proceedings of the SIGGRAPH '87 conference* (1987) pp. 25–34

82. J. Wilhelms, A. Van Gelder: "Anatomically Based Modeling," in *SIGGRAPH '97: Proceedings of the SIGGRAPH '97 conference* (1997) pp. 173–80

83. G. Ridsdale: "Connectionist Modelling of Skill Dynamics," *J. of Visualization and Computer Animation* **1**(2), 66–72 (1990)

84. H. Noser, R. Turner, D. Thalmann: "Interaction between L-systems and Vector Force-Field," in *CGI92: Proceedings of the Computer Graphics International '92 conference* (1992) pp. 747–61

85. N. Magnenat-Thalmann, D. Thalmann: "The Direction of Synthetic Actors in the Film "Rendez-vous à Montreal"," *IEEE Computer Graphics and Applications* **7**(12), 9–19 (1987)

86. N. Magnenat-Thalmann, R. Laperriere, D. Thalmann: "Joint-dependent local deformations for hand animation and object grasping," in *Proceeeding of the Graphics Interface 88* (1988) pp. 26–33

87. A. Mohr, M. Gleicher: "Building efficient, accurate character skins from examples," *ACM Transactions on Graphics* **22**(3), 562–8 (2003)

88. X. Wang, C. Phillips: "Multi-weight enveloping: least-squares approximation techniques for skin animation," in *Proceedings of the Symposium on Computer Animation, SCA02* (2002) pp. 129–38

89. J. Chadwick, D. Haumann, R. Parent: "Layered construction for deformable animated characters," in *SIGGRAPH '89: Proceedings of the SIGGRAPH '89 conference* (1989) pp. 243–52

90. D. Thalmann, S. Jianhua, E. Chauvineau: "Fast realistic human body deformations for animation and VR applications," in *Proceedings of Computer Graphics International* (IEEE Comput. Soc. Press, 1996) pp. 166–74

91. F. Scheepers, R. Parent, W. Carlson, S. May: "Anatomy-based modeling of the human musculature," in *SIGGRAPH '97: Proceedings of the SIGGRAPH '97 conference* (1997) pp. 163–72

92. L. Porcher-Nedel, D. Thalmann: "Real Time Muscle Deformations Using Mass- Spring Systems," in *CGI98: Proceedings of the Computer Graphics International '98 conference* (IEEE Computer Society Press, 1998) pp. 156–65

93. A. Aubel, D. Thalmann: "Interactive Modeling of the Human Musculature," in *Proceedings of the Computer Animation 2001 conference*Seoul, Korea (2001) pp. 167–73

94. V. Blanz, T. Vetter: "A morphable model for the synthesis of 3D faces," in *SIGGRAPH '99: Proceedings of the SIGGRAPH '99 conference* (1999) pp. 187–94

95. D.L. James, C.D. Twigg: "Skinning mesh animations," *ACM Transactions on Graphics* **24**(3), 399–407 (2005)

96. P. Faloutsos, M.V. de Panne, D. Terzopoulos: "Dynamic freeform deformations for animation synthesis," *IEEE Transactions on Visualization and Computer Graphics* **3**(3), 201–14 (1997)

97. S. Capell, S. Green, B. Curless, T. Duchamp, Z. Popovic: "Interactive skeleton-driven dynamic deformations," in *SIGGRAPH '02: Proceedings of the SIGGRAPH '02 conference* (2002) pp. 41–7

98. R. Boulic, N. Magnenat-Thalmann, D. Thalmann: "A Global Human Walking Model with Real-time Kinematics Personification," *The Visual Computer* **6**(6), 344–58 (1990)

99. D. Thalmann, S.R. Musse: *Crowd Simulation* (Springer, 2007)

100. F. Multon, L. France, M. Cani-Gascuel, G. Debunne: "Computer animation of human walking: a survey," *The J. of Visualization and Computer Animation* **10**(1), 39–54 (1999)

101. M. van de Panne: "From Footprints to Animation," *Computer Graphics Forum* pp. 211–23 (1997)

102. M.G. Choi, J. Lee, S.Y. Shin: "Planning biped locomotion using motion capture data and probabilistic roadmaps," *ACM Transactions on Graphics* **22**(2), 182–203 (2003)

103. W. Wooten, J. Hodgins: "Simulating leaping, tumbling, landing and balancing humans," in *Proceedings of the IEEE International Conference on Robotics and Automation* (2000) pp. 656–62

104. R. Boulic, B. Ulciny, D. Thalmann: "Versatile walk engine," *J. Of Game Development* pp. 29–50 (2004)

105. A. Bruderlin, T. Calvert: "Knowledge-driven, interactive animation of human running," in *Proceedings of the Graphics Interface 96 conference* (1996) pp. 213–21

106. H. Sun, D. Metaxas: "Automating Gait Generation," in *SIGGRAPH '01: Proceedings of the SIGGRAPH '01 conference* (2001) pp. 261–70

107. S. Chung, J. Hahn: "Animation of Human Walking in Virtual Environments," in *Proceedings of Computer Animation 1999 conference* (1999) pp. 4–15

108. R.T. M. Unuma K. Anjyo: "Fourier principles for emotion-based human figure," in *SIGGRAPH '95: Proceedings of the SIGGRAPH '95 conference* (1995) pp. 91–6

109. C. Rose, M. Cohen, B. Bodenheimer: "Verbs and adverbs: Multidimensional motion interpolation," *IEEE Computer Graphics and Applications* **18**(5), 32–41 (1998)

110. S. Park, H. Shin, S. Shin: "On-line locomotion generation based on motion blending," in *Proceedings of the SIGGRAPH/Eurographics Symposium on Computer Animation 2002* (2002) pp. 105–11

111. L. Kovar, M. Gleicher: "Flexible automatic motion blending with registration curves," in *Proceedings of the SIGGRAPH/Eurographics Symposium on Computer Animation 2003* (2003) pp. 214–24

112. P. Glardon, R. Boulic, D. Thalmann: "A coherent locomotion engine extrapolating beyond experimental data," in *Proceedings of Computer Animation and Social Agent 2004* (2004) pp. 73–84

113. I.T. Jolliffe: *Principal Component Analysis* (Springer series in statistics. Springer- Verlag, 1986)

114. M. Alexa, W. Müller: "Representing animations by principal components," in *Proceedings of the Eurographics 2000 conference*Vol. 19 (2000) pp. 291–301

115. I. Lim, D. Thalmann: "Construction of animation models out of captured data," in *Proceedings of IEEE Confefernce Multimedia and Expo 2002* (2002) pp. 829–32

116. H-anim: "The humanoid animation working group.
http://www.h-anim.org
(accessed July, 2007),"

117. M. Alexa: "Linear combination of transformations," in *SIGGRAPH '02: Proceedings of the SIGGRAPH '02 conference* (2002) pp. 380–7

118. M.P. Murray: "Gait as a total pattern of movement," *Am J Phys Med* **46**(1), 290–333 (1967)

119. V. Inman, H. Ralston, F. Todd: *Human Walking* (Wiliams & Witkins, Baltimore, 1981)

120. D. Tolani, A. Goswami, N. Badler: "Real-time inverse kinematics techniques for anthropomorphic limbs," *Graph. Models Image Process* **62**(5), 353–88 (2000)

121. L. Levison: (1996) "Connecting planning and acting via object-specific reasoning," Ph.D. thesis Philadelphia, PA, USA

122. N. Badler, R. Bindiganavale, W.S. J. Allbeck, L. Zhao, M. Palmer: "Parameterized action representation for virtual human agents," *In Embodied Conversational Agents, MIT Press* pp. 256–84 (2000)

123. L. Goncalves, M. Kallmann, D. Thalmann: "Defining behaviors for autonomous agents based on local perception and smart objects," *Computers and Graphics* **26**(6), 887–97 (2002)

124. M. Kallmann, D. Thalmann: "Modeling behaviors of interactive objects for real-time virtual environments," *J. of Visual Languages and Computing* **13**(2), 177–95 (2002)

125. C. Peters, S. Dobbyn, B. McNamee, C. O'Sullivan: "Smart objects for attentive agents," *J. of WSCG* **11** (2003)

126. M.R. Cutkosky: "On grasp choice, grasp models, and the design of hands for manufacturing tasks," *IEEE Transactions on Robotics and Automation* **5**(3), 269–79 (1989)

127. R. Mas, R. Boulic, D. Thalmann: "Extended grasping behavior for autonomous human agents," in *AGENTS '97: Proceedings of the first*

international conference on Autonomous agents (ACM Press, New York, 1997) pp. 494–5

128. R. Mas, D. Thalmann: "A Hand Control and Automatic Grasping System for Synthetic Actors," *Comput. Graph. Forum* **13**(3), 167–77 (1994)

129. P. Baerlocher: (2001) "Inverse kinematics Techniques for the Interactive Posture Control of Articulated Figures," Ph.D. thesis École Polytechnique Fédérale de Lausanne (EPFL)

130. X. Wang, J.P. Verriest: "A geometric algorithm to predict the arm reach posture for computer-aided ergonomic evaluation," *J. of Visualization and Computer Animation* **9**(1), 33–47 (1998)

131. D.J. Wiley, J.K. Hahn: "Interpolation Synthesis of Articulated Figure Motion," *IEEE Comput. Graph. Appl.* **17**(6), 39–45 (1997)

132. Z. Huang, R. Boulic, N.M. Thalmann, D. Thalmann: "A multi-sensor approach for grasping and 3D interaction," *Computer graphics: developments in virtual environments* pp. 235–53 (1995)

133. B. Espiau, R. Boulic: "Collision avoidance for redondants robots with proximity sensors," in *Third International Symposium of Robotics Research* (1985)

134. M. van de Panne, E. Fiume: "Sensor-Actuator Networks," in *Proceedings of the of SIGGRAPH-93: Computer Graphics* Anaheim, CA (1993) pp. 335–42

135. C.B. Phillips, N.I. Badler: "JACK: a toolkit for manipulating articulated figures," in *UIST '88: Proceedings of the 1st annual ACM SIGGRAPH symposium on User Interface Software* (ACM Press, New York, 1988) pp. 221–9

136. N.I. Badler, C.B. Phillips, B.L. Webber: *Simulating humans: computer graphics animation and control* (Oxford University Press, Inc., New York, 1993)

137. B. Douville, L. Levison, N.I. Badler: "Task-Level Object Grasping for Simulated Agents," *Presence* **5**(4), 416–30 (1996)

138. T.S. Trias, S. Chopra, B.D. Reich, M.B. Moore, N.I. Badler, B.L. Webber, C.W. Geib: "Decision Networks for Integrating the Behaviors of Virtual Agents and Avatars," in *VRAIS '96: Proceedings of the 1996 Virtual Reality Annual International Symposium (VRAIS 96)* (IEEE Computer Society, Washington, DC, USA, 1996) p. 156

139. N.S. Pollard, V.B. Zordan: "Physically based grasping control from example," in *SCA '05: Proceedings of the 2005 ACM SIGGRAPH/Eurographics symposium on Computer animation* (ACM Press, New York, 2005) pp. 311–8

140. J. Ciger, T. Abaci, D. Thalmann: "Planning with Smart Objects," in *WSCG '2005* (2005)

141. M. Mortara, G. Patane, M. Spagnuolo, B. Falcidieno, J. Rossignac: "Blowing bubbles for the multi-scale analysis and decomposition of triangle meshes," *Algorithmica, Special Issues on Shape Algorithms, 38(2):227-248* (2004)

142. M. Mortara, G. Patane, M. Spagnuolo, B. Falcidieno, J. Rossignac: "Plumber: a method for a multi-scale decomposition of 3D shapes into tubular primitives and bodies," in *SMI '04: Proceedings of the ninth ACM symposium on Solid modeling and applications* (Eurographics Association, Aire-la-Ville, Switzerland, Switzerland, 2004) pp. 339–44

143. J. Latombe: *Robot Motion Planning* (Kluwer Academic Publishers, Norwell, MA, USA, 1991)

144. L. Kavraki, P. Svestka, J. Latombe, M. Overmars: (1994) "Probabilistic roadmaps for path planning in high-dimensional configuration spaces," Tech. rep. Stanford University Stanford, CA, USA

145. S.M. LaValle: (1998) "Rapidly-exploring random trees: A new tool for path planning," Tech. Rep. 98-11 Dept. of Computer Science, Iowa State University

146. T. Simon, J. Laumond, C. Nissoux: "Visibility based probabilistic roadmaps for motion planning," *Advanced Robotics J.* **14**(2) (2000)

147. J.J. Kuffner, S.M. LaValle: "RT-connect: An efficient approach to single-query path planning," in *Proceedings of the ICRA 2000 conference* (2000) pp. 995–1001

148. M. Kallmann, A. Aubel, T. Abaci, D. Thalmann: "Planning Collision-Free Reaching Motions for Interactive Object Manipulation and Grasping," in *Proceedings of the Eurographics 2003 conference*Vol. 22 (2003) pp. 313–22

149. K. Yamane, J.J. Kuffner, J.K. Hodgins: "Synthesizing animations of human manipulation tasks," *ACM Transactions on Graphics* **23**(3), 532–9 (2004)

150. M. Kallmann, M. Mataric: "Motion planning using dynamic roadmaps," in *Proceedings of the ICRA 2004 conference* (2004) pp. 4399–404

151. P. Leven, S. Hutchinson: "Motion planning using dynamic roadmaps," in *Proceedings of the Fourth International Workshop on the Algorithmic Foundations of Robotics (WAFR)* (2000) pp. 363–76

152. K. Waters: "A Muscle Model for Animating Three-Dimensional Facial Expression," in *SIGGRAPH '87: Proceedings of the SIGGRAPH '87 conference* (1987) pp. 17–24

153. D. Terzopoulos, K. Waters: "Physically Based Facial Modelling, Analysis and Animation," *J. of Visualization and Computer Animation* **1**(2), 73–90 (1990)

154. P. Ekman, W.V. Friesen: *Facial Action Coding System: A Technique for the Measurement of Facial Movement* (Consulting Psychologists Press, 1978)

155. D.R. Hill, A. Pearce, B. Wyvill: "Animating speech: an automated approach using speech synthesized by rule," *The Visual Computer* **3**, 277–89 (1988)

156. C. Pelachaud: (1991) "Communication and Coarticulation in Facial Animation," Ph.D. thesis University of Pennsylvania

157. M.M. Cohen, D.W. Massaro: *N. M. Thalmann and D. Thalmann, Models and techniques in Computer Animation* (Springer-Verlag, 1993) Chap. Modelling coarticulation in synthetic visual speech, pp. 139–56

158. S. Kshirsagar, S. Garchery, N. Magnenat-Thalmann: "Feature Point Based Mesh Deformation Applied to MPEG-4 Facial Animation," in *DEFORM '00/AVATARS '00: Proceedings of the IFIP TC5/WG5.10 DEFORM'2000 Workshop and AVATARS'2000 Workshop on Deformable Avatars* (Kluwer, B.V., Deventer, The Netherlands, The Netherlands, 2001) pp. 24–34

159. S. Kshirsagar, N. Magnenat-Thalmann: "Principal Components of Expressive Speech Animation," in *Proceedings of the Computer Graphics International 2001 conference* (IEEE Computer Society, 2001) pp. 38–44

160. S. Kshirsagar, N. Magnenat-Thalmann: "Virtual Humans Personified," in *Proceedings of the Autonomous Agents Conference (AAMAS) 2002* (2002) pp. 356–9

161. O. Renault, N. Magnenat-Thalmann, D. Thalmann: "A Vision-Based Approach to Behavioural Animation," *J. of Visualization and Computer Animation* **1**(1), 18–21 (1990)

162. H. Noser, O. Renault, D. Thalmann, N.M. Thalmann: "Navigation for Digital Actors based on Synthetic Vision, Memory and Learning," *Computers and Graphics, Pergamon Press* **19**, 7–19 (1990)

163. A. Garcia-Rojas, F. Vexo, D. Thalmann: "Semantic Representation of Individualized Reaction Movements for Virtual Human," *International Journal of Virtual Reality* **6**(1), 25–32 (2007)

164. E. de Sevin, D. Thalmann: "A motivational Model of Action Selection for Virtual Humans," in *Proceedings of the Computer Graphics International (CGI2005) conference* (IEEE Computer Society Press, New York, 2005) pp. 213–20

165. T. Tyrrell: "The use of hierarchies for action selection," *Adapt. Behav.* **1**(4), 387–420 (1993)

166. J.Y. Donnart, J.A. Meyer: "Learning Reactive and Planning Rules in a Motivationally Autonomous Animal," *IEEE Transactions on Systems, Man, and Cybernetics* **26**(3), 381–95 (1996)

167. S. Musse, D. Thalmann: "A Behavioral Model for Real-Time Simulation of Virtual Human Crowds," *IEEE Transactions on Visualization and Computer Graphics* **7**(2), 152–64 (2001)

168. L. Emering, R. Boulic, T. Molet, D. Thalmann: "Versatile Tuning of Humanoid Agent Activity," *Computer Graphics Forum* **19**(4), 231–42 (2000)

169. E. Bouvier, P. Guilloteau: "Crowd Simulation in Immersive Space Management," in *Eurographics Workshop on Virtual Environments and Scientific Visualization '96* (pringer-Verlag, 1996) pp. 104–10

170. E. Bouvier, E. Cohen, L. Najman: "From crowd simulation to airbag deployment: particle systems, a new paradigm of simulation," *J. of Electrical Imaging* **6**(1), 94–107 (1997)

171. D. Brogan, J. Hodgins: "Robot Herds: Group Behaviors for Systems with Significant Dynamics," in *Proceedings of. Artificial Life IV* (1994) pp. 319–24

172. S. Musse, C. Babski, T. Capin, D. Thalmann: "Crowd Modeling in Collaborative Virtual Environments," in *Proceedings of the ACM VRST 98* Taiwan (1998) pp. 115–23

173. B. Ulicny, D. Thalmann: "Crowd simulation for interactive virtual environments and VR training systems," in *Proceedings of the Eurographics Workshop on Animation and Simulation* (Springer-Verlag, 2001) pp. 163–70

174. J. Cremer, J. Kearney, Y. Papelis: "HCSM: Framework for Behavior and Scenario Control in Virtual Environments," *ACM Transactions on Modeling and Computer Simulation* **5**(3), 242–67 (1995)

175. R. Boulic, P. Becheiraz, L. Emering, D. Thalmann: "Integration of Motion Control Techniques for Virtual Human and Avatar Real-Time Animation," in *Proceedings of the ACM VRST '97* (1997) pp. 111–8

176. J. Pettre, P. de Heras, J. Maim, B. Yersin, J. Laumond, D.Thalmann: "Real-Time Navigating Crowds: Scalable Simulation and Rendering," in *Computer Animation and Virtual Worlds* Vol. 16 (2006) pp. 445–56

177. A. Treuille, S. Cooper, Z. Popovic: "Continuum crowds," in *Proceedings of the SIGGRAPH 06 conference* (2006) pp. 1160–8

178. F. Morini, J. Mam, B. Yersin, D. Thalmann: "Real-Time Scalable Motion Planning for Crowds," in *Proceedings of the CyberWorlds 2007 conference* (2007) pp. 144–51

179. M. Oliveira, J. Crowcroft, M. Slater: "An innovative design approach to build virtual environment systems," in *EGVE '03: Proceedings of the workshop on Virtual environments 2003* (ACM Press, 2003) pp. 143–51

180. O. Hagsand: "Interactive multiuser VEs in the DIVE system," *IEEE Multimedia* **3**(1), 30–9 (1996)

181. C. Greenhalgh, J. Purbrick, D. Snowdon: "Inside MASSIVE-3: flexible support for data consistency and world structuring," in *CVE '00: Proceedings of the third international conference on Collaborative virtual environments* (ACM Press, 2000) pp. 119–27

182. M.R. Macedonia, D.P. Brutzman, M.J. Zyda, D.R. Pratt, P.T. Barham, J. Falby, J. Locke: "NPSNET: a multi-player 3D virtual environment over the Internet," in *SI3D '95: Proceedings of the 1995 symposium on Interactive 3D graphics* (ACM Press, 1995) pp. 93–4

183. D. Anderson, J. Barrus, J. Howard, C. Rich, R. Waters: "Building multiuser interactive multimedia environments at MERL," *IEEE Multimedia* **2**(4), 77–82 (1995)

184. C. Grimsdale: "dVS-Distributed Virtual Environment System," in *Proceedings of Computer Graphics'91, London, UK, Bleinheim Online* (1991) pp. 163–70

185. Sense8 Corporation: (1998) "WorldToolkit Reference Manual – Release 7. Mill Valley, CA,"

186. H. Tramberend: "Avocado: A Distributed Virtual Reality Framework," in *VR '99: Proceedings of the IEEE Virtual Reality* (IEEE Computer Society, 1999) pp. 14–21

187. A. Bierbaum, C. Just, P. Hartling, K. Meinert, A. Baker, C. Cruz-Neira: "VR Juggler: A Virtual Platform for Virtual Reality Application Development," in *Proceedings of the Virtual Reality 2001 Conference (VR'01)* (IEEE Computer Society, 2001) pp. 89–96

188. M. Ponder, G. Papagiannakis, T. Molet, N. Magnenat-Thalmann, D. Thalmann: "VHD++ Development Framework: Towards Extendible, Component Based VR/AR Simulation Engine Featuring Advanced Virtual Character Technologies," in *Proceedings of Computer Graphics International (CGI)* (IEEE Computer Society Press, 2003) pp. 96–104

189. S. Huang, R. Baimouratov, W.L. Nowinski: "Building virtual anatomic models using Java3D," in *VRCAI '04: Proceedings of the 2004 ACM SIGGRAPH international conference on Virtual Reality continuum and its applications in industry* (ACM Press, 2004) pp. 402–5

190. R. Dörner, P. Grimm: "Three-dimensional Beans–creating Web content using 3D components in a 3D authoring environment," in *VRML '00: Proceedings of the fifth symposium on Virtual reality modeling language (Web3D-VRML)* (ACM Press, 2000) pp. 69–74

191. C. Yimin, Z. Tao, W. Di, H. Yongyi: "A robot simulation, monitoring and control system based on network and Java3D," in *Proceedings of the 4th World Congress on Intelligent Control and Automation* (2002) pp. 139–43

192. M. Kallmann, D. Thalmann: "Direct 3D interaction with smart objects," in *VRST '99: Proceedings of the ACM symposium on Virtual reality software and technology* (ACM Press, 1999) pp. 124–30

193. M. Gutiérrez: (2005) "Semantic Virtual Environments," Ph.D. thesis École Polytechnique Fédérale de Lausanne (EPFL)

194. M. Gutiérrez, D. Thalmann, F. Vexo: "Semantic Virtual Environments with Adaptive Multimodal Interfaces," in *Proceedings of the 11th International Conference on Multimedia Modelling (MMM2005)* (2005) pp. 277–83

195. M. Gutiérrez, P. Lemoine, D. Thalmann, F. Vexo: "Telerehabilitation: controlling haptic virtual environments through handheld interfaces," in *VRST '04: Proceedings of the ACM symposium on Virtual reality software and technology* (ACM Press, New York, 2004) pp. 195–200

196. F. Steinicke, T. Ropinski, K. Hinrichs: "A generic virtual reality software system's architecture and application," in *ICAT '05: Proceedings of the 2005 international conference on Augmented tele-existence* (ACM Press, New York, 2005) pp. 220–7

197. D. Lee, M. Lim, S. Han, K. Lee: "ATLAS: A Scalable Network Framework for Distributed Virtual Environments," *Presence: Teleoper. Virtual Environ.* **16**(2), 125–56 (2007)

198. D. Lee, M. Lim, S. Han: "ATLAS: a scalable network framework for distributed virtual environments," in *CVE '02: Proceedings of the 4th international conference on Collaborative virtual environments* (ACM Press, New York, 2002) pp. 47–54

199. T. Molet, A. Aubel, T. Capin, S. Carion, E. Lee, N.M. Thalmann, H. Noser, I. Pandzic, G. Sannier, D. Thalmann: "Anyone for Tennis?," *Presence, MIT* **8**(2), 140–56 (1999)

200. S. Bneford, J. Bowers, L. Fahldn, G. Greenhalgh, J. Mariani, T. Rodden: "Networked Virtual Reality and Cooperative Work," *Presence, MIT* **4**(4), 364–86 (1995)

201. W. Pasman, C. Woodward, M. Hakkarainen, P. Honkamaa, J. Hyväkkä: "Augmented reality with large 3D models on a PDA: implementation, performance and use experiences," in *VRCAI '04: Proceedings of the 2004 ACM SIGGRAPH international conference on Virtual Reality continuum and its applications in industry* (ACM Press, New York, 2004) pp. 344–51

202. B. Lucas, T. Kanade: "An iterative image registration technique with an application to stereo vision," in *International Joint Conference on Artificial Intelligence* (1981) pp. 674–9

203. S. Baker, I. Matthews: "Lucas-Kanade 20 years on: A unifying framework," in *International J. of Computer Vision* (2004) pp. 221–55

204. L. Vacchetti, V. Lepetit, P. Fua: "Stable Real-Time 3D Tracking Using Online and Offline Information," *IEEE Transactions on Pattern Analysis and Machine Intelligence* **26**(10), 1385–91 (2004)

205. D. Nister, O. Naroditsky, J. Bergen: "Visual odometry," in *Conference on Computer Vision and Pattern Recognition* (2004) pp. 652–9

206. B. Williams, G. Narasimham, B. Rump, T.P. McNamara, T.H. Carr, J. Rieser, B. Bodenheimer: "Exploring large virtual environments with an HMD when physical space is limited," in *APGV '07: Proceedings of the 4th symposium on Applied perception in graphics and visualization* (ACM Press, New York, 2007) pp. 41–8

207. C. Ware, K. Arthur, K.S. Booth: "Fish tank virtual reality," in *CHI '93: Proceedings of the INTERACT '93 and CHI '93 conference on Human factors in computing systems* (ACM Press, New York, 1993) pp. 37–42

208. K.W. Arthur, K.S. Booth, C. Ware: "Evaluating 3D task performance for fish tank virtual worlds," *ACM Transactions on Information Systems* **11**(3), 239–65 (1993)

209. W. Qi, I. Russell M. Taylor, C.G. Healey, J.B. Martens: "A comparison of immersive HMD, fish tank VR and fish tank with haptics displays for volume visualization," in *APGV '06: Proceedings of the 3rd symposium on Applied perception in graphics and visualization* (ACM Press, New York, 2006) pp. 51–8

210. G.W. Fitzmaurice, S. Zhai, M.H. Chignell: "Virtual reality for palmtop computers," *ACM Transactions on Information Systems* **11**(3), 197–218 (1993)

211. K. Watsen, R. Darken, W. Capps: "A Handheld Computer as an Interaction Device to a Virtual Environment," in *Proceedings of Third International Immersive Projection Technology Workshop (IPT 1999)*Stuttgart, Germany (1999)

212. L. Hill, C. Cruz-Neira: "Palmtop interaction methods for immersive projection technology systems," in *Fourth International Immersive Projection Technology Workshop (IPT 2000)* (2000)

213. E. Farella, D. Brunelli, M. Bonfigli, L. Benini, B. Ricco: "Using Palmtop Computers and Immersive Virtual Reality for Cooperative archaeological analysis: the Appian Way case study," in *International Conference on Virtual Systems and Multimedia (VSMM)*Gyeongju, Korea (2002)

214. E. Farella, D. Brunelli, M. Bonfigli, L. Benini, B. Ricco: "Multi-client cooperation and wireless PDA interaction in immersive virtual environment," in *Euromedia 2003 Conference*Plymouth, United Kingdom (2003)

215. A. Cheok, X. Yang, Z. Ying, M. Billinghurst, H. Kato: "Touch-Space: Mixed Reality Game Space Based on Ubiquitous, Tangible, and Social Computing," in *Personal and Ubiquitous Computing*Vol. 6 (2002) pp. 430–42

216. O. Bimber, R. Raskar: "Modern approaches to augmented reality," in *SIGGRAPH '07: ACM SIGGRAPH 2007 courses* (ACM Press, New York, 2007)

217. M. Mine: "Towards virtual reality for the masses: 10 years of research at Disney's VR studio," in *EGVE '03: Proceedings of the workshop on Virtual environments 2003* (ACM Press, New York, 2003) pp. 11–7

218. T. Höllerer, J. Kuchera-Morin, X. Amatriain: "The allosphere: a large-scale immersive surround-view instrument," in *EDT '07: Proceedings of the 2007 workshop on Emerging displays technologies* (ACM Press, New York, 2007) p. 3

219. C. Cruz-Neira, D.J. Sandin, T.A. DeFanti: "Surround-screen projection-based virtual reality: the design and implementation of the CAVE," in *SIGGRAPH '93: Proceedings of the 20th Annual Conference on Computer Graphics and Interactive Techniques* (ACM Press, New York, 1993) pp. 135–42

220. J. Jacobson, Z. Hwang: "Unreal tournament for immersive interactive theater," *Commun. ACM* **45**(1), 39–42 (2002)

221. A. Peternier, S. Cardin, F. Vexo, D. Thalmann: "Practical Design and Implementation of a CAVE Environment," in *International Conference on Computer Graphics, Theory and Applications GRAPP* (2007) pp. 129–36

222. P. Larsson, D. Vstfjll, M. Kleiner: "Better presence and performance in virtual environments by improved binaural sound rendering," in *Proceedings of the AES 22nd Intl. Conf. on virtual, synthetic and entertainment audio* (2002) pp. 31–8

223. D.A. Burgess: "Techniques for low cost spatial audio," in *UIST '92: Proceedings of the 5th annual ACM symposium on User interface software and technology* (ACM Press, New York, 1992) pp. 53–9

224. B. Kapralos, N. Mekuz: "Application of dimensionality reduction techniques to HRTFS for interactive virtual environments," in *ACE '07: Proceedings of the international conference on Advances in computer entertainment technology* (ACM Press, New York, 2007) pp. 256–7

225. M. Naef, O. Staadt, M. Gross: "Spatialized audio rendering for immersive virtual environments," in *VRST '02: Proceedings of the ACM symposium on Virtual reality software and technology* (ACM Press, New York, 2002) pp. 65–72

226. R.D. Shilling, B. Shinn-Cunningham: *Handbook of virtual environments: Design, implementation, and applications* (Lawrence Erlbaum Associates, Mahwah, NJ, 2002) Chap. Virtual Auditory Displays, pp. 65–92

227. B. Insko: (2001) "Passive Hapics Significantly Enhance Virtual Environments," Ph.D. thesis University of North Carolina, Department of Computer Science

228. H.Z. Tan, A. Pentland: *Fundamentals of Wearable Computers and Augmented Reality* (Lawrence Erlbaum Associates, Mahwah, NJ, 2001) Chap. Tactual Displays for Sensory Substitution and Wearable Computers, pp. 579–98

229. G. Robles-De-La-Torre: "The Importance of the Sense of Touch in Virtual and Real Environments," *IEEE MultiMedia* **13**(3), 24–30 (2006)

230. K. Salisbury, D. Brock, T. Massie, N. Swarup, C. Zilles: "Haptic rendering: programming touch interaction with virtual objects," in *SI3D '95: Proceedings of the 1995 symposium on Interactive 3D graphics* (ACM Press, New York, 1995) pp. 123–30

231. A. Bejczy, J.K. Salisbury: "Kinematic coupling between operator and remote manipulator," *Advances in Computer Technology* **1**, 197–211 (1980)

232. W. Kim, A. Bejczy: "Graphical displays for operator aid in telemanipulation," in *Proceedings of the IEEE Int. Conf. on Systems, Man and Cybernetics* (1991) pp. 1059–67

233. N. Patrick: (1990) "Design, Construction, and Testing of a Fingertip Tactile Display for Interaction with Virtual and Remote Environments," Master's thesis Department of Mechanical Engineering, MIT

234. M. Minsky, O. young Ming, O. Steele, F.P. Brooks, M. Behensky: "Feeling and seeing: issues in force display," in *SI3D '90: Proceedings of the 1990 symposium on Interactive 3D graphics* (ACM Press, New York, 1990) pp. 235–41

235. G. Burdea, J. Zhuang, E. Roskos, D. Silver, N. Langrana: "A Portable Dextrous Master with Force Feedback," *Presence - Teleoperators and Virtual Environments* **1**(1), 18–27 (1992)

236. T. Massie, J.K. Salisbury: "The PHANTOM® haptic interface: A device for probing virtual objects," in *Proceedings of the ASME Winter Annual Meeting: Symposium on Haptic Interfaces for Virtual Environment and Teleoperator Systems* (1994) pp. 295–300

237. B. Jackson, L. Rosenberg: *Interactive Technology and the New Paradigm for Healthcare* (IOS Press, 1995) Chap. Force Feedback and Medical Simulation, pp. 147–51

238. V. Hayward, O.R. Astley, M. Cruz-Hernandez, D. Grant, G. Robles-De-La-Torre: "Haptic Interfaces and Devices," *Sensor Review* **4**(1), 16–29 (2004)

239. D. Caldwell, C. Gosney: "Enhanced tactile feedback (tele-taction) using a multi-functional sensory system," in *Proceedings of the IEEE International Conference on Robotics and Automation* (1993) pp. 955–60

240. S. Cardin, F. Vexo, D. Thalmann: "Vibro-Tactile Interface for Enhancing Piloting Abilities During Long Term Flight," *J. of Robotics and Mechatronics* **18**(4), 381–91 (2006)

241. S. Cardin, F. Vexo, D. Thalmann: "Wearable System for Mobility Improvement of Visually Impaired People," *Visual Computer J.* **23**, 109 – 18 (2006)

242. A. Cassinelli, C. Reynolds, M. Ishikawa: "Haptic radar / extended skin project," in *SIGGRAPH '06: ACM SIGGRAPH 2006 Sketches* (ACM Press, New York, 2006) p. 34

243. A. Yamamoto, S. Nagasawa, H. Yamamoto, T. Higuchitokyo: "Electrostatic tactile display with thin film slider and its application to tactile telepresentation systems," in *VRST '04: Proceedings of the ACM symposium on Virtual reality software and technology* (ACM Press, New York, 2004) pp. 209–16

244. H.N. Ho, L.A. Jones: "Development and evaluation of a thermal display for material identification and discrimination," *ACM Trans. Appl. Percept.* **4**(2), 13 (2007)

245. D. Caldwell, S. Lawther, A. Wardle: "Tactile perception and its application to the design of multi-modal cutaneous feedback systems," in *Proceedings of the IEEE International Conference on Robotics and Automation* (1996) pp. 3215–21

246. S.A. Wall, S. Brewster: "Sensory substitution using tactile pin arrays: Human factors, technology and applications," *Signal Process.* **86**(12), 3674–95 (2006)

247. R.D. Howe: "The shape of things to come: pin-based tactile shape displays," in *Proceedings of the 4th International Conference Eurohaptics 2004, Munich, Germany, 5-7 June 2004* (1996) pp. 2–11

248. I.R. Summers, C.M. Chanter: "A broadband tactile array on the fingertip," *J. of the Acoustical Society of America* **112**(5), 2118–26 (2002)

249. J.C. Bliss, M.H. Katcher, C.H. Rogers, R.P. Shepard: "Optical-to-Tactile Image Conversion for the Blind," *IEEE Transactions on Man Machine Systems* **11**(1), 58–65 (1970)

250. K. Minamizawa, S. Fukamachi, H. Kajimoto, N. Kawakami, S. Tachi: "Gravity grabber: wearable haptic display to present virtual mass sensation," in *SIGGRAPH '07: ACM SIGGRAPH 2007 emerging technologies* (ACM Press, New York, 2007) p. 8

251. H. Iwata: "Art and technology in interface devices," in *VRST '05: Proceedings of the ACM symposium on Virtual reality software and technology* (ACM Press, New York, 2005) pp. 1–7

252. M. Solazzi, A. Frisoli, F. Salsedo, M. Bergamasco: "A fingertip haptic display for improving local perception of shape cues," in *WHC '07: Proceedings of the Second Joint EuroHaptics Conference and Symposium on Haptic Interfaces for Virtual Environment and Teleoperator Systems* (IEEE Computer Society, Washington, DC, USA, 2007) pp. 409–14

253. M. Sato: "SPIDAR and Virtual Reality," in *Proceedings of the 5th Biannual World Automation Congress* (2002) pp. 17–23

254. J. Murayama, L. Bougrila, Y. Luo, K. Akahane, S. Hasegawa, B. Hirsbrunner, M. Sato: "SPIDAR G&G: a Two-Handed Haptic Interface for Bimanual VR Interaction," in *Proceedings of the 4th International Conference Eurohaptics 2004, Munich, Germany, 5-7 June 2004* (2004)

255. J. Solis, C.A. Avizzano, M. Bergamasco: "Teaching to Write Japanese Characters using a Haptic Interface," in *HAPTICS '02: Proceedings of the 10th Symposium on Haptic Interfaces for Virtual Environment and Teleoperator Systems* (IEEE Computer Society, Washington, DC, USA, 2002) pp. 255–62

256. C. Avizzano, O. Portillo-Rodriguez, M. Bergamasco: "Assisting to Sketch Unskilled People with Fixed and Interactive Virtual Templates," in *Proceedings of IEEE International Conference on Robotics and Automation* (2007) pp. 4013–17

257. O. Portillo-Rodriguez, C. Avizzano, A. Chavez-Aguilar, M. Raspolli, S. Marcheschi, M. Bergamasco: "Haptic Desktop: The Virtual Assistant Designer," in

Proceedings of the 2nd IEEE/ASME International Conference on Mechatronic and Embedded Systems and Applications (2006) pp. 1–6

258. H. Iwata: "Artificial reality with force-feedback: development of desktop virtual space with compact master manipulator," in *SIGGRAPH '90: Proceedings of the 17th Annual Conference on Computer Graphics and Interactive Techniques* (ACM Press, New York, 1990) pp. 165–70

259. R. Ott, D. Thalmann, F. Vexo: "Organic shape modeling through haptic devices," *Computer-Aided Design and Applications* **3**(1-4), 79–88 (2006)

260. R. Ott, M. Gutiérrez, D. Thalmann, F. Vexo: "Advanced virtual reality technologies for surveillance and security applications," in *VRCIA '06: Proceedings of the 2006 ACM international conference on Virtual reality continuum and its applications* (ACM Press, New York, 2006) pp. 163–70

261. A. Frisoli, F. Rocchi, S. Marcheschi, A. Dettori, F. Salsedo, M. Bergamasco: "A new force-feedback arm exoskeleton for haptic interaction in virtual environments," in *WHC 2005: First Joint Eurohaptics Conference and Symposium on Haptic Interfaces for Virtual Environment and Teleoperator Systems* (2005) pp. 195–201

262. M. Bergamasco, A. Frisoli, F. Barbagli: "Haptics Technologies and Cultural Heritage Applications," in *CA '02: Proceedings of the Computer Animation* (IEEE Computer Society, Washington, DC, USA, 2002) p. 25

263. H. Iwata, H. Yano, F. Nakaizumi, R. Kawamura: "Project FEELEX: adding haptic surface to graphics," in *SIGGRAPH '01: Proceedings of the 28th Annual Conference on Computer Graphics and Interactive Techniques* (ACM Press, New York, 2001) pp. 469–76

264. I. Poupyrev, T. Nashida, S. Maruyama, J. Rekimoto, Y. Yamaji: "Lumen: interactive visual and shape display for calm computing," in *SIGGRAPH '04: ACM SIGGRAPH 2004 Emerging technologies* (ACM Press, New York, 2004) p. 17

265. I. Poupyrev, T. Nashida, M. Okabe: "Actuation and tangible user interfaces: the Vaucanson duck, robots, and shape displays," in *TEI '07: Proceedings of the 1st international conference on Tangible and embedded interaction* (ACM Press, New York, 2007) pp. 205–12

266. B. Rasch, C. Büchel, S. Gais, J. Born: "Odor Cues During Slow-Wave Sleep Prompt Declarative Memory Consolidation," *Science* **315**(5817), 1426–9 (2007)

267. G. Michael, L. Jacquot, J. Millot, G. Brand: "Ambient odors modulate visual attentional capture," *Neuroscience Letters* **352**(3), 221–5 (2003)

268. S.A. Simon, R.G. Ivan E. de Araujo, M.A.L. Nicolelis: "The neural mechanisms of gustation: A distributed processing code," *Nature Reviews Neuroscience* **7**, 890–901 (2006)

269. D. Drayna: "Human Taste Genetics," *Annual Review of Genomics and Human Genetics* **6**, 217–35 (2005)

270. L. Bartoshuk, V. Duffy, I. Miller: "PTC/PROP tasting: Anatomy, psychophysics and sex effects," *Physiol. Behav.* **56**, 1165–71 (1994)

271. T.P. Heath, J.K. Melichar, D.J. Nutt, L.F. Donaldson: "Human Taste Thresholds Are Modulated by Serotonin and Noradrenaline," *The J. of Neuroscience* **26**(49), 12 664–71 (2006)

272. R. Gutierrez-Osuna: *Encyclopedia of human-computer interaction* (Berkshire Pub., 2004) Chap. Olfactory Interaction, pp. 507–11

273. J.J. Kaye: "Making Scents: Aromatic output for HCI," *Interactions* **11**(1), 48–61 (2004)

274. D.A. Washburn, L.M. Jones: "Could Olfactory Displays Improve Data Visualization?," *Computing in Science and Engg.* **6**(6), 80–3 (2004)

275. Y. Yanagida, S. Kawato, H. Noma, A. Tomono, N. Tetsutani: "Projection-Based Olfactory Display with Nose Tracking," in *VR '04: Proceedings of the IEEE Virtual Reality 2004 (VR'04)* (IEEE Computer Society, Washington, DC, USA, 2004) p. 43

276. S. Brewster, D. McGookin, C. Miller: "Olfoto: designing a smell-based interaction," in *CHI '06: Proceedings of the SIGCHI conference on Human Factors in computing systems* (ACM Press, New York, 2006) pp. 653–62

277. K. Tominaga, S. Honda, T. Ohsawa, H. Shigeno, K. ichi Okada, Y. Matsushita: ""Friend Park"-Expression of the Wind and the Scent on Virtual Space," in *VSMM '01: Proceedings of the Seventh International Conference on Virtual Systems and Multimedia (VSMM'01)* (IEEE Computer Society, Washington, DC, USA, 2001) p. 507

278. H. Iwata, H. Yano, T. Uemura, T. Moriya: "Food Simulator: A Haptic Interface for Biting," in *VR '04: Proceedings of the IEEE Virtual Reality 2004 (VR'04)* (IEEE Computer Society, Washington, DC, USA, 2004) pp. 51–7

279. Y. Hashimoto, N. Nagaya, M. Kojima, S. Miyajima, J. Ohtaki, A. Yamamoto, T. Mitani, M. Inami: "Straw-like user interface: Virtual experience of the sensation of drinking using a straw," in *ACE '06: Proceedings of the 2006 ACM SIGCHI international conference on Advances in computer entertainment technology* (ACM Press, New York, 2006) p. 50

280. B.I. Resner: (2001) "Rover@Home: Computer Mediated Remote Interaction between Humans and Dogs," Master's thesis Program in Media Arts and Sciences, School of Architecture and Planning, MIT

281. D. Maynes-Aminzade: "Edible Bits: Seamless Interfaces between People, Data and Food," in *CHI 2005: alt.chi, Extended Abstracts* (2005)

282. N.E. Seymour, A.G. Gallagher, S.A. Roman, M.K. OBrien, V.K. Bansal, D.K. Andersen, R.M. Satava: "Virtual Reality Training Improves Operating Room Performance: Results of a Randomized, Double-Blinded Study," *Annals of Surgery* **236**(4), 458–64 (2002)

283. G. Sela, J. Subag, A. Lindblad, D. Albocher, S. Schein, G. Elber: "Real-time haptic incision simulation using FEM-based discontinuous free-form deformation," *Computer Aided Design* **39**(8), 685–93 (2007)

284. P. Wang, A.A. Becker, I.A. Jones, A.T. Glover, S.D. Benford, C.M. Greenhalgh, M. Vloeberghs: "Virtual reality simulation of surgery with haptic feedback based on the boundary element method," *Computers & Structures* **85**(7-8), 331–9 (2007)

285. G. Székely, C. Brechbühler, J. Dual, R. Enzler, J. Hug, R. Hutter, N. Ironmonger, M. Kauer, V. Meier, P. Niederer, A. Rhomberg, P. Schmid, G. Schweitzer, M. Thaler, V. Vuskovic, G. Tröster, U. Haller, M. Bajka: "Virtual Reality-Based Simulation of Endoscopic Surgery," *Presence: Teleoper. Virtual Environ.* **9**(3), 310–33 (2000)

286. O. Körner, R. Männer: "Implementation of a Haptic Interface for a Virtual Reality Simulator for Flexible Endoscopy," in *HAPTICS '03: Proceedings of the 11th Symposium on Haptic Interfaces for Virtual Environment and Teleoperator Systems (HAPTICS'03)* (IEEE Computer Society, Washington, DC, USA, 2003) p. 278

287. C. Wagner, M. Schill, R. Männer: "Intraocular surgery on a virtual eye," *Commun. ACM* **45**(7), 45–9 (2002)
288. S.K. Warfield, M. Ferrant, X. Gallez, A. Nabavi, F.A. Jolesz: "Real-time biomechanical simulation of volumetric brain deformation for image guided neurosurgery," in *Supercomputing '00: Proceedings of the 2000 ACM/IEEE conference on Supercomputing (CDROM)* (IEEE Computer Society, Washington, DC, USA, 2000) p. 23
289. S.C. Yeh, A. Rizzo, W. Zhu, J. Stewart, M. McLaughlin, I. Cohen, Y. Jung, W. Peng: "An integrated system: Virtual reality, haptics and modern sensing technique (VHS) for post-stroke rehabilitation," in *VRST '05: Proceedings of the ACM symposium on Virtual reality software and technology* (ACM Press, New York, 2005) pp. 59–62
290. Y. Jung, S.C. Yeh, J. Stewart: "Tailoring virtual reality technology for stroke rehabilitation: A human factors design," in *CHI '06: CHI '06 extended abstracts on Human factors in computing systems* (ACM Press, New York, 2006) pp. 929–34
291. D. Jack, R. Boian, A. Merians, S.V. Adamovich, M. Tremaine, M. Recce, G.C. Burdea, H. Poizner: "A virtual reality-based exercise program for stroke rehabilitation," in *Assets '00: Proceedings of the fourth international ACM conference on Assistive technologies* (ACM Press, New York, 2000) pp. 56–63
292. J. Jacobson, M.S. Redfern, J.M. Furman, S.L. Whitney, P.J. Sparto, J.B. Wilson, L.F. Hodges: "Balance NAVE: A virtual reality facility for research and rehabilitation of balance disorders," in *VRST '01: Proceedings of the ACM symposium on Virtual reality software and technology* (ACM Press, New York, 2001) pp. 103–9
293. J.E. Deutsch, J. Latonio, G.C. Burdea, R. Boian: "Post-Stroke Rehabilitation with the Rutgers Ankle System: A Case Study," *Presence: Teleoper. Virtual Environ.* **10**(4), 416–30 (2001)
294. M. Krijn, P.M.G. Emmelkamp, R.P. Ólafsson, M. Bouwman, L.J. van Gerwen, P. Spinhoven, M.J. Schuemie, C.A.P.G. van der Mast: "Fear of Flying Treatment Methods: Virtual Reality Exposure vs. Cognitive Behavioral Therapy," *Aviation, Space, and Environmental Medicine* **78**(2), 121–8 (2007)
295. S. Bouchard, S. Côté, J. St-Jacques, G. Robillard, P. Renaud: "Effectiveness of virtual reality exposure in the treatment of arachnophobia using 3D games," *Technol. Health Care* **14**(1), 19–27 (2006)
296. A. Garcia-Palacios, H.G. Hoffman, T.R. Richards, E.J. Seibel, S.R. Sharar: "Use of Virtual Reality Distraction to Reduce Claustrophobia Symptoms during a Mock Magnetic Resonance Imaging Brain Scan: A Case Report," *CyberPsychology & Behavior* **10**(3), 485–8 (2007)
297. H. Grillon, F. Riquier, B. Herbelin, D. Thalmann: "Virtual Reality as Therapeutic Tool in the Confines of Social Anxiety Disorder Treatment," *International Journal on Disability and Human Development* **5**(3) (2006)
298. B. Herbelin, P. Benzaki, F. Riquier, O. Renault, H. Grillon, D. Thalmann: "Using physiological measures for emotional assessment: A computer-aided tool for Cognitive and Behavioural Therapy," *International J. on Disability and Human Development* **4**(4), 269–77 (2005)
299. L.M. Wilcox, R.S. Allison, S. Elfassy, C. Grelik: "Personal space in virtual reality," *ACM Trans. Appl. Percept.* **3**(4), 412–28 (2006)
300. B. Herbelin, F. Riquier, F. Vexo, D. Thalmann: "Virtual Reality in Cognitive Behavioral Therapy : A preliminary study on Social Anxiety Disorder," in

8th International Conference on Virtual Systems and Multimedia, VSMM2002 (2002)

301. M.J. Ackerman: "The Visible Human Project," *Proceedings of the IEEE* **86**(3), 504–11 (1998)

302. C. North, B. Shneiderman, C. Plaisant: "User controlled overviews of an image library: a case study of the visible human," in *DL '96: Proceedings of the first ACM international conference on Digital libraries* (ACM Press, New York, 1996) pp. 74–82

303. M. López-Cano, J. Rodríguez-Navarro, A. Rodríguez-Baeza, M. Armengol-Carrasco, A. Susín: "A real-time dynamic 3D model of the human inguinal region for surgical education," *Comput. Biol. Med.* **37**(9), 1321–6 (2007)

304. A. Aubel, D. Thalmann: "MuscleBuilder: a modeling tool for human anatomy," *J. Comput. Sci. Technol.* **19**(5), 585–95 (2004)

305. A. Maciel, R. Boulic, D. Thalmann: "Efficient Collision Detection within Deforming Spherical Sliding Contact," *IEEE Transactions on Visualization and Computer Graphics* **13**(3), 518–29 (2007)

306. A. Maciel, S. Sarni, R. Boulic, D. Thalmann: "Stress Distribution Visualization on Pre- and Post-Operative Virtual Hip Joint," in *Computer Aided Orthopedic Surgery 2005* (2005) pp. 298–301

307. Virtual Physiological Human: "Towards Virtual Physiological Human: Multilevel Modelling and Simulation of the Human Anatomy and Physiology - WHITE PAPER, November 2005,"

308. J. Zara, B. Benes, R.R. Rodarte: "Virtual Campeche: A Web Based Virtual Three-Dimensional Tour," in *Proceedings of the Fifth Mexican International Conference in Computer Science (ENC 2004)* (IEEE Press, 2004) pp. 133–40

309. R. Ruiz, S. Weghorst, J. Savage, P. Oppenheimer, T.F. III, Y. Dozal: "Virtual Reality for Archeological Maya Cities," in *Congreso Virtual, INAH-UNESCO)*Ciudad de Mexico (2002)

310. B. Lutz, M. Weintke: "Virtual Dunhuang Art Cave: A Cave within a CAVE," *EG '99: Computer Graphics Forum* **18**(3), 257–64 (1999)

311. N. Magnenat-Thalmann, I. Pandzic, J-C.Moussaly: "The Making of the Terra-Cotta Xian Soldiers," in *Digitalized'97: Proceedings in Digital Creativity* (1997) pp. 66–73

312. P. Kalra, N. Magnenat-Thalmann, L. Moccozet, G. Sannier, A. Aubel, D. Thalmann: "Real-time animation of realistic virtual humans," *IEEE Computer Graphics and Applications* **18**(5), 42–56 (1998)

313. K.T. Erim: "De Aphrodisiade," *American J. of Archaeology* **71**, 233–43 (1967)

314. J. Rogers: *Sinan: Makers of Islamic Civilization* (I. B. Tauris, London, 2006)

315. P. de Heras Ciechomski, S. Schertenleib, J. Maim, D. Thalmann: "Reviving the Roman Odeon of Aphrodisias: Dynamic Animation and Variety Control of Crowds in Virtual Heritage," in *VSMM'05* (2005)

316. J.H. Rindel, A.C. Gade, M. Lisa: "The Virtual Reconstruction of the Ancient Roman Concert Hall in Aphrodisias, Turkey," in *Proceedings of the Institute of Acoustics: The 6th International Conference on Auditorium Acoustics*Vol. 28 (5-7 May 2006) pp. 316–23

317. V. Vlahakis, N. Ioannidis, J. Karigiannis, M. Tsotros, M. Gounaris, D. Stricker, T. Gleue, P. Daehne, L. Almeida: "Archeoguide: An Augmented Reality Guide for Archaeological Sites," *IEEE Comput. Graph. Appl.* **22**(5), 52–60 (2002)

318. V. Vlahakis, J. Karigiannis, M. Tsotros, M. Gounaris, L. Almeida, D. Stricker, T. Gleue, I.T. Christou, R. Carlucci, N. Ioannidis: "Archeoguide: First results of an augmented reality, mobile computing system in cultural heritage sites," in *VAST '01: Proceedings of the 2001 conference on Virtual reality, archeology, and cultural heritage* (ACM Press, New York, 2001) pp. 131–40

319. P. Dähne, J.N. Karigiannis: "Archeoguide: System Architecture of a Mobile Outdoor Augmented Reality System," in *ISMAR '02: Proceedings of the International Symposium on Mixed and Augmented Reality (ISMAR'02)* (IEEE Computer Society, Washington, DC, USA, 2002) p. 263

320. T. Gleue, P. Daehne: "Design and Implementation of a Mobile Device for Outdoor Augmented Reality in the ARCHEOGUIDE Project," in *VAST '01: Proceedings of the 2001 conference on Virtual reality, archeology, and cultural heritage* (ACM Press, 2001)

321. D. Stricker, T. Kettenbach: "Real-time Markerless Vision-based Tracking for Outdoor Augmented Reality Applications," in *IEEE and ACM International Symposium on Augmented Reality (ISAR 2001)* (IEEE Computer Society, New York, USA, 2001) pp. 29–30

322. G. Papagiannakis, S. Schertenleib, B. O'Kennedy, M. Arevalo-Poizat, N. Magnenat-Thalmann, A. Stoddart, D. Thalmann: "Mixing virtual and real scenes in the site of ancient Pompeii," *Computer Animation & Virtual Worlds* **16**(1), 11–24 (2005)

323. N. Magnenat-Thalmann, G. Papagiannakis, A. Foni, M. Arevalo-Poizat, N. Cadi-Yazli: "Simulating life in ancient sites using mixed reality technology," in *CEIG'04: XIV Congreso Español de Informática Gráfica* (2004)

324. F. Cordier, N. Magnenat-Thalmann: "Real-time Animation of Dressed Virtual Humans," in *Eurographics Conference Proceedings* (Blackwell, 2002) pp. 327–35

325. M. Kallmann, P. Lemoine, D. Thalmann, F. Cordier, N. Magnenat-Thalmann, C. Ruspa, S. Quattrocolo: "Immersive vehicle simulators for prototyping, training and ergonomics," in *Proceedings of Computer Graphics International* (2003) pp. 90–5

326. R. Ott, M. Gutiérrez, D. Thalmann, F. Vexo: "VR haptic interfaces for teleoperation: an evaluation study," in *IV'2005* (2005) pp. 788–93

327. P. Salamin, D. Thalmann, F. Vexo: "Visualization Learning for Visually Impaired People," in *The 2nd International Conference of E-Learning and Games: Edutainment 2007* (2007) pp. 171–81

328. R. Ott, M. Gutiérrez, D. Thalmann, F. Vexo: "Improving user comfort in haptic virtual environments through gravity compensation," in *Proceedings. First Joint Eurohaptics Conference and Symposium on Haptic Interfaces for Virtual Environment and Teleoperator Systems. World Haptics Conference* (2005) pp. 401–9

329. S.C. Ou, W.T. Sung, S.J. Hsiao: "Development of intelligent virtual reality web-based robotics for manufacturing applications," in *IEEE International Conference on Industrial Technology (IEEE ICIT'02)* (2002) pp. 348–53

330. L. Jin, Z. Wen, I.A. Oraifige: "Distributed VR for Collaborative Design and Manufacturing," in *IV '07: Proceedings of the 11th International Conference Information Visualization* (IEEE Computer Society, Washington, DC, USA, 2007) pp. 792–7

331. T. Salonen, J. Sääski, M. Hakkarainen, T. Kannetis, M. Perakakis, S. Siltanen, A. Potamianos, O. Korkalo, C. Woodward: "Demonstration of assembly work

using augmented reality," in *CIVR '07: Proceedings of the 6th ACM international conference on Image and video retrieval* (ACM Press, New York, 2007) pp. 120–3

332. A. Liverani, G. Amati, G. Caligiana: "Interactive control of manufacturing assemblies with Mixed Reality," *Integrated Computer-Aided Engineering* **13**(2), 163–72 (2006)

333. L. Vacchetti, V. Lepetit, M. Ponder, G. Papagiannakis, D. Thalmann, N. Magnenat-Thalmann, P. Fua: "A Stable Real-Time AR Framework for Training and Planning in Industrial Environments," in *Virtual and Augmented Reality Applications in Manufacturing*, ed. by S. Ong, A. Nee (Springer, New York, 2004) pp. 129–46

334. A. Shirai, E. Geslin, S. Richir: "WiiMedia: Motion analysis methods and applications using a consumer video game controller," in *Sandbox '07: Proceedings of the 2007 ACM SIGGRAPH symposium on Video games* (ACM Press, New York, 2007) pp. 133–40

335. T. Abaci, R. de Bondeli, J. Ciger, M. Clavien, F. Erol, M. Gutiérrez, S. Noverraz, O. Renault, F. Vexo, D. Thalmann: "Magic Wand and the Enigma of the Sphinx," *Computers & Graphics* **28**(4), 477–84 (2004)

336. S. Blackman: "Serious games...and less!," *SIGGRAPH Comput. Graph.* **39**(1), 12–16 (2005)

Index

"Enigma of the Sphinx", 187
3D sound imaging, 141

ambient reflection, 35
angular representations, 17
ARM, 149, 153
Aroma Aura, 159
artificial reality, 5
Ascension Technology, 6
augmented reality, 7, 178, 180, 184
augmented reality toolkit (ARToolkit), 184
augmented virtuality, 8
axis angle, 19

B-Splines, 31
Bézier curves, 29
behavioral animation, 52
Bernstein polynomials, 29
binaural sound, 140
Brooks, Frederick, 6

Cardano angles, 18
cartesian coordinate system, 12
cathode-ray tubes, 125
CAVE, 3, 6, 135, 175
color, 36
    CIE model, 36
    HSV model, 36
    RGB model, 36
computer animation, 49
computer vision, 53
convolvotron, 141
coordinate systems, 11

cultural heritage, 173
CyberForce^{TM}, 154
CyberGlove^{TM}, 6, 154
CyberGrasp^{TM}, 148, 149, 154
cybersickness, 2
CyberTouch^{TM}, 148
CyberTrack^{TM}, 154

data glove, 1, 6, 54, 148
diffuse reflection, 35
direct kinematics method, 57
Disney, Walt, 186
dynamic animation, 65
dynamic simulation, 52

entertainment, 185
Euclidean space, 11
Euler angles, 18
exponential maps, 23
eye-tracking, 168

facial animation parameters, 90
Fantasound, 144
FAP, 90
FDP, 90
FEELEX, 155
fish tank VR, 133
Fisher, Scott, 5
Flock of Birds, 55
free-form deformation, 74

gesture, 52
gimbal lock, 18
global illumination, 37

Gouraud shading, 36
GPU programing techniques, 177
grasping, 82
GROPE, 6, 149, 153

H-anim, 51
haptic interfaces, 149
  active interfaces, 150
  kinesthetic displays, 152
    exoskeletons, 153
    haptic surfaces, 155
    single point force-feedback, 153
  passive interfaces, 150
  tactile displays, 151
    electrotactile displays, 151
    mechanical displays, 152
    thermal displays, 151
    vibrotactile displays, 151
Haptic Master, 153
haptic rendering, 148
haptic sensory system, 147
Haptic Workstation™, 154
haptics, 147
head-mounted display (HMD), 1, 2, 5,
  54, 130, 179
  field of view, 131
  see-through, 131
head-related transfer function (HRTF),
  141
health sciences, 165
Heilig, Morton, 4
history of Virtual Reality, 4
homogeneous coordinates, 14
human localization cues (sound), 142

illumination models, 34
immersion, 2
Immersion Corporation, 6
in-between frame, 57
individuality, 62
interactive 3D software, 187
  OpenSceneGraph, 188
  Quest3D, 188
  Unreal game engine, 188
  Virtools, 188
interpolation, 58
interpolation between frames, 57
interpupillary distance, 130
inverse kinematics, 60

joint angles, 51

key-frame, 51
key-frame animation, 51, 57
kinesthetic system, 147

Lambert's cosine law, 35
Lanier, Jaron, 6
Laposky, Ben, 125
level of detail, 173
Liquid Crystal Displays
  active display area, 128
  active-matrix, 127
  aspect ratio, 128
  brightness, 128
  color support, 128
  contrast ratio, 128
  dot pitch, 128
  input ports, 128
  passive-matrix, 127
  resolution, 128
  response time, 128
  viewing angle, 128
liquid crystal displays, 126
local illumination, 35
loudspeaker location, 142

magnetic motion capture, 53
manufacturing, 183
meta-ball, 74
mixed reality, 7
mobile animator, 111, 134
monaural sound, 140
motion capture, 51, 52, 55
motion control, 51
motion retargeting, 62
MotionStart, 55
MPEG4, 90
multimodal interaction, 178
multimodal interface, 187
  Magic Wand, 187

Nintendo Wii, 185
nonparametric curves, 27
nonrational B-splines, 32
NURB, 32

olfactory displays, 158
optical motion capture, 53
orthographic projection, 24

PHANTOM®, 149, 153
Phong shading, 37
photon mapping, 40
Physiome project, 170
plasma displays, 129
polar coordinate system, 12
Polhemus, 6
posture, 52
presence, 3
principal component analysis (PCA),
        62, 73, 78
procedural animation, 64
projection matrices, 24
proprioception, 147
psychological therapy, 168

quaternions, 21

radiosity, 39
raster images, 30
rational B-splines, 32
ray tracing, 38
real-time tracking, 179
real-time tracking, 180
reality continuum, 7
rendering, 13
rendering equation, 38
rendering pipeline, 44
    fixed pipeline, 44
    programmable pipeline, 46
Rutgers ankle, 166
Rutgers Master, 149

sensorama, 4, 157
shaders, 46
    fragment shaders, 46
    vertex shaders, 46
shutter glasses, 133
skinning, 72, 177
smart object, 82
smell interfaces, 158
smell, sense of, 157
sound cards, 145
sound engines, 146
sound rendering, 140
spatial sound, 139, 140
specular reflection, 35
spherical coordinate system, 12
SPIDAR, 153

splines, 28, 58
    bias, 58
    continuity, 58
    tension, 58
stereo sound, 140
surround-sound, 144
Sutherland, Ivan, 5

Tait-Bryan angles, 18
taste interfaces, 159
    drink simulator, 160
    edible user interfaces, 160
    food simulator, 159
taste, sense of, 157
teleoperation, 149, 154, 182
teleoperator, 149
telerehabilitation, 154, 167
texture mapping, 41
    bump mapping, 41
    displacement mapping, 43
    environment mapping, 41
textures, 41, 173
transformation matrices, 13
transformations
    modeling transformations, 45
    modelview matrix, 45
    viewing transformations, 45
trigonometric identities, 17

vector, 14
vector graphics, 30
vehicle simulators, 181
VIEW system, 5
virtual anatomy, 169
virtual assembly, 184
virtual characters, 71
    locomotion, 76
virtual cockpits, 183
virtual guide, 173
virtual humans, 71
    clothes simulation, 180
    hair simulation, 180
virtual life, 180
virtual physiological human (VPH), 170
Virtual Reality exposure system (VRE),
        168
Virtual Reality modeling language
        (VRML), 183
virtual rehabilitation, 166

virtual storytelling, 180
virtual surgery, 165
Virtual Technologies Inc., 6
virtual training, 185
Visible Human Project, 169

vision, 125
VPL Research, 6

wearable computer, 179

X3D, 184

Printed in the United States